T0305401

Habitual Entrepreneurs

Deniz Ucbasaran

Associate Professor in Entrepreneurship, Nottingham University Business School, UK

Paul Westhead

Professor of Enterprise, Warwick Business School, UK and Visiting Professor at Bodø Graduate School of Business, Norway

Mike Wright

Professor of Financial Studies, Director of the Centre for Management Buy-out Research, Nottingham University Business School, UK and Visiting Professor at Erasmus University, The Netherlands

Edward Elgar
Cheltenham, UK • Northampton, MA, USA

Published by
Edward Elgar Publishing Limited
Glensanda House
Montpellier Parade
Cheltenham
Glos GL50 1UA
UK

Edward Elgar Publishing, Inc.
William Pratt House
9 Dewey Court
Northampton
Massachusetts 01060
USA

A catalogue record for this book
is available from the British Library

Library of Congress Cataloguing in Publication Data
Ucbasaran, Deniz.
    Habitual entrepreneurs / Deniz Ucbasaran, Paul Westhead, Mike Wright.
        p. cm.
    Includes bibliographical references and index.
    1. Entrepreneurship. 2. Entrepreneurship—Research. 3.
    Businesspeople—Research. I. Westhead, Paul, 1962– II. Wright, Mike, 1952–
    III. Title.

    HB615.U33   2006
    338'.04—dc22

                                                            2006008422

ISBN-13: 978 1 84542 249 3
ISBN-10: 1 84542 249 X

Typeset by Manton Typesetters, Louth, Lincolnshire, UK.
Printed and bound in Great Britain by MPG Books Ltd, Bodmin, Cornwall.

Contents

Preface

An important feature of the response to increasingly turbulent market conditions is a renewed focus on entrepreneurs and entrepreneurship as central drivers of economic development. Entrepreneurs, however, are not a homogeneous entity. A distinction can be made between entrepreneurs with regard to their prior business ownership experience. Entrepreneurs with prior business ownership experience who have started or acquired two or more independent businesses can be labelled habitual entrepreneurs. Some have successfully owned several businesses (such as Sir Richard Branson, the founder of the Virgin group and Stelios Haji-Ioannou, the founder of Easyjet). While habitual entrepreneurs have been able to move down the experience curve with respect to the problems and processes of owning a business, not all are consistently successful. There is a need, therefore, to understand the contributions and potential liabilities that prior entrepreneurial experience can bring. This book represents the first systematic study of habitual entrepreneurs. We use a blend of theoretical perspectives to explore the behaviour and contribution of habitual entrepreneurs relative to novice entrepreneurs who have no prior business ownership to draw upon. Evidence from a large representative sample of entrepreneurs is used to highlight similarities and differences between habitual and novice entrepreneurs.

If habitual entrepreneurs are distinctive in their behaviour and performance there may be important implications for advisers, providers of finance, policymakers seeking to stimulate economic growth, and other newer entrepreneurs seeking to identify opportunities and develop their ventures. If on the other hand, habitual entrepreneurs do not outperform their novice counterparts, it is important to understand why and address potential barriers to learning from experience.

We view business ownership experience as one component of an entrepreneur's human capital, that is, the achieved attributes, accumulated work experience and habits of individuals that affect their productivity (Becker, 1993). Habitual entrepreneurs' experience may mean they have had opportunity to develop other aspects of their human capital to a greater extent than novice entrepreneurs. The evidence from our study shows that while similarities exist, habitual entrepreneurs do indeed display different human capital characteristics from novice entrepreneurs.

The evidence presented indicates that habitual entrepreneurs use different sources of information as well as identifying and pursuing a significantly greater number of opportunities. However, habitual entrepreneurs do not appear to out-perform their novice counterparts. Neither those habitual entrepreneurs who had been consistently successful, nor those who had previously failed, report superior performance to novice entrepreneurs. In seeking to explain this result, we high-light the heterogeneity of habitual entrepreneurs by distinguishing between portfolio entrepreneurs (those who own multiple businesses simultaneously) and serial entrepreneurs (those who have owned multiple businesses sequentially). Empirical evidence is presented, highlighting the similarities and differences in attitudes, behaviour and contributions reported by serial and portfolio entrepreneurs as well as between novice entrepreneurs.

Our findings of differences in the human capital and behavioural profile of novice and habitual (serial and portfolio) entrepreneurs, suggest a need for tai-lored policy support for different types of entrepreneur. The implications of the analysis contained in this book are not confined to the policy arena. In our view, the distinctiveness that we identify in relation to habitual entrepreneurs is worthy of further research attention. To this end we outline an agenda for future research in the concluding chapter.

Acknowledgements

As with all books, this one owes its transition from an identified to an exploited opportunity to a number of people. A pilot study relating to the habitual entrepreneur phenomenon was pursued in collaboration with Frank Martin (University of Stirling) who conducted several in-depth interviews with novice, serial and portfolio entrepreneurs. Frank's bridging role with the support network is appreciated. The insightful support of Brian McVey and Scottish Enterprise is warmly acknowledged. We are also grateful for the financial sponsorship from the Institute of Enterprise and Innovation at Nottingham University Business School that enabled additional interviews to be conducted in England and Wales. A number of colleagues provided helpful comments during the development of the research and suggestions on earlier versions of the study, notably David Storey, Colin Mason and Richard Harrison, Andy Lockett, Dave Paton, Sue Birley, Per Davidsson, Dean Shepherd, Lowell Busenitz, Jim Fiet, Rita McGrath, Lars Kolvereid, Jerome Katz, Peter Rosa, Johan Wiklund and Shaker Zahra, as well as participants at the Global Entrepreneurship Conference, Babson Entrepreneurship Conference, the Academy of Management Conferences and various seminars and workshops, provided helpful insights on earlier versions of some of the material presented here. Most importantly, we thank the respondents to the study who took time out from running their businesses to complete our questionnaire; we hope they will find some useful insights. Thanks also to Francine O'Sullivan and Jo Betteridge of Edward Elgar for their encouragement and forbearance.

On a personal note, Deniz Ucbasaran would like to thank her husband for his involvement in football, which allowed her to write the book in peace, but more importantly for his endless patience, support and encouragement. She would also like to thank her family for their love and for providing her with opportunities and invaluable guidance in life. She would like to thank her father in particular for her Goethean upbringing: 'Treat people as if they were what they ought to be and you will help them become what they are capable of being'. Paul Westhead warmly thanks Sue Birley with whom some of his initial work on habitual entrepreneurs was conducted. He would also like to thank Benjamin and Tracy for allowing him to pursue his serial/portfolio academic career away from home. Mike Wright thanks Barclays Private Equity and Deloitte for sponsorship of the Centre for Management Buy-out Research and for insights into the financing of serial entrepreneurs that originally helped to identify this research opportunity. He would also like to thank AF and BD, two of the greatest serial entrepreneurs, for their inspiration.

Deniz Ucbasaran, Paul Westhead and Mike Wright
January 2006

1.   Introduction

Experience is not what happens to a man; it is what a man does with what happens to him.

Aldous Huxley (1932)

THE HABITUAL ENTREPRENEUR PHENOMENON

Considerable debate continues to surround the notion of entrepreneurs and entrepreneurship. Numerous theories have been developed to explain the activities of entrepreneurs and the organizations they own (Cuevas, 1994; Westhead and Wright, 2000). It is very difficult to present an overarching theory of entrepreneurship, because there is no consensus surrounding the definition of entrepreneurs or the entrepreneurial process. Definitions have focused upon 'what the entrepreneur is' (that is, the entrepreneur as a particular type of person or the entrepreneur as the product of a particular environment) or 'what the entrepreneur does' (that is, the entrepreneur as the performer of a particular role in society; entrepreneurship as a specific input in the economy; entrepreneurial events or entrepreneurial processes) (Gartner, 1990). Beyond definitional problems, an additional source of difficulty in understanding entrepreneurship stems from the heterogeneity of entrepreneurs.

One notable source of heterogeneity is the variation in the level and nature of entrepreneurs' experience. The nature and impact of entrepreneurial experience is attracting increasing attention (Chandler and Jansen, 1992; Reuber and Fischer, 1999; Westhead et al., 2005a, b, c, d). This has led to the distinction between experienced ('habitual') entrepreneurs and first-time ('novice') entrepreneurs. Empirical evidence suggests habitual entrepreneurs are a widespread phenomenon. The proportion of habitual entrepreneurs identified in UK studies ranges from 12 per cent (Cross, 1981) to 52 per cent (Ucbasaran, 2004a). High proportions of habitual entrepreneurs have also been detected in the US (51 per cent to 63 per cent) (Schollhammer, 1991; Ronstadt, 1986); Australia (49 per cent) (Taylor, 1999), Malaysia (38 per cent) (Taylor, 1999); and Norway (34 per cent) (Kolvereid and Bullvåg, 1993). Practitioners (such as financial institutions and enterprise agencies) use information relating to the experience accumulated by an entrepreneur to screen applications for assistance (MacMillan et al., 1985). Further, the financial press has drawn attention to a number of high profile entrepreneurs who have successfully owned several businesses (for example, Sir Richard Branson in a variety of sectors; biotech entrepreneur Sir Chris Evans; Dr Herman Hauser of Acorn Computers and Arm Holdings; and Stelios Haji-Ioannou of easyGroup) (Wheatley, 2004). These habitual entrepreneurs own more than one business, either sequentially (as serial entrepreneurs) or concurrently (as portfolio entrepreneurs).

While the above high profile habitual entrepreneurs have successfully started numerous businesses, success is not a necessary condition for habitual entrepreneurship. Less successfully Rachel Elnaugh's initial business Red Letter Days, which offered adults the opportunity to experience special events such as fast-car driving and helicopter flying, failed before she subsequently bought into and became CEO of Easyart.com (Parkhouse, 2005).

These contrasting experiences of habitual entrepreneurs highlight a number of major questions concerning the link between business ownership experience and entrepreneurial behaviour, such as: What do habitual entrepreneurs learn from their business ownership experiences? How do habitual entrepreneurs search for and identify new opportunities? What factors influence whether they pursue such opportunities? Do entrepreneurs with business ownership experience perform better than those without such experience?

Although habitual entrepreneurs are widespread and many have received media attention, there has been limited conceptual and theoretical understanding of this group. In this book we seek to address this void by utilizing human capital theory to provide a framework for studying habitual entrepreneurs. Due to their ownership of multiple businesses, habitual entrepreneurs may have had an opportunity to develop additional knowledge and skills resulting in potentially more diverse human capital (Becker, 1975) than novice entrepreneurs. With only one experience, novice entrepreneurs are unable to move down the experience curve with respect to the problems and processes of identifying and exploiting entrepreneurial opportunities (that is, to start or purchase a business) (MacMillan, 1986). As a result of their experience and associated human capital, habitual entrepreneurs need to be considered as an important sub-group of entrepreneurs who have the potential to make a fundamental contribution to the process of wealth creation in society (Scott and Rosa, 1996) and aid our understanding of entrepreneurship.

Despite calls for studies to focus on the experience profiles of entrepreneurs (Wright et al., 1998; Reuber and Fischer, 1999), there remains a dearth of systematic evidence relating to the relationship between an entrepreneur's prior business ownership experience and their behaviour. Additional evidence relating to the habitual entrepreneur phenomenon warrants the stimulation of academic and practitioner debate relating to the allocation of resources to inexperienced novice entrepreneurs with no prior business ownership experience and to experienced habitual (serial and portfolio) entrepreneurs with prior business ownership experience. This book provides such evidence.

The remainder of this introductory chapter is structured as follows. First, we clarify and justify our definitions of novice and habitual (serial and portfolio) entrepreneurs. This is followed by an explanation of why a distinction between these groups of entrepreneurs is warranted. A theoretical and policy case for distinguishing between different types of entrepreneurs is made. The contributions to knowledge that this book seeks to make are then highlighted. Finally, an outline of the book is provided.

DEFINING NOVICE AND HABITUAL (SERIAL AND PORTFOLIO) ENTREPRENEURS

Debate continues to surround the notion of entrepreneurs and entrepreneurship. In this book, we define entrepreneurs based on three well-established criteria: business ownership; a decision-making role; and an ability to identify and exploit opportunities.

Business ownership is recognized as an important dimension of entrepreneurship (Hawley, 1907; Fama and Jensen, 1983). Fama and Jensen (1983) argue that classic entrepreneurial firms are those that are owned by individuals who combine the roles of residual risk bearer and decision-maker. Ownership (that is, being the residual risk bearer) is seen as providing the incentive and right to earn entrepreneurial profits. Entrepreneurial profit is the reward for bearing the uncertainty associated with combining and coordinating the resources owned (Hawley, 1907). The decision-making role of the entrepreneur is also deemed important (Marshall, 1920). Further, given the prevalence of team-based entrepreneurship (Birley and Stockley, 2000; Ucbasaran et al., 2003a), ownership may involve minority or majority equity stakes. Finally, some entrepreneurship scholars suggest that entrepreneurship involves the identification and exploitation of at least one business opportunity (Venkataraman, 1997; Shane and Venkataraman, 2000; Ardichvili et al., 2003). A business opportunity can relate to new firm formation or the purchase of an existing private firm (Cooper and Dunkelberg, 1986). We therefore define entrepreneurs as having a minority or majority ownership stake in at least one business that they have either created or purchased, within which they are a key decision-maker.

A categorization of the nature of entrepreneurship by type of entrepreneur is summarized in Table 1.1. The entrepreneurs covered by cells 1, 2 and 3 are involved in the founding of a new independent business. Novice founders (cell 1) have only founded one business, while serial founders (cell 2) and portfolio founders (cell 3) have founded more than one business sequentially or concurrently/simultaneously, respectively. The entrepreneurs in cells 4, 5 and 6 have acquired an ownership stake in an established independent business. The term 'acquirer' is used to reflect the fact that ownership in the existing business is

Table 1.1   A categorization of the nature of entrepreneurship by type of entrepreneur

	Single activity	*Multiple* activity	
	Novice entrepreneurs	Habitual entrepreneurs	
Nature of entrepreneurship		**Sequential**	**Simultaneous**
		Serial entrepreneurs	Portfolio entrepreneurs
Involving *new* business(es)	Novice founders 1	Serial founders 2	Portfolio founders 3
Involving *existing* business(es)	Novice acquirers 4	Serial acquirers 5	Portfolio acquirers 6

acquired even though this may take a variety of forms. Acquirers include individuals from outside, who undertake a straight purchase or a management buy-in (MBI), and individuals from inside the firm who undertake a management buy-out (MBO). While novice acquirers (cell 4) may have only acquired a single business, serial acquirers (cell 5) and portfolio acquirers (cell 6) purchase more than one business sequentially or simultaneously, respectively. In the remainder of this book, while we include both founder and acquirer entrepreneurs, we do not make an explicit distinction between the two in our analysis.

On the basis of the above discussion, the following definitions of novice and habitual (serial and portfolio) entrepreneurs are operationalized in this book:

Novice entrepreneurs

These are individuals with no prior minority or majority business ownership experience, either as a business founder or purchaser of an independent business, who currently own a minority or majority equity stake in an independent business that is either new or purchased.

Habitual entrepreneurs

These are individuals who hold or have held a minority or majority ownership stake in two or more businesses, at least one of which was established or purchased. Habitual entrepreneurs are subdivided as follows:

Serial entrepreneurs   Individuals who have sold or closed at least one business in which they had a minority or majority ownership stake, and currently have a minority or majority ownership stake in a single independent business; and

Portfolio entrepreneurs   Individuals who currently have minority or majority ownership stakes in two or more independent businesses.

THE THEORETICAL CASE FOR DISTINGUISHING BETWEEN DIFFERENT TYPES OF ENTREPRENEUR

Differences in Mindset?

Just as managerial work experience is seen as a key empirical indicator of managerial human capital (Castanias and Helfat, 2001), business ownership experience can be viewed as a significant contributor to entrepreneurial human capital (Gimeno et al., 1997). Human capital includes achieved attributes, accumulated work experience and habits that may have a positive or negative effect on productivity (Becker, 1993). Business ownership experience may provide entrepreneurs with a variety of resources that can be utilized in identifying and exploiting subsequent ventures, such as direct entrepreneurial experience; additional managerial experience; an enhanced reputation; better access to and understanding of the requirements of finance institutions; and access to broader social and business networks (Shane and Khurana, 2003). As a result of these benefits accruing from business ownership experience, the development of subsequent businesses owned by habitual entrepreneurs can be enhanced by overcoming the liabilities of newness and attaining developmental milestones quicker (Starr and Bygrave, 1991). Habitual entrepreneurs can obtain financial resources for their subsequent ventures from a variety of sources such as banks, venture capitalists and informal investors, and possibly on better terms (Wright et al., 1997a). This discussion suggests that business ownership experience can lead to the accumulation/development of human capital as well as other types of capital (such as social and financial capital). It follows that habitual entrepreneurs who may have more diverse human capital and access to other resources need to be distinguished from novice entrepreneurs.

Alvarez and Busenitz (2001) argue that entrepreneurs' human capital should include an understanding of their cognitive characteristics. As a result of their business ownership experience, habitual entrepreneurs may display different cognitive characteristics (in terms of how they think, process information and learn) than novice entrepreneurs. Experience provides a framework for processing information and can allow experienced entrepreneurs with diverse skills and competencies (such as networks, knowledge, and so on) to foresee and take advantage of disequilibrium profit opportunities, either proactively or reactively (Kaish and Gilad, 1991). Habitual entrepreneurs, who have multiple experiences to draw from, may be more likely to rely on information processing based on heuristics[1] than their novice counterparts (Ucbasaran et al., 2003c). Novice entrepreneurs may have fewer experience-related benchmarks or mental short cuts to draw upon.

The expertise literature also offers a potential theoretical basis for distinguishing between novice and habitual entrepreneurs. Expert information-processing literature suggests that there are differences in the cognition of novices and 'experts'. A large body of this research attributes differences between novices and 'experts' to the quantity and organization of knowledge gained through experience (Shanteau, 1992). 'Experts' are viewed as being able to manipulate incoming information into recognizable patterns, and then match the information to appropriate actions (Lord and Maher, 1990). This capacity reduces the burden of cognitive processing, which can allow the 'expert' to concentrate on novel or unique material (Hillerbrand, 1989). It is possible that entrepreneurs who have the benefit of additional entrepreneurial experience (habitual entrepreneurs) are more reliant on information processing methods that resemble those of an expert.

While the above discussion suggests that habitual entrepreneurs have an advantage over novice entrepreneurs in terms of their human capital and cognitive skills, assuming that all habitual entrepreneurs will outperform novice entrepreneurs because of their experience may be too simplistic (Ucbasaran et al., 2003c). In the context of habitual entrepreneurs, there is an understanding that business ownership experience may result in the acquisition of assets and liabilities (Starr and Bygrave, 1991). While business ownership experience can result in the acquisition of human capital enhancing assets as discussed above, it may also lead to the acquisition of several liabilities. These liabilities can include hubris and staleness, whereby the entrepreneur becomes either overconfident and/or relies on routines that appeared to work well in his or her previous venture even though the circumstances may have changed (Starr and Bygrave, 1991; Wright et al., 1997b). Further, some of the more traditional views on the value of entrepreneurial experience (for example, Jovanovic, 1982) are based on the assumption that experience is associated with learning. While individuals generally adjust their judgement by learning from feedback based on experience, due to delays in feedback individuals may be prone to errors and biases (Bazerman, 1990).

There appears to be a theoretical case for distinguishing between habitual and novice entrepreneurs on the grounds that they have different human capital endowments and think differently. As highlighted above, habitual entrepreneurs themselves can also be heterogeneous. A distinction has been made between serial and portfolio entrepreneurs. Schein (1978) found that self-employed individuals fell into one of two career anchors. A career anchor is defined as 'the pattern of self-perceived talents, motives, and values [which] serves to guide, constrain, stabilise and integrate the person's career' (Schein, 1978: 127). The first anchor is that of autonomy/independence, which represents a desire for freedom from rules and the control of others. The second is the entrepreneurship anchor, which focuses on the creation of something new, involving the motivation to overcome obstacles, the willingness to run risks, and the desire for personal prominence (Schein, 1978). The autonomy-oriented individual is more likely to be driven by the desire to have freedom from control by others and is likely to be involved in ventures one at a time (Katz, 1994). Serial entrepreneurs are often motivated by autonomy, independence and an interest in gaining and maintaining control (Wright et al., 1997a, b). To maintain a position of control, serial entrepreneurs may feel a greater need for information and, therefore, be less reliant on heuristic-based thinking. In contrast, those with an entrepreneurship anchor are driven by the opportunity-recognition process and/or wealth creation (Katz, 1994). These entrepreneurs tend to be involved in multiple ventures simultaneously. These characteristics resemble more closely those of portfolio entrepreneurs. The fact that they are involved in multiple ventures suggests that they do not require complete information to the same extent as serial entrepreneurs. Portfolio entrepreneurs may be associated more strongly with a heuristic mode of cognition.

The above discussion suggests that scholars may benefit from distinguishing between novice and experienced habitual entrepreneurs on the grounds that their human capital and cognitive profiles are different, which in turn may explain differences in behaviour and performance. Furthermore it is suggested that among habitual entrepreneurs there are differences in the mindset, attitudes and motives of serial entrepreneurs and portfolio entrepreneurs. The next section explores the implications of these differences in mindset by exploring potential differences in entrepreneurial behaviour.

Differences in Behaviour?

Numerous theoretical approaches to entrepreneurship have been proposed with the purpose of explaining what entrepreneurs do, how they behave and the outcomes of their actions (Ucbasaran et al., 2001). These approaches have had limited success in explaining entrepreneurial behaviour and processes. For example, the psychological 'trait' approach sought to distinguish entrepreneurs from non-entrepreneurs in terms of dispositional character traits such as need for achievement, locus of control and risk-taking propensity. This approach met with considerable criticism partly due to the limited evidence that entrepreneurs were associated with distinct traits and partly due to insufficient explanation of entrepreneurial behaviour (Gartner, 1988; Robinson et al, 1991). In contrast to

the trait approach, the economic approach focused on the outcomes of entrepreneurship. However, this approach was criticized on grounds that too much
emphasis was placed on the economic outcomes of entrepreneurship at the expense of explaining how those outcomes were achieved. Finally, the sociological
and environmental approaches have sought to explain entrepreneurship by focusing on the context (economic and social) within which entrepreneurship
takes place. Once again, these approaches failed to explain what it is that the
entrepreneur does and how the entrepreneur acts.

Opportunity-based conceptualizations of entrepreneurship (Hitt et al., 2001;
Shane and Venkataraman, 2000) have been presented more recently to address
the limitations of previous approaches. Accordingly, it has been argued that
entrepreneurship research should focus on explaining the entrepreneurial process, which is largely viewed as involving the identification and exploitation of
opportunities (Venkataraman, 1997; Shane and Venkataraman, 2000). Explanations of opportunity identification and exploitation have focused on the role of
knowledge and the acquisition and processing of information by the entrepreneur (Venkataraman, 1997; Fiet, 1996). Given differences in the human capital
and mindset of novice and habitual entrepreneurs proposed in the previous section, it is reasonable to expect differences in the behaviour of these two groups
of entrepreneur, in terms of opportunity identification and exploitation. Further,
given differences in the endowment of knowledge, novice and habitual entrepreneurs may search for different quantities and types of information with a
view to identifying opportunities. If novice and habitual entrepreneurs behave
differently in the way they utilize information and identify opportunities, this
may have implications for the performance of the ventures they own.

THE 'POLICY' CASE FOR DISTINGUISHING BETWEEN
DIFFERENT TYPES OF ENTREPRENEUR

Policymakers have increasingly recognized that the entrepreneurial function is
a vital component in the process of economic growth (Baumol, 1968; Casson,
1982; Reynolds et al., 1994; OECD, 1998; DTI, 2004) and a means of combat-
ing unemployment and poverty (Storey, 1982, 1994). This viewpoint is
supported in the OECD (1998) document entitled 'Fostering Entrepreneurship',
which stated that:

> Entrepreneurship is central to the functioning of market economies. Entrepreneurs
> are agents of change and growth in a market economy and they can act to accelerate
> the generation, dissemination and application of innovative ideas. In doing so, they
> not only ensure that efficient use is made of resources, but also expand the boundaries
> of economic activity. (p. 12)

Support for entrepreneurship has manifested itself in various forms. During the late 1970s and 1980s the British government, for example, encouraged new firm formation (Westhead and Moyes, 1992), and the growth of self-employment (Storey, 1994). This policy shifted during the 1990s, however, toward supporting growth firms (Storey, 1994; Westhead, 1995). To maximize returns on public policy investments, attempts have been made to 'target' external support to 'winning businesses' (that is businesses with significant wealth-creation potential) (Storey, 1994). In response to a slowdown in business start-ups, the British government realized the need for a balanced policy agenda (Gavron et al., 1998; DTI, 2004), and continues to encourage business formation (Reynolds, 1997), as well as supporting the growth of some 'types' of existing firms (Reynolds et al., 1994).

Policymakers and practitioners need to appreciate that the processes of enterprise are much broader than the processes associated with enterprise formation (Taylor, 1999). The entrepreneurial process can be explored in relation to the skills of practising (and potential) entrepreneurs with reference to imagination and creativity, idea generation, opportunity identification, pursuit and exploitation, as well as resource assemblage and utilization. The accumulation and utilization of 'entrepreneur/entrepreneurial team' resources and capabilities, rather than solely 'business' resources and capabilities, can provide fresh insights into the entrepreneurial process and entrepreneurial events relating to the creation of new private ventures, and the development of purchased and inherited private ventures. However, the 'firm' rather than 'entrepreneur' still appears to be the focus of much policy seeking to achieve sustainable increases in prosperity. In 2004 the Department of Trade and Industry (DTI) in the UK published a report entitled *A Government Action Plan for Small Business: Making the UK the Best Place in the World to Start and Grow a Business: The Evidence Base*. As intimated above, it is assumed that if an enterprise culture is fostered, this policy choice will be associated with several beneficial outcomes. Entrepreneurs and the new or established (smaller) private firms they have equity stakes in may, however, face internal and external environmental obstacles. The latter obstacles may retard the realization of the economic and social outcomes and benefits assumed to be associated with entrepreneurship. The DTI's (2004) action plan for small businesses does, however, appear to show some recognition of the importance of the individual entrepreneur.

Policymakers, practitioners, enterprise and development agencies and local government must understand their 'target' groups (Westhead and Wright, 1999; Westhead et al., 2003b, 2005a). If support for entrepreneurship is to be effective, it is vital that issues relating to the entrepreneurial process are well understood (Ucbasaran et al., 2001). The refocusing of external support away from the entrepreneur, towards the more visible business, fails to fully appreciate the crucial role played by the entrepreneur (or the entrepreneurial team) in relation to the entrepreneurial process. While both research and policy have hitherto tended to focus on the business, it may be more appropriate to consider the entrepreneur as the unit of analysis (Birley and Westhead, 1993b; Scott and Rosa, 1996). Entrepreneurs and entrepreneurial teams establish, purchase and inherit private firms. Their aspirations, resources, strategies and capabilities may impact on business development. Concern has therefore been raised surrounding whether the firm alone should be the unit of policy and academic analysis (Westhead and Wright, 1998a, b, 1999).

In considering the entrepreneur as a unit of policy analysis, however, it is necessary to appreciate that entrepreneurs are not a homogeneous entity (Woo et al., 1991) with regard to their characteristics, resources, motivations, behaviour and performance. An increase in the number (stock) of businesses in an economy may not necessarily be a reliable indicator of the development of entrepreneurship since both new and established businesses are owned by different types of entrepreneur. Policymakers and practitioners monitoring the growth in the supply of new firms need to be aware that habitual (serial and portfolio) entrepreneurs with business ownership experience own a sizeable proportion of new firms. Studies which judge the scale of entrepreneurship in terms of the number of new firms but ignore the scale of serial and portfolio entrepreneur activity may overestimate the gross number of entrepreneurs, and underestimate the contribution made by particular types of entrepreneur.

A shift in the allocation of resources towards experienced habitual entrepreneurs, instead of the provision of initiatives solely to increase the pool of first-time entrepreneurs may yield greater returns. An unresolved question remains: should policy support be directed to 'winning entrepreneurs'? If experienced habitual entrepreneurs are found to report superior entrepreneur and/or firm performance than inexperienced novice entrepreneurs, there is a case to target assistance to habitual entrepreneurs to maximize returns from public policy investments. Moreover, if inexperienced novice entrepreneurs report poorer entrepreneur and/or firm performance, there is a case to encourage them to adopt some of the skills and the behavioural characteristics of experienced habitual entrepreneurs.

Policymakers and practitioners also need to understand the resource profiles and objectives of different types of entrepreneurs. An understanding of habitual entrepreneurs has implications for the investment behaviour of financial institutions. Financial institutions and professional advisers (for example, accountants, lawyers, management consultants, and so on) are aware that they have different types of customers and some customers may be more 'risky' than others. Moreover they may be prepared to provide additional advantage to customers (such as habitual entrepreneurs) who have a proven track record of success. Nevertheless, as will be discussed below, prior entrepreneurial success (that is, number and quality of businesses previously and currently owned and wealth accumulated) may not be an appropriate indicator of higher current entrepreneurial performance, as previous entrepreneurial experience may be associated with a set of liabilities and biases. Assuming that all habitual entrepreneurs will outperform novice entrepreneurs (for example, with regard to a variety of entrepreneur and firm outcome indicators) because of their experience may be too simplistic (Ucbasaran, et al., 2003c). There may also be a downside to prior business ownership experience; some habitual entrepreneurs may become overconfident in their abilities and less attentive to the venture-creation process. In addition, some serial entrepreneurs may be unable to accumulate the financial (and non-financial) resources required to exploit a business opportunity. Further, some serial entrepreneurs may have failed to learn from previous entrepreneurial experiences and are unable to adapt to changing environmental conditions with regard to their subsequent ventures. Examination of habitual entrepreneurs in relation to other less experienced novice entrepreneurs may, therefore, aid insights into entrepreneurship and the process of wealth creation (Rosa, 1998; Westhead and Wright, 1999). Analysis of the heterogeneity of entrepreneurs may contribute towards the development of policies tailored to different types of entrepreneur, rather than provide broad 'blanket' policies to all types of entrepreneur, irrespective of need or ability (Westhead et al., 2003a, 2003b, 2005a).

Evaluations seeking to monitor the 'success in building an enterprise culture' need to monitor more clearly the contributions made by different types of entrepreneurs. Most notably, habitual entrepreneurs with prior business ownership experience may distort 'headline measures' relating to new firm formation rates and self-employment and business ownership stock data. In our concluding chapter we revisit these issues to assess the implications of the findings presented in this book for the policymaker and practitioner audience.

THE STRUCTURE OF THE BOOK

Previous studies focusing upon habitual entrepreneurs have generally been conducted in a theoretical vacuum. In Chapter 2 an integrative human capital framework is presented to explore the human capital of the entrepreneur, the entrepreneurial process and outcomes. This framework is then used to develop hypotheses suggesting differences between inexperienced novice entrepreneurs and experienced habitual (serial and portfolio) entrepreneurs in relation to general and specific human capital resource profiles, motivations, behaviour (that is, information search, opportunity identification and exploitation) and financial and non-financial outcomes.

Chapter 3 details the data and methodology utilized to examine the differences between novice and habitual (serial and portfolio) entrepreneurs. The measures operationalized are reported; data quality issues (such as representativeness, validity and reliability) are discussed; and the profiles of the respondents and their surveyed businesses are reported.

In Chapters 4, 5 and 6 the hypotheses developed in Chapter 2 are tested using a variety of bivariate and multivariate statistical techniques. In Chapter 4 hypotheses relating to human capital based differences between the groups of entrepreneurs are tested. The extent to which novice and habitual entrepreneurs display different profiles in terms of their general and specific human capital is established. Specific human capital is explored with reference to entrepreneurship-specific and venture-specific human capital. Among the habitual entrepreneurs, the human capital profiles of serial and portfolio entrepreneurs are also identified.

Following a similar pattern, Chapter 5 presents the results of the hypothesis testing relating to behavioural differences between the groups of entrepreneur. Despite recent consensus amongst scholars that the study of entrepreneurship should focus on the identification and exploitation of opportunities (Venkataraman, 1997; Shane and Venkataraman, 2000; Hitt et al., 2001; Ardichvili et al., 2003), there has been limited empirical work in this area. To address this gap, differences between novice and habitual (and then serial and portfolio) entrepreneurs with regard to their information search patterns, their attitudes towards opportunity identification and extent of their opportunity identification are presented. Novice and habitual (serial and portfolio) entrepreneurs are also compared in terms of the extent to which they pursued business opportunities (that is, the time and effort invested into evaluating the feasibility of the identified opportunity) and the mode of exploitation they selected for the surveyed business (such as a start-up or the purchase of an existing business).

Differences between the groups of entrepreneurs in terms of entrepreneur-level and firm-level performance are presented in Chapter 6. Most previous studies focusing upon the entrepreneur have solely focused on 'firm' rather than 'entrepreneur' outcomes. Several objective and subjective performance indicators were selected. A key objective was to explore whether experienced habitual entrepreneurs reported superior levels of performance than novice entrepreneurs. Here the refinement of some of the definitions relating to habitual entrepreneurs was deemed necessary. Novice entrepreneurs were compared with those habitual entrepreneurs who had consistently failed or were consistently successful. This feeds into an emerging debate surrounding whether the barriers to subsequent business ownership imposed on people whose earlier business(es) had failed should be relaxed to encourage the supply of experienced habitual entrepreneurs (Enterprise Act, 2002). Though arguments to the contrary exist, it has been suggested that those entrepreneurs who have failed may have an advantage over others because they are forced to reflect on what went wrong and modify their subsequent actions (Sitkin, 1992). It would, therefore, make sense to explore if prior business failure had implications for subsequent venture performance.

In the final chapter (Chapter 7) the key findings of our study are summarized. Presented empirical evidence may enable policymakers to understand the aspirations and needs of different types of entrepreneurs. It may also allow practitioners to better understand the strengths and weakness of novice, serial and portfolio entrepreneurs. The implications of our findings for policymakers and practitioners are discussed at length. Further, while the research presented in this book seeks to draw attention to the importance of examining different types of entrepreneurs, it is not possible to examine all aspects of the habitual entrepreneurship phenomenon in one study. In our final chapter we conclude by mapping out an agenda for further research.

NOTE

1. Heuristics are simplifying strategies that individuals use to make strategic decisions, especially in complex situations where less complete information is available.

2.   A human capital approach to entrepreneurship

INTRODUCTION

The vast and diverse body of entrepreneurship research lacks agreement on the definition, scope and theory of the field (Gartner, 1990, 2001; Low, 2001). One source of confusion stems from the heterogeneity of entrepreneurship. For example, as intimated in the previous chapter, entrepreneurship can involve the creation, purchase and even inheritance of a business. Further, there is a need to acknowledge heterogeneity among entrepreneurs resulting from variations in their experience. We have argued therefore, that it is important to distinguish between novice (individuals with no prior business ownership experience) and habitual entrepreneurs (individuals with prior business ownership experience). In the previous chapter, a theory and policy case for distinguishing between these groups of entrepreneurs was provided. In this chapter we develop a theoretical framework that will allow us to explore and understand differences between these entrepreneurs.

One of the difficulties faced by entrepreneurship scholars in developing an appropriate theory arises from the multi-disciplinary nature of the phenomenon. Any theory of entrepreneurship must be rooted in the social sciences of psychology, sociology, economics and politics (Amit et al., 1993; Bygrave, 1993). 'There is no doubt that a theory of entrepreneurship should reflect a range of decision theoretic, economic and psychological and other dimensions. It is unclear, however, what core aspects of entrepreneurship should be reflected in such a theory and how the various perspectives can be effectively integrated' (Amit et al., 1993: 824). Low and MacMillan (1988) argued that any theoretical model or research design should integrate the outcomes of entrepreneurial efforts and the processes that led to those outcomes. Given the difficulties associated with trying to integrate various disciplinary perspectives to provide a complete theoretical model, several scholars have attempted to identify key themes or areas that entrepreneurship scholars should focus upon. Stevenson and Jarillo (1990) propose that three main categories of research have emerged:

1.   Research attempting to explain *what* happens when the entrepreneur acts

and the effect upon the general economic system and the development of the market system.

2. Research attempting to explain *why* they act.
3. Research attempting to explain *how* they act.

With varying degrees of emphasis over time, entrepreneurship research has attempted to address these questions. The extent to which emphasis has been placed on addressing one or more of the above questions has been influenced by the dominant discipline guiding the approach. For example, the economic approach has tended to explore the first question, while the psychological and sociological approaches have tended to focus on the second question. Until recently, much less work has been undertaken to address the third question. Entrepreneurship scholars are now increasingly trying to understand entrepreneurial behaviour. Opportunity-based conceptualizations of entrepreneurship have recently been presented to explain entrepreneurial behaviour (Hitt et al., 2001, Shane and Venkataraman, 2000; Venkataraman, 1997). Accordingly, it has been argued that entrepreneurship research should seek to explain the entrepreneurial process by focusing on the 'scholarly examination of how, by whom, and with what effect opportunities to create future goods and services are discovered, evaluated and exploited' (Shane and Venkataraman, 2000: 218). To this end in this chapter we develop a theoretical framework that will allow us to understand how entrepreneurs act. Specifically this framework builds on but also addresses some of the limitations of previous theoretical approaches; it builds on and extends traditional human capital theory. Our human capital framework will then be used to help understand variations in the characteristics, behaviour and performance of novice and habitual entrepreneurs. In particular, guided by the human capital framework, a set of hypotheses proposing differences between novice and habitual, and then serial and portfolio entrepreneurs, will be presented.

The structure of this chapter is as follows: first, we provide an overview of a human capital framework for understanding entrepreneurship. This framework is used to identify the themes that will guide our exploration of differences between novice and habitual entrepreneurs (and serial and portfolio entrepreneurs). Second, we develop each of the themes and develop a set of hypotheses. The different types of entrepreneur are presumed to display distinct human capital profiles with regard to their general human capital (for example, education and managerial human capital); entrepreneurship-specific human capital (for example, entrepreneurial capability); and venture-specific human capital (for example, motivations and prior knowledge of the venture domain). This is followed by hypotheses relating to behavioural differences between the entrepreneurs in terms of information search, opportunity identification, opportunity pursuit and opportunity exploitation. Finally, hypotheses are derived which suggest that habitual entrepreneurs (particularly portfolio entrepreneurs) will report superior levels of entrepreneur and firm performance. Within this section, a distinction is also made between those habitual entrepreneurs who have been previously successful and those who have failed. Finally, concluding comments are presented.

AN INTEGRATIVE HUMAN CAPITAL FRAMEWORK

A review of the literature suggests four core dimensions associated with entrepreneurship (Cooper, 1993; Gartner, 1985; Low and MacMillan, 1988; Ucbasaran et al., 2001): the individual; the process; outcomes; and the context. In an attempt to incorporate these core dimensions and address the limitations of previous work, an integrating framework is developed. The human capital framework discussed within this section addresses several concerns directed towards the economic, trait and sociological/environmental theoretical approaches to entrepreneurship (highlighted in the Introduction). First, it focuses on the individual entrepreneur, as well as the firm, as the unit of analysis. As intimated earlier, since ventures cannot be initiated without an individual (or group of individuals) (Davidson and Wiklund, 2001; Shook et al., 2003), ignoring the entrepreneur would provide an incomplete model of entrepreneurship. Furthermore, by focusing on the human capital of the entrepreneur (discussed below), it moves beyond personality characteristics (such as traits) and allows for the incorporation of cognition. Human capital can include cognition and can be modified over time. Unlike most traits or personality characteristics, human capital can be developed and can change. Second, the framework includes the entrepreneurial process, broadly defined in terms of opportunity identification and exploitation (Ucbasaran et al., 2001). Consequently the model allows for the exploration of the behaviour of entrepreneurs. Third, the human capital framework described below meets the criteria stipulated by Low and MacMillan (1988) that any research design should integrate the outcomes of entrepreneurial effort and the processes that led to those outcomes. Finally, the framework offers a means of identifying heterogeneous groups among entrepreneurs. In particular this study utilizes the human capital framework to distinguish between novice and habitual (experienced) entrepreneurs. The remainder of this section offers an overview of the human capital framework, which will guide the remainder of this study.

This study focuses mainly on the relationship between the individual entrepreneur and opportunity identification, exploitation behaviour and subsequent outcomes. This approach is not uncommon (see Shook et al., 2003, for example). However the environment may be a source of opportunity (Kirzner, 1973; Gartner, 1985) and opportunity identification may be a function of the interaction between the individual and the environment (Shane and Venkataraman, 2000). Where the empirical evidence is presented, therefore, the external environment is controlled for where deemed important.

Human capital includes achieved attributes (Becker, 1975), accumulated work and habits that may have a positive or negative effect on productivity (Becker, 1993) and the cognitive characteristics of entrepreneurs (Alvarez and Busenitz, 2001). Within the economics literature, productivity has been largely viewed in terms of earnings and human capital in terms of education and training (Mincer, 1974; Bates, 1990; Becker, 1993). This view of productivity and human capital may be too narrow for the context of entrepreneurship. First, as the definition of human capital provided above implies, it can comprise dimensions beyond just education and training. Second, productivity within an entrepreneurial context may relate to a variety of outcomes and behaviours. A considerable amount of research suggests that the human capital of the entrepreneur is central to the development and survival of his or her venture (Brüderl, et al., 1992; Gimeno et al., 1997; Mosakowski, 1993; Bates, 1995). However, limited research has been conducted surrounding the relationship between human capital and behaviour (that is, opportunity identification and exploitation). Further, the relationship between human capital and various outcomes associated with entrepreneurship may be mediated (Baron and Kenny, 1986; Cohen et al., 2003) by entrepreneurial behaviour. Since human capital can be viewed as an input, this section provides a framework that allows us to explore its relationship with various 'outputs' ranging from entrepreneurial behaviour to other outcomes.

Figure 2.1 below illustrates the relationships proposed within the framework. Accordingly, the entrepreneur is viewed in terms of his or her human capital endowment (theme 1). This is consistent with studies that view entrepreneurs with respect to their resource endowments. In many businesses (especially smaller ones), the entrepreneur may be the key resource of the organization (or a key constraint) (Castanias and Helfat, 1991; Brown and Kirchhoff, 1997). Furthermore, the entrepreneur can be viewed as both the 'foundation and fountainhead' for all other resources that will become the organization (Greene et al., 1999).

The nature and composition of the entrepreneur's human capital is expected to be associated with both the processes (that is, behaviours) and outcomes associated with entrepreneurship. Sarasvathy (2001) argues that entrepreneurship is best viewed from an effectuation perspective. She argues that effectual reasoning is different from causal reasoning where the individual has a given goal to achieve. Effectual reasoning begins with a given set of means and allows goals to emerge contingently over time from the varied imagination and diverse aspirations of the entrepreneur. What individuals know (the human capital associated with their education, expertise and experience) constitutes (at least partly) the means available to them. Accordingly, the composition and nature

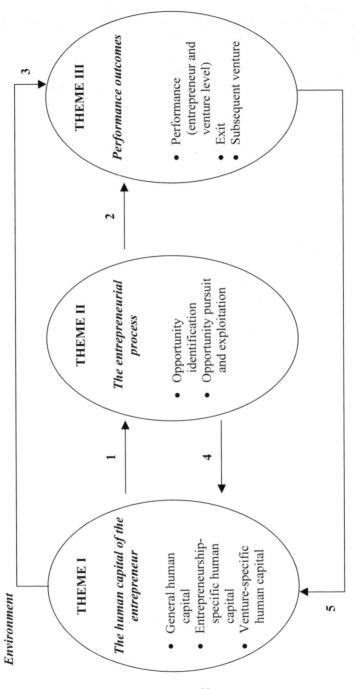

Figure 2.1   A human capital framework for understanding entrepreneurship

of an individual's human capital is central in determining the 'imagined ends'. The human capital of the entrepreneur, for example, is likely to be a central determinant of the likelihood, extent and nature of opportunity identification. Entrepreneurs with superior levels of human capital (in terms of amount and diversity) may be in a better position to both identify an opportunity and then subsequently exploit it (path 1). Indeed though there is limited evidence, Venkataraman (1997) argues that opportunity identification may be a function of the individual's capacity to process information. This capacity in turn is likely to be associated with their level of human capital. Shane (2000) found that prior knowledge (one aspect of human capital) influenced the ability of entrepreneurs to identify opportunities. Further, the nature and extent of the entrepreneur's human capital may be crucial in accessing and leveraging resources such as the social, financial, physical and organizational resources necessary to exploit an identified opportunity.

The experiences, skills and competencies associated with the entrepreneur's human capital are widely regarded as influencing organizational development, survival and performance (Mosakowski, 1993; Chandler and Hanks, 1994; Storey, 1994; Westhead, 1995; Gimeno et al., 1997; Bates, 1998) (path 3). Alongside the human capital characteristics of the entrepreneur, however, the actual decisions made by the entrepreneur (their behaviours) are likely to influence the outcomes of entrepreneurship (path 2). Furthermore, behaviours may mediate the relationship between human capital and outcomes.

Once the venture has come into fruition (that is, the opportunity has been exploited), the entrepreneur is in a position to evaluate it. As a result of this evaluation, the entrepreneur may modify his or her behaviour (the way the opportunity is being exploited) (back to path 1). For example, if the entrepreneur is not satisfied with the growth rate of the business having followed organic growth, he or she may opt for an acquisition-based growth strategy. Alternatively, depending on their performance threshold (Gimeno et al., 1997), the entrepreneur may choose to exit from the venture (for example, to close the business or sell it). In both situations (the decision to terminate the venture or modify behaviour), the course of action will be determined by the entrepreneur and therefore by the nature and composition of his or her human capital. This suggests that the entrepreneurial process is by no means static: it involves continuous reassessment and modification of behaviour. Furthermore, at every stage of the entrepreneurial process, the entrepreneur is accumulating knowledge and experience, which feeds back into his or her initial endowment of human capital (paths 4 and 5).

An additional source of dynamism relates to re-entry into the entrepreneurial cycle. Entrepreneurs may identify subsequent ventures, suggesting that entrepreneurship is not a single-event action (Birley and Westhead, 1993b; Scott and Rosa, 1996; Rosa and Scott, 1998; Westhead and Wright, 1998a, 1998b, 1999).

While involvement in a single venture offers experience and insights to the entrepreneur, involvement in additional ventures may allow the entrepreneur to gain access to more diverse experiences and also to put into practice what they have learnt from the previous venture.

The three core themes illustrated in Figure 2.1 (that is, the entrepreneur, behaviour and outcomes) and discussed above are now explored in greater depth. For each theme we develop a set of hypotheses which suggest differences between novice and habitual entrepreneurs and then between serial and portfolio entrepreneurs.

THEME I: HUMAN CAPITAL OF THE ENTREPRENEUR

Human capital may comprise a range of aspects: the owner-founder's achieved attributes (Becker, 1975); family background characteristics (Greene and Brown, 1997); attitudes and motivations (Birley and Westhead, 1990b); education, gender and ethnic origin (Cooper et al., 1994); industry-specific know-how (Cooper et al., 1994); competencies or capabilities (Chandler and Jansen, 1992); age (Bates, 1995); and cognition (Alvarez and Busenitz, 2001). Entrepreneurs can develop their human capital over time, which can then determine the extent to which other resources (financial, social, technological and so on) necessary for the identification and exploitation of a venture idea can be accessed and leveraged.

Becker (1993) argues that one of the most influential theoretical concepts in human capital analysis is the distinction between general and specific knowledge. In most cases, human capital has been viewed as consisting of a hierarchy of skills and knowledge with varying degrees of transferability across firms (Castanias and Helfat, 1992). These skills and knowledge can either be firm-specific, which are difficult to transfer across firms, or generic, which are transferable across all industries and firms. This hierarchy can be adapted to reflect the entrepreneur as the unit of analysis.

General human capital is generic to all types of economic activity and includes aspects of individual human capital such as education, age, gender, and managerial and technical know-how. General human capital may provide access to general networks and may increase the problem-solving ability of the entrepreneur (Cooper et al., 1994). In contrast, an entrepreneur's specific human capital has a relatively more limited scope of applicability (Gimeno et al., 1997). While there is no consistent delineation between general and specific human capital in the entrepreneurship literature (with the exception of Gimeno et al., 1997), two aspects of an entrepreneur's specific human capital can be proposed. First, there is human capital that has most applicability in the domain of entrepreneurship (entrepreneurship-specific human capital). Entrepreneurship-specific human capital includes: business ownership experience; attitudes towards entrepreneurship; parental business ownership and entrepreneurial capabilities. Gimeno et al. (1997) focus on human capital that is specific to the venture in which the entrepreneur is involved. As such, human capital specific to the venture comprises motivations specific to the venture (especially in terms of the motives for the purchase or start-up) and the level of business similarity (reflecting the level of experience or prior knowledge the entrepreneur has about the industry and skills needed). Table 2.1 below provides a summary of the key types and components of human capital utilized in this study. We now explore these components in greater depth and propose differences between novice and habitual (serial and portfolio) entrepreneurs in terms of these components.

Table 2.1   Types and components of human capital

Type of human capital	Components
General human capital (GHK)	Education Gender and age Managerial human capital Managerial and technical capabilities
Human capital specific to entrepreneurship (SHK_E)	Business ownership experience Parental business ownership Entrepreneurial capability
Human capital specific to the venture (SHK_V)	Motivations for starting or purchasing the venture Knowledge of the venture domain

General Human Capital

Cooper et al. (1994) argue that an examination of general human capital provides for a more controlled evaluation of the effects of specific types of human capital. In this section, differences between novice and habitual entrepreneurs are discussed with regard to their general human capital. Also, hypotheses are derived suggesting differences between serial and portfolio entrepreneurs.

Education
Education is one of the most frequently examined components of human capital (particularly by economists such as Mincer, 1974 and Becker, 1975). Education can be an important source of knowledge, skills, problem-solving ability, discipline, motivation and self-confidence (Cooper et al., 1994). These attributes

enable highly educated entrepreneurs to cope better with problems. They can also use their knowledge to search for and acquire additional resources. There is extensive evidence that education is positively related to individual earnings (Becker, 1993). Furthermore, Evans and Leighton (1989) suggest that education has greater returns for self-employment than for waged employment. Higher levels of education can give habitual entrepreneurs the confidence, motivation and skills to own more than one business. It is expected, therefore, that habitual entrepreneurs will be associated with higher levels of education than novice entrepreneurs. Indeed, evidence from Donckels et al., (1987) and Kolvereid and Bullvåg (1993) shows that habitual entrepreneurs were more likely to have obtained higher education qualifications. Westhead and Wright (1998b), however, revealed that while there were no differences in the education level of novice and serial entrepreneurs, portfolio entrepreneurs reported higher levels of education than the other two groups. One interpretation of this finding is that portfolio entrepreneurs who own several businesses at once may require a greater level of knowledge to control multiple businesses simultaneously. This discussion suggests the following hypotheses:

H_{1a} *Habitual entrepreneurs will report a higher level of education than novice entrepreneurs.*

H_{1b} *Portfolio entrepreneurs will report a higher level of education than serial entrepreneurs.*

Managerial human capital

Managerial human capital refers to innate and learned abilities, expertise, and knowledge (Castanias and Helfat, 2001). It can be acquired and perfected through substantial investment of time in observing, studying, and making business decisions (Cooper et al. 1994). Westhead and Wright (1998a) found no significant difference between novice and habitual entrepreneurs with regard to their managerial background. This finding was based on a relatively simple measure of managerial human capital. Further examination of the relationship between business ownership experience and managerial human capital is therefore warranted.

Managerial human capital has frequently been operationalized in terms of the number of years of work experience (Evans and Leighton, 1989; Brüderl et al., 1992; Bates, 1995). The number of years of experience may not, however, closely reflect the skills and knowledge developed. Gimeno et al. (1997) suggest two alternative indicators of managerial human capital. One of these relates to the number of prior full-time jobs held; the latter is an appropriate proxy for the level of work experience. These suggest a breadth of different experiences. On the one hand, individuals who have been in more job settings are likely to develop a diverse range of managerial knowledge: that the individual has held multiple jobs may signal that they are moving up the corporate ladder. Conversely, many job changes may signal poor performance on the part of the individual, indicating lower levels of managerial human capital. For entrepreneurs, and in particular habitual entrepreneurs, many previous jobs may be symptomatic of their tendency to get restless quickly and their attraction to changing contexts.

The quality or nature of work experience also needs to be considered. Gimeno et al., (1997) argue that the second indicator of managerial human capital relates to the achievement level attained by the entrepreneur. Individuals who have held a managerial position or were self-employed may be endowed with superior levels of managerial human capital. Further, individuals who report high numbers of previous jobs and a managerial status are likely to possess higher levels of managerial human capital than those who report a lower level of attainment alongside many previous jobs.

Habitual entrepreneurs may be psychologically attracted to the thrill of initiating a venture (Gimeno et al., 1997; Ucbasaran et al., 2003c). They may place less emphasis on ensuring that they have sufficient managerial knowledge than novice entrepreneurs. However, as a result of their business ownership experience, habitual entrepreneurs may have learned the importance of managerial human capital. Most notably, it can be crucial for exploiting and developing an opportunity into a successful business. Portfolio entrepreneurs may need higher levels of managerial human capital to coordinate their multiple businesses and facilitate simultaneous ownership relative to their serial counterparts.

Based on the above discussion, the following hypotheses are presented:

H_{2a} *Habitual entrepreneurs will report higher levels of managerial human capital than novice entrepreneurs.*

H_{2b} *Portfolio entrepreneurs will report higher levels of managerial human capital than serial entrepreneurs.*

Capabilities

The various dimensions of human capital discussed so far represent stocks of human capital. Recent work on capabilities (Chandler and Hanks, 1994; Teece et al., 1997; Eisenhardt and Martin, 2000) suggests the need to supplement the stock-based (or static) view of capital or resources with a more process-oriented view. Calls have been made to examine the functional roles and capabilities of entrepreneurs that are action-oriented. In the context of the firm, (dynamic) capabilities are viewed as antecedent organizational and strategic routines by which managers alter their resource base. They acquire and shed resources, integrate them and recombine them to generate new value-creating strategies

(Eisenhardt and Martin, 2000). The entrepreneur must demonstrate capabilities in three functional areas: entrepreneurial, managerial and technical (Penrose, 1959; Mintzberg and Waters, 1982; Schein, 1978; Chandler and Jansen, 1992). Entrepreneurial capabilities will be discussed in greater detail in the next section where human capital specific to entrepreneurship is the focus. Here, managerial and technical capabilities will be explored.

The discussion in the previous section relating to the managerial human capital of different types of entrepreneurs is likely to hold for managerial capabilities. We can reasonably infer that novice and habitual (serial and portfolio) entrepreneurs will differ with regard to the importance they give to managerial capabilities. Managerial human capital is crucial for the survival and development of a business. Consequently, habitual entrepreneurs will appreciate its importance and will have sought to acquire this capability in order to own multiple businesses. Owning multiple businesses simultaneously may put more pressure on portfolio entrepreneurs to develop their managerial capabilities. Serial entrepreneurs, who own only one business at a time, may be less likely to appreciate the value of managerial capabilities. The following hypotheses can be derived from the above discussion:

H_{3a} *Habitual entrepreneurs will report a higher managerial capability than novice entrepreneurs.*

H_{3b} *Portfolio entrepreneurs will report a higher managerial capability than serial entrepreneurs.*

Technical knowledge and capabilities (Chandler and Jansen, 1992) in a particular domain may facilitate the identification of an opportunity. In particular, many novice entrepreneurs may have developed technical knowledge when employed in another business and utilized this knowledge to start or purchase their current business. Hoy and Hellriegel (1982) found that small business founders preferred technical-functional tasks to managerial tasks. As intimated earlier, entrepreneurs are likely to need technical as well as other capabilities (such as managerial and entrepreneurial). Due to business ownership experience habitual entrepreneurs may be more aware of the need for a variety of capabilities.

Technical knowledge, on which technical capabilities are based, represents a form of articulable knowledge (that is, knowledge that can be codified and that can be written and easily transferred or acquired) (Teece et al., 1997). As such, it may be possible to acquire technical capability via employees who have technical knowledge. In contrast to technical capabilities, managerial and entrepreneurial capabilities are likely to be based on tacit knowledge and personal experience, and are consequently more difficult to imitate or acquire externally.

Habitual entrepreneurs may be in a better position to appreciate this difference. Given the difference in the relative importance likely to be given to technical capabilities by novice and habitual entrepreneurs, one would expect this to influence the level of perceived technical capability reported by each type of entrepreneur. Even though habitual entrepreneurs may have reported high technical capability for their first venture, technical knowledge and capability may erode over time and across ventures. To maintain their level of technical capability, entrepreneurs would have to update and upgrade their technical knowledge. Habitual entrepreneurs may be less likely than novice entrepreneurs to focus on developing their technical capability, especially if they believe that technical knowledge can be acquired through employees. In contrast, the former group may place greater emphasis on developing their managerial and entrepreneurial capabilities, which may be more difficult to acquire externally. Among habitual entrepreneurs, portfolio entrepreneurs may be more likely to report higher levels of technical capability than serial entrepreneurs, because of the potential for technical synergies across ventures. This discussion leads to the following hypotheses:

H_{4a} *Habitual entrepreneurs will report a lower technical capability than novice entrepreneurs.*

H_{4b} *Portfolio entrepreneurs will report a higher technical capability than serial entrepreneurs.*

Demographic Control Variables

Several demographic variables have been used as proxies for human capital. Gender and age variables are stock level measures of human capital; they do not represent aspects that can be developed or changed. In this study they are viewed as control variables.

Though the situation is changing, traditionally women have been associated with lower levels of human capital. Women are more likely to work part-time and withdraw, at least temporarily, from the labour force to have and raise children (Becker, 1993). Consequently, female entrepreneurs may have fewer opportunities to develop the relevant experience that allows them to acquire the resources necessary for business ownership (Sexton and Robinson, 1989; Cooper et al., 1994). Therefore, the likelihood of women becoming habitual entrepreneurs may be lower than that for male entrepreneurs. Indeed, empirical evidence supports this view (Kolvereid and Bullvåg, 1993; Rosa and Hamilton, 1994; Westhead and Wright, 1998a). Given the traditional earnings pattern of women, female entrepreneurs who become habitual entrepreneurs may be more likely to adopt the serial entrepreneur route (where business ownership takes place one at a time), rather than portfolio entrepreneurship.

Aldrich (1999) highlights that the age of an individual is strongly and positively correlated with work experience. Bates (1995) finds that age is expected to contribute to human capital and hence benefit the entrepreneur until diminishing effort associated with old age sets in. Kolvereid and Bullvåg (1993) as well as Westhead and Wright (1998a, b) found that habitual entrepreneurs started their first business at a younger age than novice entrepreneurs. However, not surprisingly, habitual entrepreneurs (serial entrepreneurs in particular) were older than their novice counterparts. Because serial entrepreneurs own businesses one at a time, there are likely to be gaps between business ownership. These gaps may explain why serial entrepreneurs were found to be older than portfolio entrepreneurs.

Entrepreneurship-Specific Human Capital

Entrepreneurial capability

The classical entrepreneurial role is seen as one where the entrepreneur scans the environment, selects promising opportunities and formulates strategies accordingly (Mintzberg, 1988; Thompson and Strickland, 1989). Penrose (1959) saw the entrepreneurial role as relating to the creation or acceptance of proposals for innovation, and for initiating and making decisions on proposals for expansion. The ability to recognize and envision taking advantage of opportunities (Timmons et al., 1987; Chandler and Jansen, 1992) appears to be at the heart of the entrepreneurial role, describing what is termed in this study as the entrepreneurial capability. In Chapter 1 it was suggested that habitual entrepreneurs display stronger entrepreneurial cognition and expert information processing. Greater reliance on heuristics (entrepreneurial cognition), it was argued, would allow habitual entrepreneurs to take advantage of brief windows of opportunity. Further, expert information processing involves unifying superficially disparate information, in turn facilitating the generation of opportunities. One would therefore expect habitual entrepreneurs possessing such cognitive qualities to display higher levels of entrepreneurial capability. Moreover their experience may give habitual entrepreneurs (over)confidence, suggesting higher reported levels of entrepreneurial capability than their novice counterparts.

As intimated in Chapter 1, we would expect habitual (and in particular portfolio) entrepreneurs to report higher levels of entrepreneurial cognition than novice entrepreneurs. The emphasis on novelty, the desire for personal prominence, the opportunity and wealth-creation drive (Katz, 1994) and strong entrepreneurial cognition provide a mix that would suggest that portfolio entrepreneurs will demonstrate entrepreneurial capability superior to their serial counterparts. From the above discussion, the following hypotheses can be derived:

H_{5a} *Habitual entrepreneurs will report a higher entrepreneurial capability than novice entrepreneurs.*

H_{5b} *Portfolio entrepreneurs will report a higher entrepreneurial capability than serial entrepreneurs.*

Parental background

Cooper et al. (1994) argued that human capital can be acquired directly through personal experience or through observing others, such as parents. Knowledge acquired this way (by observing others) is known as vicarious experience (Bandura, 1995). The occupation(s) of parents can influence the extent to which an individual is exposed to management and entrepreneurship. Having at least one business-owner parent can help to develop the human capital of the individual but also to modify one's expectations about what business ownership entails. Individuals whose parents are business owners appear to be much more likely to follow their parent's footsteps and become business owners themselves (Evans and Leighton, 1989; Curran et al., 1991; Brüderl et al., 1992). It has been argued that habitual entrepreneurs display stronger entrepreneurial cognition. This cognition can be formed in the early years, being reinforced through subsequent activities. When people have gained certain preferences and standards of behaviour, they tend to choose activities based on those preferences (Bandura, 1982; Deci, 1992a, b). Consequently, those individuals whose parents are business owners may be more likely to have developed an entrepreneurial cognition and are, therefore, more likely to become habitual entrepreneurs. Among habitual entrepreneurs, portfolio entrepreneurs who appear to be driven by opportunity identification and wealth creation to a greater extent than serial entrepreneurs may be more likely to be drawn from a background where their parents were business owners. The following hypotheses can be presented:

H_{6a} *Habitual entrepreneurs are more likely to have parent(s) who are business owners than novice entrepreneurs.*

H_{6b} *Portfolio entrepreneurs are more likely to have parent(s) who are business owners than serial entrepreneurs.*

Attitudes

Attitudes represent one aspect of cognition (Delmar, 2000). Behaviour in a given situation can be viewed as a function of the individual's attitude towards the situation (Fazio et al., 1983; Fiske and Taylor, 1991). Furthermore, Delmar (2000) argues that attitudes are proximal determinants of behaviour (that is, they are more specific and because of their specificity they are considered to be important determinants of behaviour). Given earlier definitions of entrepreneurial behaviour as involving the identification of opportunities, attitudes towards opportunity identification are important and represent one dimension of an entrepreneur's entrepreneurship-specific human capital.

Two broad approaches to opportunity identification are presented in the literature (discussed further below): the development/process approach and the alertness approach to opportunity identification. According to the developmental/process approach, opportunities are identified through search (Stigler, 1961), or through some kind of creative process. The search-based approach relies on the assumption that entrepreneurs know *a priori* where an opportunity can be found, and can accurately weigh the costs and benefits of acquiring new information relevant to the invention. Fiet (1996) argues that entrepreneurs invest in specific information surrounding a targeted invention, enabling them to be in a better position to discover the new opportunities. The creativity approach relies on the individual combining their existing knowledge and experiences with current information to create, or identify an opportunity (Long and McMullan, 1984; Witt, 1998).

The alertness perspective argues that the discovery of opportunities cannot be accurately modelled as a rational process. Rather, the focus of attention needs to be on 'entrepreneurial alertness'; the ability to see where products (or services) do not exist, or have unsuspectedly emerged as valuable. Alertness exists when one individual has an ability to recognize the value of an opportunity when it presents itself, while others do not (Kirzner, 1997). This perspective suggests a much less proactive approach to opportunity identification.

While there has been increasing interest in opportunity identification, there is limited consensus as to whether one perspective is superior to or more widely used than the other. It is possible that the search and alertness approaches to opportunity identification are not mutually exclusive. Circumstances may dictate when and where one approach is used over another. Further, the level and nature of business ownership experience may shape attitudes towards opportunity identification.

Expert information processing theory may provide some insight into the role of experience in shaping attitudes towards the approach to opportunity identification. Evidence from the expert information processing literature suggests there are differences between novices and experts in the way they process information. As intimated in Chapter 1, habitual entrepreneurs may display an information processing style (cognition) resembling that of an expert. Accordingly it was argued that habitual entrepreneurs were more likely to be able to manipulate incoming information into recognizable patterns and then match the information more strongly to appropriate actions (Lord and Maher, 1990). If habitual entrepreneurs are indeed similar to experts in this respect, they may be in a more favourable position to be alert to opportunities. This is because they are more able to make sense of the information and opportunities surrounding them.

While the above discussion suggests that habitual entrepreneurs may display a favourable attitude towards an alertness-based approach to opportunity identification, Long and McMullan (1984) argue that opportunity identification is a process, whereby social, personal (including knowledge and experience), cultural and technological forces come together, and result in the eventual development of an opportunity. In the early stages of the process, Long and McMullan emphasize the importance of experience, knowledge and education in the development of an opportunity. Due to their experience, habitual entrepreneurs may be in an advantageous position relative to their novice counterparts in adopting a developmental approach also. Furthermore their experience may allow them to be more effective in searching for and selecting the information that is most useful for the identification and development of an opportunity. There is no direct guidance in the literature to suggest that there are variations between portfolio and serial entrepreneurs with regards to the emphasis placed on developmental and alertness approaches to entrepreneurship. Some serial entrepreneurs report a 'reflective' period between ventures (Wright et al., 1997a), which may facilitate the 'development' of an opportunity. Conversely, portfolio entrepreneurs may be less likely to have time to develop an opportunity, but may be more alert to opportunities in the internal (within the businesses) and external environments. Based on this discussion, the following hypotheses are derived:

H_{7a} *Habitual entrepreneurs will place greater emphasis on being alert to opportunities than novice entrepreneurs.*

H_{7b} *Portfolio entrepreneurs will place greater emphasis on being alert to opportunities than serial entrepreneurs.*

H_{7c} *Habitual entrepreneurs will place greater emphasis on a developmental approach to identifying opportunities than novice entrepreneurs.*

H_{7d} *Portfolio entrepreneurs will place less emphasis on a developmental approach to identifying opportunities than serial entrepreneurs.*

Venture-Specific Human Capital

Knowledge of the venture domain
A measure of specific human capital is an entrepreneur's knowledge of the venture domain relating to customers, suppliers, products, and services (Gimeno et al., 1997). Yet such knowledge and associated ties largely lose their value outside their original context. This knowledge should be directly related to the degree of similarity between the new venture and the organization where the

entrepreneur was previous employed, or had an ownership stake. The level of business similarity may be critical to venture success, favouring those entrepreneurs who have been exposed to it (Sandberg, 1986; Cooper et al., 1994). In addition, similarity between the new venture and the prior experience may allow the entrepreneur to build on prior relationships with relevant stakeholders. Consequently, this may minimize the 'liability of (organizational) newness' (Stinchcombe, 1965; Aldrich and Auster, 1986).

Knowledge of the venture domain is likely to be important for both novice and habitual entrepreneurs. Habitual entrepreneurs who have been through the process of business ownership may have the confidence to venture into areas where they have relatively limited knowledge (Wright et al., 1997a). This may be facilitated by their strong reliance on entrepreneurial cognition, which allows habitual entrepreneurs to make decisions with limited information. Alternatively, hubris may lead experienced habitual entrepreneurs to venture into a territory where they have limited knowledge. However Shane (2000) found that knowledge relating to a particular market is crucial to identifying opportunities in that area. Furthermore an entrepreneur's previous investments and repertoire of routines (that is their history) can constrain future behaviour (Minniti and Bygrave, 2001). Path dependency may be more of an issue for habitual entrepreneurs, such that they choose activities that reinforce their previous inclinations (Bandura, 1982).

To reduce business risk, portfolio entrepreneurs may choose to have a 'diversified portfolio' of businesses, suggesting lower levels of business similarity. On the other hand, portfolio entrepreneurs may be more likely to benefit from ensuring some similarity between their previous background and the several businesses they own. By doing so, similar resources can be used to manage and develop their businesses. Further, there may be benefits accruing from potential synergies between the businesses owned.

Chandler and Jansen (1992) argue that a distinction needs to be made between task environment similarity (as described above) and skills similarity. The latter is associated with: the level of knowledge, skills and abilities; managerial duties; technical–functional duties and tasks performed. One would expect the nature of the relationship between prior business ownership experience and task environment similarity to hold for skills similarity. Therefore, based on the above discussion, the following hypotheses are derived:

H_{8a} *Habitual entrepreneurs will report higher levels of task environment similarity between their current business venture and their previous main business activity than novice entrepreneurs.*

H_{8b} *Portfolio entrepreneurs will report higher levels of task environment similarity between their current business venture and their previous main business activity than serial entrepreneurs.*

H_{8c} *Habitual entrepreneurs will report higher levels of skills similarity between their current business venture and their previous main business activity than novice entrepreneurs.*

H_{8d} *Portfolio entrepreneurs will report higher levels of skills similarity between their current business venture and their previous main business activity than serial entrepreneurs.*

Motivations

Motivations also represent an important aspect of cognition. Attitudes differ from motivation in that attitudes refer to what the individual finds important or unimportant, whilst motivation relates to what the individual likes or dislikes. Together, attitudes and motivations tend to form a set of preferences that guide our choices (Delmar, 2000). Two types of motivation can be observed: intrinsic and extrinsic motivation. Intrinsic motivation is closely related to interest and enjoyment. Intrinsically motivated behaviours are ones for which there is no apparent reward except for the activity itself. In contrast, extrinsic motivation is based on external motivators (such as acting to reap some reward, not necessarily because the task is attractive) (Deci, 1992b; Amabile et al., 1994). Extrinsically motivated behaviours involve behaviours where an external controlling variable (for example, approval or money) can be readily identified by the person acting. Individuals driven by extrinsic motivation tend to do less well than those driven by intrinsic motivation (Delmar, 2000). Furthermore, intrinsic motivation is seen as both an antecedent and a consequence of high self-efficacy (that is, a high perception of personal capabilities) (Bandura, 1991, 1995).

There are a variety of intrinsic and extrinsic motivations for entrepreneurship (Scheinberg and MacMillan, 1988; Birley and Westhead, 1994). Common intrinsic motivations include personal development independence/autonomy (Gimeno et al., 1997). In contrast motivations based on financial considerations, a need for approval and the welfare of others represent extrinsic motivations. While there is some consensus regarding the key motivations for entrepreneurship, there is conflicting evidence about the motives of novice and habitual entrepreneurs. Hence despite there being previous work on this theme, there is still a need to resolve the debate. While Donckels et al. (1987), Gray (1993) and Hall (1995) found autonomy to be a key motivation for novice entrepreneurs and less so for habitual entrepreneurs, Wright et al. (1997b) and Westhead and Wright (1998a) found that this was a key motivation for novice as well as habitual entrepreneurs. In addition, while earlier studies (Donckels et al., 1987; Gray, 1993; Hall, 1995) found that wealth and materialistic motives become predominant in subsequent ventures owned by habitual entrepreneurs Wright et al. (1997b) found that this extrinsic motive was less important for habitual entrepreneurs in subsequent ventures. Habitual entrepreneurs who have been through the experience of owning a business must be sufficiently motivated to want to continue their career in entrepreneurship. While extrinsic motivations such as wealth may be important for them, it is most likely that they enjoy and achieve personal satisfaction from entrepreneurship to justify their involvement in subsequent ventures. Enjoyment and personal satisfaction (and development) represent intrinsic motivations and are likely to be more stable than extrinsic motivations, which are dependent on an external driver that may change. As intimated above, intrinsic motivation is both an antecedent and consequence of self-efficacy. Habitual entrepreneurs associated with higher levels of self-efficacy (see earlier sections on capabilities and entrepreneurial capability) can re-enforce their intrinsic motivations. Thus, the following hypothesis can be derived:

> H_{9a} *Habitual entrepreneurs will place greater importance on intrinsic motivations for entrepreneurship than novice entrepreneurs*

It is not obvious *a priori* why and if there would be a difference between serial and portfolio entrepreneurs with respect to intrinsic and extrinsic motivations. Some of the earlier discussion on the distinction between serial and portfolio entrepreneurs in Chapter 1 offers some insight. Based on their career anchor, serial entrepreneurs are more likely to be associated with the autonomy/independence motive, and are more likely to be driven by the desire to have freedom from the control of others. Moreover they are likely to be involved in ventures one at a time so as to ensure that autonomy resides with them. Autonomy and the desire for independence have been cited as a form of intrinsic motivation (Gimeno et al., 1997). In contrast, it was argued that portfolio entrepreneurs are characterized as having an entrepreneurship anchor. This anchor induces portfolio entrepreneurs to be motivated by the opportunity-recognition process and wealth creation. Supporting this view, Westhead and Wright (1998b) found that portfolio entrepreneurs were more likely than novice or serial entrepreneurs to emphasize wealth-related motives for establishing a business. This discussion suggests that portfolio entrepreneurs are more likely to be driven by extrinsic motives. In contrast, serial entrepreneurs are more likely to be driven by intrinsic motives. However, this difference between serial and portfolio entrepreneurs may not be so clear. The entrepreneurship anchor may also be interpreted in another way, whereby the entrepreneur is motivated by the entrepreneurial process itself (an intrinsic motivation). If the entrepreneurial process is seen as involving opportunity identification, it may simply be the case that portfolio entrepreneurs select opportunities on the basis of their wealth creating potential, even though wealth may not be the dominant driver. Nonetheless, the following speculative hypothesis is presented:

H_{9b} *Serial entrepreneurs will place greater importance on intrinsic motivations for entrepreneurship than portfolio entrepreneurs, who will place greater emphasis on extrinsic motivations.*

THEME II: THE ENTREPRENEURIAL PROCESS

While novice, serial and portfolio entrepreneurs may be distinguished on the basis of their human capital characteristics, how they utilize their human capital is also important. In this section, three key dimensions of the entrepreneurial process are explored: information search, opportunity identification and opportunity pursuit/exploitation.

One of the fundamental reasons for the fascination with entrepreneurs centres around why and how they spot new business opportunities. An entrepreneurial opportunity invariably involves the development of some new idea that most others overlook. In the context of environmental change, those with entrepreneurial intentions (Bird, 1992; Krueger, 1993; Krueger and Brazeal, 1994) and (cognitive) orientation (Busenitz and Lau, 1996; Sarasvathy, 2001) often see new opportunities where most others are concerned with protecting themselves from emerging threats and changes resulting from uncertainty. While stocks of information (knowledge) create mental schemas providing a framework for recognizing new information, opportunity recognition and information search by entrepreneurs may be a function of an individual's capacity to handle complex information (Venkataraman, 1997). Various components of human capital may aid the development of mental schemata (in other words the cumulative experience; learning and meanings an individual has encountered and constructed about a specific domain) conducive to the identification and exploitation of opportunities. For example, individuals with higher levels of human capital (especially entrepreneurship-specific human capital) may have a more developed mental schema that they can use to make assessments, judgements or decisions surrounding opportunity identification and exploitation (Mitchell et al., 2002). Further, human capital endowments may influence the extent and nature of information search. As such, it can be argued that the information search patterns of entrepreneurs and their ability to identify and exploit opportunities will be a function of their human capital. In the following subsections the relationship between human capital (in particular business ownership experience) and the three aforementioned aspects of entrepreneurial behaviour are discussed: information search, opportunity identification and opportunity exploitation.

Information Search

Debate surrounds the matter of how entrepreneurs identify business opportunities. From an inductive viewpoint (as adopted by Kirzner), business opportunities are available in the environment and are waiting to be discovered. Conversely, from a deductive viewpoint, imaginative entrepreneurs can make use of their experience, subjective understanding and current information to identify business opportunities (Witt, 1998). The former view parallels Kirzner's (1973) modern Austrian tradition, whereby the possession of idiosyncratic information allows people to see particular opportunities that others cannot see, even if they are not actively searching for opportunities. Irrespective of which viewpoint is taken, information in some format is necessary, but not sufficient, for the identification of a business opportunity.

Why some people identify opportunities and others do not is related to the information (and knowledge) they possess (Venkataraman, 1997). Information plays a key role in the identification and exploitation of opportunities (Casson, 1982; Gilad et al., 1989; Shane, 2000). If information facilitates the identification of an opportunity, individuals may choose to increase their access to opportunities by searching for information. The level and nature of experience (and knowledge) acquired over time may influence the search for information. Individuals with no prior business ownership experience have fewer benchmarks to assess whether the information they have collected is appropriate to identify and exploit a business opportunity.

Cooper et al. (1995) suggested that novice entrepreneurs would search for less information, due to their limited understanding of what is needed. Conversely, habitual entrepreneurs would attend to more signals and have a better appreciation of the value of information being sought than novice entrepreneurs. Consequently, habitual entrepreneurs would generally seek more information than novice entrepreneurs. Contrary to expectation, Cooper et al. (1995) detected that novice entrepreneurs, on average, sought more information than habitual entrepreneurs. McGrath and MacMillan (2000: 3) argue that habitual entrepreneurs avoid 'analyzing ideas to death' and, therefore avoid deliberate, time-consuming and analytically correct models. Fiet et al. (2001) suggest that habitual entrepreneurs may be less likely to engage in extensive search strategies. They may be more likely to concentrate on searching within a more specific domain of venture ideas based on routines that worked well in the past. By focusing on a smaller number of more diagnostic items of information, experienced entrepreneurs can avoid information overload, which can degrade their decision-making capabilities (Jacoby et al., 2001).

Evidence elsewhere suggests that when an ill-structured problem is encountered individuals with high levels of knowledge will attempt to add structure by making inferences and drawing on existing knowledge (Simon, 1973). In addition, highly knowledgeable and experienced individuals in a particular domain ('experts') have been found to be more selective in the information they acquire, are better able to acquire information in a less structured environment, and exhibit more flexible information search behaviour (Spence and Brucks, 1997)[1].

Over time, habitual entrepreneurs may acquire contacts that provide them with a flow of information relating to business opportunities (Kaish and Gilad, 1991; Rosa, 1998), implying that they may need to be less proactive in the search for opportunities and information. Having earned a reputation as a successful entrepreneur, financiers, advisers, other entrepreneurs and business contacts may present business proposals to some habitual entrepreneurs (Ucbasaran et al., 2003b).

Ronstadt (1988) asserted that the best new venture opportunities may only be revealed when the individual is involved in a venture. This is because greater information becomes available about relevant contacts, viable markets, product availability and competitive resources during this process. Similarly McGrath (1999) has argued that habitual entrepreneurs (particularly portfolio entrepreneurs) may be more likely to pursue ventures as a means of gaining access to a wider range of 'shadow options' (that is, business opportunities that had not been previously recognized) than novice entrepreneurs. Since by definition portfolio entrepreneurs are involved in a number of ventures simultaneously they may be more likely to be presented with an opportunity without having to proactively search for it. Further, serial entrepreneurs may have a longer 'reflective' period between their ventures, which allows them to search for opportunities and relevant information.

Based on the above discussion the following hypotheses are derived:

H_{10a} *Habitual entrepreneurs will search for less information than novice entrepreneurs.*

H_{10b} *Portfolio entrepreneurs will search for less information than serial entrepreneurs.*

Opportunity Identification

Several conceptual views of opportunity identification exist. Two broad approaches will be discussed here: the 'instantaneous' view and the 'process' view of opportunity identification. The 'instantaneous' view is largely based on Austrian economist Kirzner's (1973) 'entrepreneurial alertness' concept. This 'alertness' approach to opportunity identification is an inductive one (Witt, 1998), where opportunities are available in the environment and are waiting to be discovered. Kirzner (1973) used the term entrepreneurial alertness to describe the ability of certain individuals to see where products (or services) do not exist, or have unexpectedly emerged as valuable. Alertness exists when one individual has an insight into the value of a given resource when others do not. From this perspective, entrepreneurial alertness refers to 'flashes of superior insight' that enable one to recognize an opportunity when it presents itself (Kirzner, 1997). Research in the field of cognitive science has shown that people vary in their abilities to combine existing concepts and information into new ideas (see Ward et al., 1997 for a review). Recently Gaglio and Katz (2001) have suggested that like most psychological constructs alertness may also lie on a continuum, with 'non-alert' and 'alert' being the two extremes. This suggests that there may be variations among entrepreneurs in terms of their ability to be alert. This ability may in turn be determined by the make-up of the individual's human capital. Indeed, adopting an Austrian view of opportunity identification, Shane (2000) found that those individuals with higher levels of prior knowledge (human capital) were more likely to discover opportunities.

Long and McMullan (1984) suggest that opportunity identification is a process that occurs over time, rather than a single moment of inspiration. Accordingly, opportunity identification is seen to be the result of a myriad of personal, social, cultural and technological forces, which somehow meld together and lead to the perception of a possible market opportunity. In this creative process the first step is preparation, which represents the knowledge an individual acquires regarding the language and rules of the salient domain (Gaglio, 1997). The amount and kind of preparation an individual has achieved is determined by their experience, knowledge and training (Long and McMullan, 1984). Opportunities are identified or created in an imaginative act by combining individual experience, subjective understanding and current information in a most complex associative way (Witt, 1998). Because human capital reflects such knowledge and experience and in turn can facilitate access to information, it is clear to see the relevance of human capital in understanding opportunity identification from a process perspective.

The view of opportunity identification as a process has a long-standing tradition in neoclassical economics. The neoclassical view is based on the notion of the entrepreneur as an economic agent searching for opportunities for profit (Stigler, 1961). According to this perspective, information search is a means of optimizing performance. Discoveries are generally modelled to be the result of an extensive search targeted in the direction of where the discovery is to be made (Stigler, 1961; Caplan, 1999). This approach generally assumes that entrepreneurs know *a priori* where the invention needs to be made and can accurately weigh the cost and benefits of acquiring new information relevant to the invention. The human capital of the entrepreneur may be critical in determining the extent to which the entrepreneur can 'know' where an invention needs to be made. Human capital may also be associated with the ability of the entrepreneur to 'accurately weigh' the costs and benefits of acquiring new information.

Building on the search perspective, Herron and Sapienza (1992) assume that an individual will engage in conscious search for a profitable business opportunity only when they are motivated properly. As this search involves costs, its extent will depend on the potential benefits. The actual opportunity is seen as emerging from some form of subconscious integration of information obtained during the search process. While Herron and Sapienza (1992) do not elaborate on how this subconscious integration occurs, those with superior levels of human capital may once again have an advantage because of their extensive knowledge, experience and skills.

This discussion suggests that irrespective of which of these two approaches is adopted, human capital is likely to be associated with opportunity identification. We now focus on the more specific relationship between business ownership experience and information search. While habitual entrepreneurs may engage in less extensive information search, this does not necessarily mean that they identify fewer opportunities. First, the limited information that they do acquire may be more useful in that it is specific to a particular opportunity (for example, knowledge of people, local conditions and special circumstances) (Hayek, 1945, Fiet, 1996). While novice entrepreneurs may conduct more intensive information searches, the information that they acquire may be more general (perhaps widely available) and not particularly useful. Second, the ability to utilize information is at least as, if not more, important than the information itself. Even if a person possesses the information necessary to identify an opportunity, he or she may fail to do so because of an inability to see new means–ends relationships (Shane and Venkataraman, 2000).

One of the limitations of the 'alertness' approach is that it has largely ignored the possibility for variations among entrepreneurs. Gaglio and Katz (2001) have argued that Kirzner's alertness theory relates to one extreme of an alertness continuum, but does not explore the possibility of other points on the continuum. Prior business ownership experience may allow habitual entrepreneurs to be more alert to opportunities than inexperienced novice entrepreneurs. Experience-based knowledge can direct an individual's attention, expectations, and interpretations of market stimuli, thus facilitating the generation of ideas (Gaglio, 1997). Habitual entrepreneurs may draw on their business ownership experience to 'see' business opportunities that are ignored, or not recognized, by inexperienced novice entrepreneurs. Further, in a given period of time portfolio entrepreneurs who are driven to a greater extent by opportunity identification and wealth creation, and who do not mind exploiting multiple opportunities simultaneously, may identify more opportunities. In contrast, serial entrepreneurs who seek to exploit opportunities one at a time, and tend to be driven more by the desire for autonomy, may be less alert to opportunities in a given time period. The following hypotheses are, therefore, presented:

H_{11a} *In a given time period, habitual entrepreneurs will identify a greater number of opportunities than novice entrepreneurs.*

H_{11b} *In a given time period, portfolio entrepreneurs will identify a greater number of opportunities than serial entrepreneurs.*

While opportunity identification is a necessary condition for entrepreneurship it is not sufficient (Day, 1987; Shane and Venkataraman, 2000). The exploitation of the opportunity is also important. The following section explores this theme.

Opportunity Pursuit/Exploitation

There is an implicit assumption in many studies on opportunity identification that identified opportunities will be automatically exploited. This is not necessarily the case. Exploitation activities are perhaps the most under-researched aspect of entrepreneurship (Shook et al., 2003). Though sparse, the literature on opportunity exploitation focuses on the decision to exploit, and the mode of exploitation (Shane and Venkataraman, 2000; Shook et al., 2003). Variations in human capital can be related to the decision to exploit an opportunity and/or how it is exploited. These themes are explored in this section with particular emphasis on their relationship to the level and nature of business ownership experience.

The decision to pursue an opportunity

Individuals consider the opportunity cost of pursuing alternative activities in reaching their decision to exploit an opportunity, and pursue an opportunity when the opportunity cost is lower (Reynolds, 1987; Amit et al., 1995). The transferability of information from prior experience to the opportunity (Cooper et al., 1989), as well as prior entrepreneurial experience (Carroll and Mosakowski, 1987), increases the probability of exploiting a business opportunity because learning reduces its cost (Shane and Venkataraman, 2000). Further, individual cognition can influence the decision to exploit an opportunity. Based on attribution theory, Ucbasaran et al. (2003c) suggest that the way in which entrepreneurs evaluate their experiences will determine their decision to exploit subsequent ventures. Palich and Bagby (1995) found that people who exploit opportunities tended to have more positive perceptions of the opportunity and information relating to it. Moreover optimism and in some cases overconfidence may increase the likelihood of an entrepreneur exploiting an opportunity (Cooper et al., 1988; Kaish and Gilad, 1991; Kahneman and Lovallo, 1994; Busenitz and Barney, 1997).

In the previous section the relationship between previous business ownership experience and the number of opportunities identified in a given time period was discussed. It would follow that here the relationship between business ownership experience and the number of opportunities exploited should be considered. This, however, would be tautological in the context of this study because the number of opportunities exploited is the basis for our definitions of novice and habitual entrepreneurs. An alternative is to examine a stage between opportunity identification and exploitation: this stage is termed the pursuit stage in this study. In deciding whether to exploit an opportunity, the expected value of the return from the venture must exceed the opportunity cost of alternatives, but also offer the individual a premium for bearing uncertainty (Kirzner, 1973; Schumpeter, 1934). The pursuit stage involves time and resource commitments to evaluate the costs and benefits of exploiting the venture idea.

Even though there is no conclusive empirical evidence, casual observation suggests that not all identified opportunities are brought into fruition (Shane and Venkataraman, 2000). The extent to which an individual invests time and resources into evaluating (pursuing) an opportunity is likely to be a function (at least partly) of the individual's human capital characteristics. Opportunity exploitation, for example, has been found to be affected by positive perceptions (Palich and Bagby, 1995); a high tolerance of ambiguity (Begley and Boyd, 1987); and the extent of the use of heuristics such as representativeness (Busenitz and Barney, 1997). Here, it is suggested an entrepreneur's human capital profile (particularly business ownership experience) will be associated with opportunity pursuit behaviour. The transferability of information from business ownership experience to the opportunity (Carroll and Mosakowski, 1987; Cooper et al., 1989) can increase the probability of pursuit, because experience and learning can reduce costs of exploitation (Shane and Venkataraman, 2000). Individuals with prior experience may expect to receive a higher return on their investment (that is, time and resources invested during the pursuit stage), thereby increasing the likelihood of pursuit.

If habitual entrepreneurs have a broader knowledge base and access to further resources, they may feel better prepared to exploit an opportunity once it has passed the evaluation (pursuit) stage. Consequently if habitual entrepreneurs are more likely to have the ability and resources to exploit an opportunity, they may be more likely to pursue it. There seems little point investing time and resources into evaluating an opportunity if one feels ill-prepared to eventually exploit it. Moreover due to their business ownership experience, habitual entrepreneurs may identify better-quality opportunities (or at least hold the belief that they have identified better-quality opportunities), in turn increasing the likelihood of their pursuit. For a set of opportunities identified in a given time period the following hypothesis is derived:

H_{12a} *Habitual entrepreneurs will pursue a greater proportion of identified opportunities in a given time period than novice entrepreneurs.*

The literature offers limited guidance that would allow a distinction between serial and portfolio entrepreneurs with respect to opportunity pursuit. However earlier discussion surrounding the mindsets of portfolio and serial entrepreneurs may offer some insights. It has been argued that serial entrepreneurs are motivated largely by autonomy and control. In contrast, portfolio entrepreneurs are motivated by opportunities for wealth creation. Out of a particular set of identified opportunities, only a few may offer wealth creating potential, suggesting that portfolio entrepreneurs will pursue a smaller proportion of identified opportunities. On the other hand, portfolio entrepreneurs may be more likely to realize that wealth cannot be created unless opportunities are exploited. They may therefore be more likely to pursue an identified opportunity relative to serial entrepreneurs. Further, portfolio entrepreneurs who already own multiple businesses may have access to a greater variety of resources (such as networks, finance, and so on) that can facilitate the pursuit and eventual exploitation of additional opportunities. The following exploratory hypothesis is presented:

H_{12b} *Portfolio entrepreneurs will pursue a greater proportion of identified opportunities than serial entrepreneurs.*

The mode of exploitation

There is considerable heterogeneity among exploitation modes selected by entrepreneurs (Venkataraman and MacMillan, 1997; Shane and Venkataraman, 2000; Ucbasaran et al., 2001). Firm creation, or the *de novo* firm start-up, is by far the most common mode of business opportunity exploitation. It has received attention from those with perspectives ranging from organizational ecology (Aldrich, 1999), economics (Gerlowski, 1995; Caves, 1988) to organizational theory (Gartner, 1985; Katz and Gartner, 1988; Low and MacMillan, 1988). Entrepreneurship can, however, involve existing organizations (Casson, 1982; Cooper and Dunkelberg, 1986; Amit et al., 1993; Shane and Venkataraman, 2000; Ucbasaran et al., 2001). An opportunity for entrepreneurship can occur through: corporate venturing/entrepreneurship; the purchase of an existing organization (including the management buy-out and buy-in of an organization) (Wright et al., 1992, 1996); franchising (Spinelli and Birley, 1996); and the inheritance and development of family firms (Westhead and Cowling, 1998). As ownership *and* opportunity identification are both considered key to entrepreneurship (see the definitions in Chapter 1) in this study the remaining discussion focuses on start-ups and purchases of businesses.

As well as influencing the initial decision to exploit an opportunity, human capital can also influence the mode of exploitation. Chandler and Hanks (1994) suggested that businesses should select strategies to generate rents based upon their resource capabilities. In a similar vein, entrepreneurs should select a mode of exploitation that best suits their human capital endowment (Harvey and

Evans, 1995). For example, an entrepreneur with limited entrepreneurial experience may be able to reduce the perceived risks involved in entrepreneurship by purchasing an existing business and transforming it as a means of exploiting a new opportunity, rather than creating a new business from scratch (Shook et al., 2003). On the other hand, entrepreneurs with prior entrepreneurial experience may be able to raise financial capital more easily and in greater quantities making the purchase of a business as a mode of exploitation more feasible. The main motivation for entrepreneurship may also influence the mode of exploitation; an entrepreneur motivated by the desire to develop an idea, the desire for a challenge and autonomy may be more likely to opt for a start-up than the acquisition of an existing business.

The purchase of a business as a means of exploiting an opportunity has often been viewed as a way to avoid the risks involved in creating a business (Shook et al., 2003). Also, it has been viewed as being less 'entrepreneurial' than a business start-up (Cooper and Dunkelberg, 1986). This view may be too simplistic and potentially misleading for several reasons. First, Cooper and Dunkelberg (1986) used rather basic measures of motivations and attitudes to determine the extent to which an entrepreneur was 'entrepreneurial', with limited attention to behaviour and outcomes. Second, transforming a business to exploit a new opportunity may involve significant risks if the business brings along with it characteristics that are difficult to change or adapt. For example, reputation and relationships with various stakeholders (such as customers and employees) may be difficult to change. Further, there is a body of empirical evidence relating to management buy-outs (involving the purchase of established businesses from within), which shows that purchasers can be highly entrepreneurial with respect to behaviour and outcomes such as new product introductions, research and development expenditure, goals and strategies, and so on. (Wright et al, 1992, 1995; Zahra, 1993). Robbie and Wright (1996) argue that management buy-ins (where an outside management team purchases an existing business) tend to be very risky, often requiring considerable entrepreneurial initiative. Finally, a greater amount of initial capital may be needed to purchase a business relative to a business start-up, where funds may be injected into the business incrementally. Hence, the view that a purchase is less risky or entrepreneurial is questionable.

Having established that both independent business start-ups and purchases are viable modes of opportunity exploitation, attention is now turned to the relationship between the choice of mode and the level and nature of prior business ownership experience reported by entrepreneurs. Entrepreneurs should select a mode of exploitation which best suits their knowledge and skills (their human capital) (Harvey and Evans, 1995). Habitual entrepreneurs with experience and access to a broader range of resources may have greater flexibility in deciding how to exploit an opportunity. Further, habitual entrepreneurs (particularly serial entrepreneurs) may be more likely to purchase a business because in many cases they have better access to financial resources (either by relying on their reputation and track record to raise external finance or through their own funds from businesses they have sold). Given their experience in owning and managing a business, habitual entrepreneurs may be in a better position to implement change in a purchased business relative to novice entrepreneurs. Portfolio entrepreneurs who may be concerned about ensuring coordination between the businesses that they own may be able to ensure a better fit by starting up a business and moulding it, to ensure that synergies across their various businesses can be reaped. The above discussion suggests the following hypotheses:

H_{13a} *Habitual entrepreneurs will be more likely to purchase a business than novice entrepreneurs.*

H_{13b} *Serial entrepreneurs will be more likely to purchase a business than portfolio entrepreneurs.*

THEME III: OUTCOMES

The entrepreneurial process can lead to numerous outcomes. In this study, outcomes are viewed largely in terms of performance. Empirical studies exploring the outcomes of entrepreneurship have focused on various financial and non-financial yardsticks to measure firm-level growth and performance (Birley and Westhead, 1990b; Chandler and Hanks, 1993; Cooper, 1993; Bridge et al., 1998). The identification of factors associated with business performance has implications for prospective and practising entrepreneurs, policymakers and investors. Firm performance studies face a number of challenges (Cooper, 1993). Entrepreneurs pursue a wide variety of goals, some of which are non-economic in nature (Birley and Westhead, 1994). Furthermore the heterogeneity of firms in terms of scale and potential complicates the task of identifying factors associated with firm-level performance. Researchers have used a variety of performance indicators, making comparisons across studies problematic. Factors associated with survival, for example, may be very different to those associated with growth or profitability. Further, firm-level performance indicators may provide an incomplete picture of the outcomes of entrepreneurship.

Whilst several studies have focused upon the personality and traits of entrepreneurs, the performance of entrepreneurs has received limited research attention. According to Cooper and Artz (1995) satisfaction is a fundamental measure of performance for the individual entrepreneur and examining the satisfaction of entrepreneurs offers a number of practical benefits. Satisfaction may bear on decisions made by entrepreneurs about whether to continue or close down their venture(s), as well as whether to invest more time and money, or cut back. Moreover greater levels of satisfaction may translate into superior business performance, as more satisfied entrepreneurs may work more effectively with their stakeholders. Indeed, satisfaction, with performance measures, have proven to show strong internal consistency and reliability (Chandler and Hanks, 1993; Cooper and Artz, 1995). Satisfaction with performance may be a function of the expectations of the founder about objective performance and may not, therefore, reflect objective performance (Chandler and Hanks, 1993). However satisfaction measures which incorporate expectations have been developed (Naman and Slevin, 1993). Furthermore even though satisfaction may not represent an objective performance measure, it does represent an outcome upon which the entrepreneur is likely to subsequently act.

Another important, though somewhat neglected, outcome of the entrepreneurial process is the issue of firm exit (Birley and Westhead, 1993a; Stokes and Blackburn, 2002). The term business exit has often been used synonymously with business failure. Brüderl et al. (1992) examined the contribution of human capital theory and organizational ecology explanations of new firm failure. Their analysis suggests that variables reflecting the latter approach, such as the number of employees, capital invested and organizational strategies, are the most important determinants of firm survival. However characteristics of the founder, notably years of schooling and work experience, were also found to be important determinants. Human capital may therefore be associated with business failure. Defining organizational closure or 'failure', however, is a major problem and a variety of definitions has been utilized (Keasey and Watson, 1991). There is no universally accepted definition of the point in time when an organization can be said to have closed (or 'failed'). For example, the development of management buy-outs of companies in receivership suggests that although a firm may have failed in terms of one configuration of resources, it may be possible to resurrect it in another form (Robbie et al, 1993).

The entrepreneur's decision to exit from the current business may not strictly be the result of 'failure', or poor financial/economic performance. The decision to exit depends on an entrepreneur's own threshold of performance, which is determined by human capital characteristics (for example, alternative employment opportunities, psychic income derived from entrepreneurship and the switching costs involved in moving to other occupations; see Gimeno et al., 1997). If economic performance falls below this threshold the entrepreneur may exit the business, but if performance is above this threshold they may continue with the business. If we accept the perspective that entrepreneurship relates largely to the recognition and exploitation of opportunities, it follows that opportunities may emerge at any time, and in various forms. The option to exit from a firm may also be viewed as the exploitation of a strategic window of opportunity by the entrepreneur. Hence, the entrepreneur may choose to sell a firm if an attractive offer is put forward. Alternatively, the entrepreneur may choose to exit a firm if a more appealing venture (opportunity) is accessible.

Although there is increasing recognition that multiple indicators of performance need to be used (that is, firm and entrepreneur level indicators), many studies still fail to appreciate the diversity of entrepreneurs and organizations owned by them. This diversity raises opportunities for researchers because there is a need to learn more about how types of entrepreneur or types of organization influence relationships between predictors and outcomes (Cooper and Artz, 1995; Chandler, 1996). The remainder of this section explores potential performance differences between novice and habitual entrepreneurs (and also serial and portfolio entrepreneurs).

As discussed in Chapter 1, previous business ownership experience is generally viewed as a positive contributor to an entrepreneur's human capital. It is reasonable to assume, therefore, that habitual entrepreneurs will own ventures with superior performance. Despite the widely held view that experience is a key asset and will lead to superior performance, the empirical evidence has not strongly supported this. Hart et al. (1997) found that both the depth and breadth of prior founding experience was an important contributor to success in garnering and maintaining access to resources. However evidence relating to the superior performance of businesses owned is less conclusive. Numerous studies have failed to detect a difference between novice and habitual entrepreneurs with regard to the performance of the surveyed or latest business owned (Chandler and Jansen, 1992; Birley and Westhead, 1993b; Kolvereid and Bullvåg, 1993; Westhead and Wright, 1998a, b, 1999). These findings cast doubt on some of the traditional economic approaches to entrepreneurial learning, for example Jovanovic (1982) who argues that experience will allow entrepreneurs to learn about their abilities and modify their subsequent behaviour accordingly. However this approach implicitly assumes that individuals are equally able to learn. Further, the approach ignores the possibility that experienced individuals in particular may be prone to a number of biases with respect to learning. Indeed, Starr and Bygrave (1991) argue that prior business ownership experience is associated with assets as well as liabilities (Table 2.2 provides a list).

Business ownership experience can be associated with several liabilities. It can reduce motivation to work as hard as in the previous venture, result in risky projects, create a fixation on previous success or failure and reduce flexibility. Some habitual entrepreneurs may be subject to biases and blind spots, such as overconfidence, that influence their decisions and goals in subsequent ventures. Furthermore, through experience an entrepreneur may develop the inertia of conventional wisdom, which may be challenged by others who bring a fresher perspective. This negative impact of experience may be considered 'the liability of staleness' (Starr and Bygrave, 1991: 222). While experience may aid the development of networks, habitual entrepreneurs who favour familiar circles and

Table 2.2 *The assets and liabilities of business ownership experience*

Assets	Liabilities
Expertise and wisdom	Biases and blinders (such as overconfidence)
Network of relationships/ access to resources	Strong ties
Reputation/legitimacy	Success syndrome
Reduces liabilities of newness and smallness	Increases liabilities of 'staleness', 'sameness', 'priciness' and 'costliness'

Source: Adapted from Starr and Bygrave (1991).

customary relationships over the unknown and obscure may be stuck in routine patterns of interpersonal interactions that hinder their ability to innovate, thereby leaving them suffering from the 'liability of sameness'. An additional liability is the 'success syndrome'. This may result from the entrepreneur becoming particularly vulnerable to the hazards of success. As the entrepreneur develops a track record, possibly allowing him or her to obtain finance more easily, un-realistic risk–return performance expectations regarding the venture may be made, creating the 'liability of priciness'. The availability of resources, or easier access to resources in subsequent ventures, may also mean that subsequent ventures built with large amounts of capital may be subject to the 'liability of costliness'.

The assets and liabilities approach to evaluating business ownership experi-ence is useful, but somewhat static (Ucbasaran et al., 2003b, c). Introducing issues relating to learning and cognition provides a more dynamic view. Cogni-tive processes are difficult to change and can therefore be a source of sustained competitive advantage or disadvantage for entrepreneurs (Busenitz and Barney, 1997; Alvarez and Busenitz, 2001). Habitual entrepreneurs who effectively reflect on and evaluate their experiences can develop expertise in various stages of the entrepreneurial process, such as opportunity recognition, or resource acquisition. However the cognitive orientation of an entrepreneur may not al-ways be an advantage. Individuals generally adjust their judgement by learning from feedback about past decisions (Bazerman, 1990). Due to delays or bias in this feedback individuals may be prone to errors in their learning. Because of this problem some entrepreneurs may exhibit basic judgemental biases that are unlikely to be corrected in the real world (Tversky and Kahneman, 1986). Hence while cognitive processes may be a source of sustained competitive advantage in certain circumstances, they may limit the ability of some entre-preneurs to adapt in response to changing or different market and technological conditions.

Habitual entrepreneurs who rely extensively on heuristics may be particularly prone to decision-making errors and bias. Nisbett and Ross (1980) argue that an indiscriminate use of heuristics can lead people into serious judgemental errors. Heuristics may influence one's perception of uncertainty and complexity, resulting in the danger that habitual entrepreneurs, particularly those operating in the same sector as their previous venture, attempt to replicate actions that were previously successful (perhaps through hubris). If experienced entrepreneurs are not aware of (or fail to respond to) changing external environmental conditions and indiscriminately use heuristics, there is a risk that they may make serious mistakes when operating their subsequent ventures. Louis and Sutton (1991) argue that individual effectiveness is not determined by how well an individual functions in a particular cognitive mode (whether heuristic-based or a more systematic mode). Rather, individuals who are able to 'switch cognitive gears' are likely to be more effective in a given domain.

This discussion illustrates the considerable debate surrounding the performance-enhancing potential of business ownership experience. It is difficult, therefore, to establish a clear direction of association between experience and performance. However, consistent with the stance adopted throughout the chapter, it will be assumed that business ownership experience will make a positive contribution to both firm and entrepreneur performance. This is based on discussions leading to previous hypotheses, which have suggested that habitual entrepreneurs will have accumulated higher levels of human capital (general and specific). Further, given the relative emphasis placed on wealth creation by portfolio entrepreneurs, one can expect them to report superior performance to that of serial entrepreneurs. Thus:

H_{14a} *Habitual entrepreneurs will report superior firm and entrepreneur performance to that of their novice counterparts.*

H_{14b} *Portfolio entrepreneurs will report superior firm and entrepreneur performance than that of their serial counterparts.*

As intimated earlier, Jovanovic (1982) suggests that experience provides a means through which an individual can assess his or her true entrepreneurial ability. If as a result of experience individuals recognize their lack of ability, the expectation is that they will eventually exit from an entrepreneurial career. This is a simplistic view however, which does not explain why certain individuals who have failed in one venture may become involved in another in the future. Further, what is deemed a success by one entrepreneur may be deemed a failure by another entrepreneur (Gimeno et al., 1997).

The evaluation of a venture as a success or a failure may influence learning by the entrepreneur as well as subsequent behaviour and performance. Attribution theories (Heider, 1958) suggest that individuals have a tendency to attribute their successes to themselves (internal attribution), and failure to external factors (external attribution). These theories suggest that individuals can display biases when learning. Success is frequently sought, while failure is avoided (McGrath, 1999). However, individuals who have failed may be able to improve their subsequent performance because they may be forced to evaluate their thinking and behaviour (Sitkin, 1992). In contrast, there may be minimal incentive to evaluate or reconsider thinking patterns and behaviours if success is the outcome (irrespective of the causes of that success). The ability of entrepreneurs to objectively reflect on and evaluate their experiences (whether they are successes or failures) may be critical in determining their future performance. The extent to which business ownership experience is associated with performance may, therefore, be influenced by the nature of previous experiences. Based on this discussion the following exploratory hypotheses are derived:

H_{14c} *Habitual entrepreneurs who have failed will report superior firm and entrepreneur performance than novice entrepreneurs.*

H_{14d} *Habitual entrepreneurs who have been successful will report superior firm and entrepreneur performance than novice entrepreneurs.*

CONCLUSION

While entrepreneurship is widely acknowledged as being a multi-disciplinary topic, an examination of the literature suggests that certain views have dominated entrepreneurship research at various points in time. Each of these approaches (for example, the economic approach, the trait approach, the sociological/environmental approach) has faced criticisms. One common criticism is that these theoretical approaches do not provide enough guidance to understand entrepreneurial behaviour and the entrepreneurial process. To address this concern, a human capital framework for viewing entrepreneurship was developed. Accordingly, the entrepreneur is viewed in terms of his or her human capital (broadly defined). These human capital characteristics in turn can influence the decisions of the entrepreneur and the outcomes associated with those decisions. The human capital framework presented allows us to respond to calls that any theoretical model should integrate the outcomes of entrepreneurial efforts and the processes that led to those outcomes (Low and MacMillan, 1988).

Guided by this human capital framework, a number of hypotheses have been developed for investigation regarding human capital, behaviour and outcomes-based differences between novice and habitual entrepreneurs, as well as serial

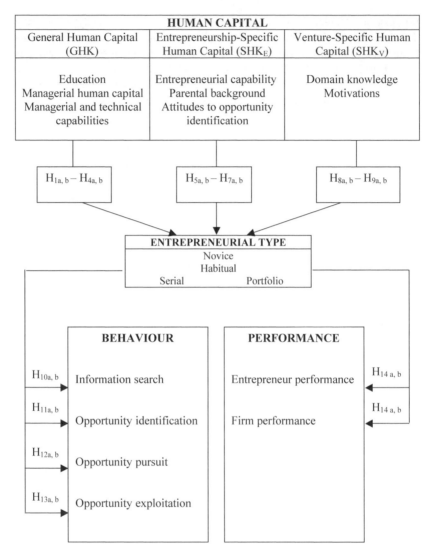

Figure 2.2   Overview of hypotheses

and portfolio entrepreneurs. A summary of these hypotheses is provided in Figure 2.2.

In the next chapter the data collection and methodology are discussed. The hypotheses are then tested in Chapters 4, 5 and 6.

NOTE

1. On the downside, confidence may limit an entrepreneur's ability to objectively assess their own strengths and weaknesses, biasing their opinions surrounding the amount of information required (Cooper et al., 1988). Indeed, one of the liabilities of experience is overconfidence.

3.   Data collection and methodology

INTRODUCTION

This chapter discusses the methodology utilized to test the hypotheses developed in the previous chapter. In the following section we explain our sampling procedure, how we collected the data and from whom. Details relating to the operationalization of the concepts used to test the hypotheses are then provided. Particular attention is given to assessing the quality of the data. The generalizability of the findings and the validity and reliability of measures and constructs used are carefully considered. An overview of the background characteristics of the sample of firms (and their owners) is then provided. Finally, concluding comments are presented.

SAMPLE, DATA COLLECTION AND RESPONDENTS

The sampling frame was constructed by obtaining sampling quotas by four broad industrial categories (agriculture, forestry and fishing, production, construction and services) and the 11 Government Official Regions from summary tables detailing the population of businesses registered for Value Added Tax in Great Britain in 1999 (Office for National Statistics 1999). After excluding non-independent businesses, industry and standard region sampling proportions were identified for a stratified random sample of independent private businesses.

A stratified random sample of 4324 independent firms was drawn from a cleaned list of business names provided by Dun and Bradstreet. A structured questionnaire was mailed during September 2000 to a single key respondent in each of the selected businesses based on two criteria: (a) possession of sufficient knowledge, and (b) adequate level of involvement with regard to the issues under investigation (Campbell 1955). Thus, the key respondent was a founder and/or principal owner who was also a key decision-maker in the business. To further ensure the validity of our data and that we had identified the correct key informant we included a number of validation items in the questionnaire. Based on these validation items, 54 respondents were identified as not being a founder and/or the principal owner of the business, and were regarded as non-respondents. Given the key issues under exploration in this study (opportunity identification and pursuit) and the emphasis on the entrepreneur as the unit of analysis, a key informant approach was adopted (Kumar et al., 1993). Although information was not available from multiple respondents, reliability checks were conducted on key firm-level variables such as business age, employment size and legal status. There was a strong correlation between these variables reported by the key informant and the archival data provided by Dunn and Bradstreet. The correlations ranged from 0.77 to 0.88 suggesting that the data collected from the key informant was reliable.

During the four-month data collection period, a further 17 responses were eliminated as they indicated the business was no longer an independent trading entity. After a three-wave mailing (the initial questionnaire and two reminders), 767 valid questionnaires were obtained from a valid sample of 4307 independent firms, producing a 17.8 per cent valid response rate. This response rate compares favourably with similar studies (Storey 1994). For example, Forbes's (2005) recent study finds an effective response rate of 16.6 per cent.

MEASURES

For clarity, Tables 3.1–3.4 provide details of the measures derived from the questionnaire. The tables are organized to reflect the three core themes high-lighted in previous chapters: human capital (general and specific); the entrepreneurial process (that is, information search, opportunity identification, pursuit and exploitation); and firm and entrepreneur performance. Tables 3.1 and 3.2 provide a description of measures relating to general human capital and specific human capital, respectively. In Table 3.3 measures relating to the entrepreneurial process, in particular information search, opportunity identification, pursuit, and exploitation are described. Finally, Table 3.4 details the measures relating to the financial and non-financial performance of the surveyed business and entrepreneur performance. The tables identify the measures used in the analysis discussed later, their description, the source of the measure (if borrowed or borrowed and amended), and finally the coding. Issues relating to the validity and reliability of scale-based measures will be discussed later.

'TRUSTWORTHINESS': GENERALIZABILITY, VALIDITY AND RELIABILITY

Three fundamental issues must be considered if research findings are to be viewed as trustworthy. Results have to be generalizable to the setting and sample population (Salkind, 2000). To ensure generalizability of findings, researchers

Table 3.1 Measures relating to general human capital

Theme	Name of variable	Description	Source (where applicable)	Value	Coding Meaning
General human capital (GHK)	Education	Highest level of education obtained		0 1 2	Pre-university qualification Undergraduate degree Postgraduate qualification
	Gender	Gender of respondent		1 0	Male Female
	Age	Age of respondent in years	Gimeno et al., (1997)		Deviation from the mean age of respondents in years[a]
	Managerial human capital	Managerial level of attainment (where 1 represented 'supervised no-one', 2 represented 'supervised others' and 3 represented 'manager or self-employed') was multiplied by the number of previous jobs held (ranging between 1 and 7, where 1 represented 'no previous jobs' and 7 represented '6 or more previous jobs'	Based on Gimeno et al., (1997)		Managerial human capital (minimum 1, maximum 21)
	Managerial capability	Perceived level of managerial capability	Chandler and Hanks (1998)		Based on PCA component scores
	Technical capability	Perceived level of technical capability	Chandler and Hanks (1998)		Based on PCA component scores

Note: [a] Deviation from the mean for this variable was used to minimize problems of multicollinearity when age^2 was included in multivariate analysis (Aiken and West, 1991).

Table 3.2 Measures relating to specific human capital

Theme	Name of variable	Description	Source (where applicable)	Value	Coding Meaning
Human capital specific to entrepreneurship (SHK_E)	Parent business owner	Principal occupation of parent (the main income earner) was business owner		1 0	Parent business owner Otherwise
	Entrepreneurial capability	Perceived level of entrepreneurial capability (opportunity identification)	Chandler and Hanks (1998)		Based on PCA component scores
	– Development – Alertness[a]	Attitudes toward opportunity identification – views opportunities as being developed over time – opportunities are identified through being alert	Hills et al., (1997)		Based on PCA component scores
	HABITUAL	Whether the respondent is a habitual entrepreneur		1 0	Habitual entrepreneur Novice entrepreneur
	TOTAL	Total number of minority and majority businesses owned			
	PORTFOLIO	Whether the respondent is a portfolio entrepreneur		1 0	Portfolio entrepreneur Serial entrepreneur
	HABITUAL_failed	Whether the respondent is a habitual entrepreneur who reported that the proportion of business which had failed (i.e., had closed/sold a business because the performance was too low in relation to the entrepreneur's expectations or had faced bankruptcy, liquidation or receivership) was greater than those which had been sold/closed because there was an opportunity to realise a capital gain or a better opportunity presented itself		1 0	Habitual entrepreneur who has failed Novice entrepreneur

53

Table 3.2 continued

Theme	Name of variable	Description	Source (where applicable)	Value	Coding Meaning
	HABITUAL$_{successful}$	Whether the respondent was a habitual entrepreneur who reported that the proportion of businesses which had failed (i.e., had sold/closed a business because the performance was too low in relation to the entrepreneur's expectations or had faced bankruptcy, liquidation or receivership) was less than those which had been sold/closed because there was an opportunity to realise a capital gain or a better opportunity presented itself		1	Habitual entrepreneur who is successful
				0	Novice entrepreneur
	HABITUAL$_{Mixed \, (no \, exit)}$	Whether the respondent was a habitual entrepreneur who had not closed or sold any businesses (a 'pure' portfolio entrepreneur).		1	Habitual entrepreneur with no exit
				0	Novice entrepreneur
	HABITUAL$_{Mixed \, (with \, exit)}$	Whether the respondent was a habitual entrepreneur who had closed or sold the same number of businesses due to failure and success.		1	Habitual entrepreneur with equal failures and successes
				0	Novice entrepreneur

Human capital specific to entrepreneurship (SHK$_E$)

Theme	Name of variable	Description	Source (where applicable)	Coding
Human capital specific to entrepreneurship (SHK$_E$)	Motivation: – Independence (intrinsic) – Personal development (intrinsic) – Approval (extrinsic) – Welfare (extrinsic) – Reactive (extrinsic) – Financial (extrinsic)	– Need for independence – Concerned with personal development – Need for approval – Concerned about welfare of others – Concerned with responding to an opportunity – Concerned with financial issues	Birley and Westhead (1994)	Based on PCA component scores
	Business similarity	Knowledge of business (such as product/service, customers, suppliers, technology and competitors)	Chandler and Jansen (1992); Chandler (1996)	Based on PCA component scores
	Task similarity	Knowledge of task (such as knowledge, skills and abilities needed; managerial duties; technical–functional duties and tasks performed)	Chandler and Jansen (1992); Chandler (1996)	Based on PCA component scores

Note: [a] This item was ignored in further analysis due to low reliability.

55

Table 3.3 Measures relating to opportunity identification

Name of variable	Description	Source	Coding	
Information search intensity	The usefulness (based on a 6-point scale, where 0 corresponded to 'did not use', 1 corresponded to 'not at all useful' and 5 corresponded to 'very useful') of 8 sources of information which were used by at least 60% of respondents (suppliers, employees, customers, friends, family, magazines/newspapers, trade publications and other business owners) were summated	Cooper et al., (1995)	Summated scale	
Opportunities identified	Number of opportunities for creating or purchasing a business identified ('spotted') within the last five years	Hills et al. (1997)	1	0 opportunities
			2	1 opportunity
			3	2 opportunities
			4	3 opportunities
			5	4 opportunities
			6	5 opportunities
			7	6–10 opportunities
			8	8 or more opportunities

Opportunities pursued	Number of opportunities for creating or purchasing a business pursued (that is, committed time and financial resources to) within the last five years	Hills et al., (1997)	As above		
Opportunities success	Number of pursued opportunities perceived as a success (in terms of meeting original expectations)	Hills et al., (1997)	As above		
Opportunities identified/ opportunities pursued	Proportion of identified opportunities pursued			0	No identified opportunities were pursued
				1	Less than 50% of identified opportunities were pursued
				2	50% or more opportunities were pursued
				3	All identified opportunities were pursued

Table 3.4 Measures relating to firm and entrepreneur performance

Name of variable	Description	Source	Coding
Weighted performance (I)	Based upon the importance attached to 6 performance indicators (sales, sales growth, cash flow, return on equity, gross profit margin, net profit from operations, each rated on a scale of 1 'very little importance' to 5 'extremely important') and the level of satisfaction with each of these indicators (on a scale of 1 'highly dissatisfied' to 5 'highly satisfied'). Importance and satisfaction scores were multiplied (Cronbach's alpha score of 0.82) and divided by 6.	Naman and Slevin (1993)	Ranges from 1–25
Weighted performance (II)	Based upon the importance attached to 12 selected performance indicators (sales, sales growth, cash flow, return on equity, gross profit margin, net profit from operations, business survival, reputation and status of business, employee security, independent ownership of business, employment of family members, maintain/enhance lifestyle, each rated on a scale of 1 'very little importance' to 5 'extremely important') and the level of satisfaction with each of these indicators (on a scale of 1 'highly dissatisfied' to 5 'highly satisfied'). Importance and satisfaction scores were multiplied (Cronbach's alpha score of 0.83) and divided by 12.	Extended version of Naman and Slevin (1993)	Ranges from 1–25
Absolute total employment change	Difference between total employment in 2001 and 1996, where total employment included full-time, part-time and casual employees, weighted as 1, 0.5 and 0.25, respectively (logged).		A constant value was added to avoid negative values so that a logarithm could be taken

Percentage change in total employment	Percentage change in total employment between 1996 and 2001, where total employment included full-time, part-time and casual employees, weighted as 1, 0.5 and 0.25, respectively.		
Absolute change in sales	Difference between the sales level reported for 1996 and 1999 (logged).		A constant value was added to avoid negative values so that a logarithm could be taken
Percentage change in sales	Percentage change in sales between 1996 and 1999.		
Profit relative to competitors	Current profit performance (i.e., operating profit) of surveyed business relative to competitors.	Birley and Westhead (1990a)	1 represents 'very poor', 5 represents 'very good'.
Money taken out	Money taken out of the business(es) owned in previous 12 months	Gimeno et al., (1997)	1 Less than £5000 2 £5001–10000 3 £10001–15000 4 £15001–25000 5 £25001–35000 6 £35001–50000 7 £50001–75000 8 £75001–100000 9 More than £100000
Money taken out (I)	Money taken out measure described above converted into an interval level measure by taking mid-points		
Money taken out (II)	Money taken out (I) standardized by the number of businesses currently owned (minority and/or majority)		

59

must seek to gather a representative random sample of respondents drawn from the specified population of respondents. Data analysis also relies on measurements and findings being both reliable and valid (Salkind, 2000). A reliable measure is one on which we can depend for obtaining consistent responses. Assessment tools must be reliable otherwise research hypotheses may be rejected even though they may actually be correct. However, even if we establish that a measure is reliable, we then face the problem of knowing whether our measures actually measure what we say they do: this problem relates to validity. A necessary but insufficient condition for validity is to ensure that reliable measures have been used in the study (Robson, 1993).

In this section, issues relating to the gathering of a representative (that is, generalizable) dataset are first discussed. This is followed by discussions of the validity and reliability of the measures operationalized in this study.

Generalizability: Population Sampling, Representativeness and Response-Bias Tests

To assess whether the results from the sample can be generalized to the population of independent businesses in Great Britain, chi-square tests were conducted to detect differences between responding and non-responding businesses. With regard to region, industry, age, legal status and size of the business in terms of employment, no statistically significant differences were detected between the two groups of businesses (Table 3.5). On these criteria it can be argued that the generalizability (also known as external validity) of this study is established.

Validity and Reliability Tests Conducted

In this section, evidence relating to validity and reliability is presented. The construct validity of the scales used in this study was investigated in a number of ways. First, face and content validity issues were considered by an extensive survey of the literature. A pilot study was conducted to test the wording of the questionnaire. The pilot questionnaire was sent to six entrepreneurs (two novice, two serial and two portfolio), and a number of academics to ensure face and content validity. The questionnaire was modified on the basis of suggestions offered by the entrepreneurs. There were no serious problems except with one item, which was subsequently removed from the questionnaire.

Convergent and discriminant validity were judged using factor analysis (Hair et al., 1995). Following common practice, factor extraction was achieved using Principal Components Analysis (PCA) whereby linear combinations of the observed variables are formed. Several PCAs were computed to identify valid constructs/measures. To achieve a simpler, theoretically more meaningful component pattern, a rotation of the component matrix was carried out using the

Table 3.5   Response bias tests by industry, region, legal status, age and employment[a] [b]

Variable	Non-responding businesses		Responding businesses		Chi-square Statistic	Sig. Level
	No.	%	No.	%		
1. Main Industrial Activity of Business					2.71	0.44
Agriculture, forestry and fishing	299	8.4	62	8.1		
Production	343	9.7	80	10.4		
Construction	379	10.7	68	8.9		
Services	2518	71.2	557	72.6		
2. Government Office Region					15.45	0.12
Scotland	258	7.3	66	8.6		
South West	325	9.2	91	11.8		
South East	553	15.6	126	16.4		
North West	360	10.2	76	9.9		
North East	93	2.6	21	2.7		
Yorkshire and the Humber	262	7.4	58	7.6		
Wales	175	4.9	36	4.7		
London	604	17.1	96	12.5		
East Midlands	243	6.9	59	7.7		
West Midlands	301	8.5	62	8.1		
East of England	365	10.3	76	9.9		
3. Legal Status of Business					1.69	0.43
Proprietorship	1722	49.8	394	51.4		
Private limited company	1034	29.9	211	27.5		
Partnership	701	20.3	161	21.0		
4. Age of Business					3.74	0.15
1–10 Years	1041	33.9	274	36.0		
11–50 years	1800	58.7	445	58.4		
51 or over	226	7.4	42	5.5		
5. Number of Employees					7.19	0.13
1–5 employees	2129	64.1	479	65.5		
6–10 employees	501	15.1	109	14.9		
11–25 employees	411	12.4	92	12.6		
26–50 employees	150	4.5	37	5.1		
51 or more employees	129	3.9	14	1.9		

Notes:
[a]   Data provided by Dun and Bradstreet in 2000.
[b]   Only valid respondents were used.

VARIMAX orthogonal rotation method. Orthogonal rotations are more widely used than oblique rotation methods, and are subject to less controversy. Among the various orthogonal approaches, VARIMAX has been found to give a clearer and more stable separation of the components (Hair et al., 1995).

Two methods were used to test the appropriateness of the PCA, both of which are reported in the presented PCA models: the Barlett test of sphericity, which provides the statistical probability that the correlation matrix has significant correlations among at least some of the variables; and the Kaiser-Meyer-Ohlin (KMO) statistic which measures the degree of intercorrelation between variables and varies between zero and one (Hair et al., 1995). The KMO measure can be interpreted with the following guidelines: 0.90 or above – marvellous; 0.80 or above – meritorious; 0.70 or above – middling; 0.60 or above – mediocre; 0.50 or above – miserable; and below 0.50 – unacceptable.

In order to determine whether the resulting PCAs were satisfactory, the significance of the component loadings and the percentage of variance explained by each PCA solution were examined. To determine whether the number of components extracted was appropriate, we considered the percentage of variance criterion. Typically, in social sciences research, a solution that accounts for 60 per cent (or in some cases even less) of the variance is considered satisfactory (Hair et al., 1995).

The most popular method for judging reliability is with the use of the Cronbach's alpha coefficient, a measure of internal consistency which attempts to calculate the correlation between scale items. Conventional practice holds that scales with a Cronach's alpha of 0.7 and above are deemed reliable. The presented tables summarizing the PCA models (Tables 3.6–3.10) also report the Cronbach's alpha values corresponding to each identified construct/measure.

The remainder of this section reports on the basic structure and statistics associated with the various constructs/measures utilized in the analysis to test the presented hypotheses. The constructs/measures discussed relate largely to the various dimensions of human capital, in particular perceived capabilities; attitudes towards opportunity identification; motivations for owning the surveyed business; and the degree of business similarity. Finally, a set of constructs/measures relating to the overall strategies of the surveyed businesses is explored, as they are used as control variables in presented multivariate regression models.

Table 3.6 shows the results of the PCA carried out on the statements relating to the self-assessed perceived capabilities of the entrepreneur. Self-assessed capabilities or competencies are the core of individuals' self-efficacy beliefs about their personal capabilities to mobilize the motivation, cognitive resources and courses of action needed to exercise control over events in their lives (Wood and Bandura, 1989). Gist (1987) has provided evidence supporting strong relationships between perceived and actual competencies.

Table 3.6 Principal components analysis relating to an entrepreneur's capabilities (n = 683) [a] [b] [c]

Statements	Component 1: Entrepreneurial capability	Component 2: Managerial capability	Component 3: Technical capability	Communality (h^2)
I accurately perceive unmet customer needs	**0.70**	0.02	−0.04	0.49
One of my greatest strengths is identifying goods and services people want	**0.79**	0.16	0.02	0.65
One of my greatest strengths is my ability to seize high quality business opportunities	**0.71**	0.29	0.15	0.61
I have a special alertness or sensitivity towards spotting opportunities	**0.65**	0.22	0.18	0.50
I can usually spot a real opportunity better than professional researchers/ analysts	**0.69**	0.14	0.13	0.51
One of my greatest strengths is achieving results by organising and motivating people	0.19	**0.85**	−0.02	0.76
One of my greatest strengths is organising resources and co-ordinating tasks	0.14	**0.74**	0.07	0.57
One of my greatest strengths is my ability to delegate effectively	0.12	**0.82**	−0.02	0.68
One of my greatest strengths is my ability to supervise, influence, and lead people	0.20	**0.83**	0.10	0.75
One of my greatest strengths is my expertise in a technical or functional area	0.01	0.05	**0.88**	0.78
One of my greatest strengths is my ability to develop goods or services that are technically superior	0.23	0.02	**0.81**	0.71
Eigenvalue	1.72	4.00	1.29	
% of variance explained	24.36	25.45	13.89	
Cronbach's alpha	0.79	0.85	0.66	

Notes:
(a) Cumulative % of variance explained is 63.7%.
(b) KMO Measure of Sampling Adequacy = 0.81.
(c) Barlett's Test of Sphericity = χ^2 = 2660.5, p < 0.0001.

The results relating to the KMO statistic (0.81) and the Barlett's test ($p <$ 0.0001) are highly satisfactory, and confirm the appropriateness of applying a PCA to this subset of data. Three components were extracted which accounted for 63.7 per cent of the variance. Component 1 highlights 'entrepreneurial capability' and relates to five statements with significant component loadings focusing upon the identification of opportunities. Component 2 contains four statements relating to the ability to manage and organize people and resources. Consistent with the literature, this component represents the 'managerial capability' of the respondent. Component 3 highlights 'technical capability', and relates to two statements focusing upon technical expertise. The pattern of components appears to be logical and consistent with previous discussions concerning the capabilities of entrepreneurs, and as a result the measurement scales can be deemed to exhibit convergent validity. The scales also appear to exhibit discriminant validity in so far as the majority of statements only load significantly on one component. In addition, the reliability of the components is highly satisfactory, ranging from 0.66 to 0.85.

Table 3.7 shows the results of the PCA used to explore six statements, relating to entrepreneurs' attitudes towards the identification of business opportunities. The results relating to both the KMO statistic (0.69) and the Barlett's test ($p <$ 0.0001) are satisfactory, and confirm the appropriateness of applying a PCA to this subset of data. Two components were extracted which accounted for 54.8 per cent of the variance. Though not ideal, as intimated earlier, values less than 60 per cent are generally acceptable in social sciences research (Diamantopoulos and Hart, 1993; Hair et al., 1995). Component 1 highlights the 'developmental approach', and relates to four statements focusing upon the view that business opportunities develop over time. The component has a Cronbach's alpha of 0.70 suggesting reasonable reliability of the measure. Component 2 relates to two statements focusing upon an alertness-based approach to business opportunity identification. This component was labelled the 'alertness approach'. The reliability of this scale was low (Cronbach's alpha of 0.27) and it was, therefore, excluded from further analysis. Overall, the results suggest that the 'developmental approach' component is sufficiently valid and reliable.

Table 3.8 reports the results relating to the PCA used to identify components relevant to the motivations cited by the respondents for starting or purchasing the surveyed business. Twenty-four statements relating to motives for business ownership were presented to the respondents. The item relating to unemployment or redundancy as a motive for business ownership was dropped from the final PCA because it had a low communality (below 0.3). Results relating to the final PCA reported in Table 3.8 suggest that the data was appropriate for a PCA, as indicated by the KMO statistic (0.84) and the Barlett's test of sphericity ($p <$ 0.0001). Six components were extracted which accounted for an acceptable 61.3 per cent of variance. Component 1 has been named 'approval'

Table 3.7 Principal components analysis relating to attitudes towards opportunity identification (n = 682) [a] [b] [c]

Statements	Component 1: Developmental approach	Component 2: Alertness approach	Communality (h^2)
Identifying opportunities is really several steps over time	**0.80**	-0.08	0.65
It is very important that the idea represents a concept which can be developed over time	**0.80**	-0.05	0.64
The consideration of one opportunity often leads to other ones	**0.67**	0.23	0.50
New business opportunities often arise in connection to a specific problem	**0.59**	0.28	0.43
The business opportunities I have identified over the years have been largely unrelated	0.05	**0.70**	0.49
Ideas for new business opportunities do not require specific market or technological knowledge	0.07	**0.76**	0.58
Eigenvalue	2.18	1.11	
% of variance explained	34.75	20.09	
Cronbach's Alpha	0.70	0.27	

Notes:
(a) Cumulative % of variance explained is 54.8%.
(b) KMO Measure of Sampling Adequacy = 0.69.
(c) Barlett's Test of Sphericity = χ^2 = 540.4, p < 0.0001.

Table 3.8 Principal components analysis of entepreneurs' motivations (n = 650) [a] [b] [c]

Statements	Comp. 1 Approval	Comp. 2 Welfare	Comp. 3 Independence	Comp. 4 Personal development	Comp. 5 Financial	Comp. 6 Reactive	Communality (h²)
To achieve something and get recognition for it	**0.51**	0.01	0.45	0.32	0.02	0.03	0.56
To achieve a higher position for myself in society	**0.86**	0.09	0.03	0.11	0.16	0.14	0.80
To increase the status and prestige of my family	**0.83**	0.20	−0.01	0.10	0.23	0.10	0.80
To be respected by my friends	**0.79**	0.30	0.09	0.06	0.13	0.05	0.74
To have more influence in my community	**0.67**	0.40	0.05	0.12	0.15	−0.04	0.65
To follow the example of a person I admire	0.15	**0.53**	0.04	0.10	−0.06	0.40	0.47
To continue a family tradition	0.01	**0.73**	−0.03	0.01	0.08	0.08	0.55
To contribute to the welfare of my relatives	0.31	**0.50**	0.03	0.02	0.31	−0.06	0.46
To contribute to the welfare of the community I live in	0.28	**0.64**	0.05	0.19	0.08	−0.07	0.53
To contribute to the welfare of people with the same background as me	0.28	**0.67**	0.03	0.14	0.06	−0.02	0.54
To have considerable freedom to adopt my own approach to my work	0.03	−0.01	**0.79**	0.24	0.03	0.19	0.70
To control my own time	0.02	0.04	**0.84**	0.01	0.16	0.12	0.74

	1	2	3	4	5	6	h²
To have greater flexibility for my personal and family life	0.08	0.11	**0.65**	-0.03	0.41	-0.15	0.62
To be challenged by the problems and opportunities of owning a business	0.09	0.08	0.34	**0.65**	-0.06	0.05	0.57
To continue learning	0.21	0.17	0.18	**0.70**	-0.04	0.03	0.60
To be innovative and be in the forefront of technological development	0.15	0.12	0.01	**0.79**	0.12	0.01	0.67
To develop an idea for a product	-0.02	0.08	-0.13	**0.72**	0.20	0.05	0.58
To have access to indirect benefits such as tax exemptions	0.10	0.32	0.12	0.18	**0.68**	-0.01	0.62
As a vehicle to reduce the burden of taxes I face	0.09	0.41	0.09	0.09	**0.57**	0.01	0.52
To give myself, my spouse, and children security	0.23	0.04	0.12	-0.07	**0.64**	0.23	0.54
To generate personal wealth (earnings or capital gain)	0.22	-0.15	0.15	0.10	**0.65**	0.18	0.55
It made sense at that time in my life	0.09	-0.02	0.43	-0.07	0.05	**0.63**	0.59
To take advantage of an opportunity that appeared	0.07	0.07	-0.01	0.15	0.28	**0.77**	0.70
% of variance explained	14.04	11.20	10.25	10.42	9.51	5.88	
Eigenvalue	6.16	2.34	1.42	1.88	1.23	1.07	
Cronbach's alpha	0.86	0.73	0.74	0.74	0.68	0.51	

Notes:
(a) Cumulative % of variance explained is 61.3%.
(b) KMO Measure of Sampling Adequacy = 0.84.
(c) Barlett's Test of Sphericity = χ^2 = 5554.3, p < 0.0001.

to reflect motives for business ownership based on the desire for recognition, respect, status and influence. Component 2 has been named 'welfare' to largely reflect motives based on the desire to ensure the welfare of others (such as family, community and people with a similar background as the respondent). Component 3 relates to statements suggesting flexibility, control, autonomy and independence as a key motivation for business ownership and has consequently been named 'independence' to reflect this. Component 4 has been named 'personal development' to reflect motives such as 'the desire to be challenged by the problems and opportunities of owning a business', 'to be innovative and at the forefront of technological developments', and 'to continue learning'. Component 5 related to financial reasons for business ownership, such as the desire for financial security, to generate personal wealth, and to reduce one's tax burden or benefit from tax exemptions. Consequently, this component was named 'financial'. Finally, Component 6 related to reactive reasons for business ownership, such as taking advantage of an opportunity that presented itself or business ownership making sense at that particular point in time. Hence, Component 6 was named 'reactive'. The pattern of components appears to be logical and consistent with the themes identified in previous research concerning the motivations for business ownership, and as a result the measurement scales are deemed to exhibit convergent validity. They appear to exhibit discriminant validity in so far as the majority of statements only load significantly on one component. The reliability of the components is also highly satisfactory ranging from 0.68 to 0.86, with one notable exception. The final component 'reactive' was associated with a Cronbach's alpha score of 0.51. Though not ideal, Cronbach's alpha scores as low as 0.5 have been deemed acceptable in exploratory social science research (Diamantopoulos and Hart, 1993).

Table 3.9 reports the findings of the PCA carried out on items relating to the degree of similarity between the surveyed business and the respondent's previous main job or business. The KMO statistic (0.93) and Barlett's test of sphericity ($p < 0.0001$) suggest that the data was highly appropriate for carrying out a PCA. The PCA produced two components consistent with previous literature. The first of these was named 'task environment similarity' to reflect the degree of knowledge relating to the product or service, customers, suppliers, technology and competitors. The second component was named 'skills similarity' to reflect the degree of knowledge the entrepreneur possesses in relation to the knowledge, skills and abilities needed: managerial duties; technical–functional duties; and tasks performed in the surveyed business. The pattern of components appears to be logical and consistent with the themes identified in previous research relating to the degree of business similarity. Consequently, the measurement scales exhibit satisfactory convergent validity. They appear to exhibit discriminant validity in so far as the majority of statements only load

Table 3.9   Principal Components Analysis of Business Similarity (n = 660)
(a) (b) (c)

Statements	Component 1 Business similarity	Component 2 Task similarity	Communality (h^2)
Product or service	**0.85**	0.32	0.82
Customers	**0.87**	0.23	0.81
Suppliers	**0.84**	0.30	0.81
Technology	**0.70**	0.43	0.68
Competitors	**0.82**	0.26	0.73
Knowledge, skills and abilities needed	0.49	**0.67**	0.69
Managerial duties	0.09	**0.89**	0.80
Technical-functional duties	0.43	**0.76**	0.76
Task performed	0.49	**0.70**	0.73
Eigenvalue	5.81	1.02	
% of variance explained	44.65	31.18	
Cronbach's alpha	0.92	0.87	

Notes:
[a]   Cumulative % of variance explained is 75.83%.
[b]   KMO Measure of Sampling Adequacy = 0.93.
[c]   Barlett's Test of Sphericity = χ^2 = 44021.1, p < 0.0001.

significantly on one component. The reliability of the two components is also highly satisfactory ranging from 0.87 to 0.92.

Finally, Table 3.10 reports the findings of the PCA conducted on a set of items relating to firm-level strategies followed by the respondents. Several additional items were developed but were subsequently excluded from the PCA due to low levels of communality. The KMO statistic (0.80) and the Barlett's test of sphericity (p < 0.0001) both confirm that the data was conducive to a PCA. Consistent with Chandler and Hanks's (1994) original work, the PCA produced three components, named 'innovation', 'differentiation', and 'cost' to reflect the three broad strategies pursued by most businesses. These measures were developed to control for the effect of strategy on firm performance (see Chapter 6). Given the coherence of the components and their consistency with previous research, there is no cause to suspect the convergent validity of the resulting measures. Furthermore, the measures display discriminant validity in that the large majority of statements only load significantly on a single component. The reliability

Table 3.10 Principal components analysis of strategies followed (n = 674) [a][b][c]

Statements	Component 1: Innovation	Component 2: Differentiation	Component 3: Cost	Communality (h^2)
We strive to be the first to have products available	**0.76**	0.23	0.08	0.64
We stress new product/service development	**0.80**	0.26	0.10	0.72
We engage in novel and innovative marketing techniques	**0.77**	0.06	0.11	0.61
We invest heavily in Research & Development (R&D)	**0.56**	−0.16	0.30	0.43
We will go to almost any length to meet customer requirements	0.07	**0.77**	0.17	0.63
We emphasise our superior customer service	0.18	**0.83**	0.04	0.72
We focus on providing only highest quality goods and services	0.12	**0.78**	0.06	0.63
We emphasise that customer needs always come first	0.02	**0.82**	0.17	0.70
We emphasise cost reduction in all facets of business operations	0.01	0.19	**0.73**	0.57
We strongly emphasise improvement in employee productivity and operations efficiency	0.21	0.18	**0.75**	0.63
We have developed lower production costs via process innovation	0.23	0.02	**0.75**	0.61
Eigenvalue	1.88	3.73	1.27	
% of variance explained	20.67	25.16	16.67	
Cronbach's alpha	0.73	0.83	0.67	

Notes:
(a) Cumulative % of variance explained is 62.51%.
(b) KMO Measure of Sampling Adequacy = 0.80.
(c) Barlett's Test of Sphericity = χ^2 = 2364.8, p < 0.0001.

of the 'innovation', 'differentiation' and 'cost' strategy variables was 0.73, 0.83 and 0.67 respectively and were consequently satisfactory.

CHARACTERISTICS OF THE RESPONDENTS AND THEIR SURVEYED BUSINESS

Several key demographic characteristics of respondents are reported in this section. As intimated earlier, only respondents who were the founder and/or principal owner of the business were included in the final valid sample. These respondents had to be key decision-makers. It should be noted that while 767 entrepreneurs returned the questionnaire complete, 37 entrepreneurs were dropped from subsequent analysis. These were respondents who had only ever inherited a business or businesses. Given the ambiguity surrounding whether these individuals have actually identified an opportunity, they were excluded from the study. The valid sample is therefore 730. The status of the respondents is summarized in Table 3.11.

Table 3.11   Status of respondents

Status	Frequency	Percentage
Founder	308	42.2
Principal owner	160	21.9
Founder and principal owner	160	21.9
Founder, principal owner and other[a]	94	12.9
Founder and other[a]	3	0.4
Principal owner and other[a]	5	0.7
Total	*730*	*100.0*

Note: [a] Other relates to managing director, chairman or 'other' as specified by the respondent.

Table 3.12 provides information relating to the background characteristics of the respondents and their surveyed businesses.

In this study, individuals who had a minority or majority ownership stake and who were involved in the start-up and/or purchase of a business or businesses were considered as valid respondents. Not surprisingly, therefore, the scale of habitual entrepreneurship detected in this study is higher than in studies reported elsewhere (see Introduction), which have tended to focus on business start-ups alone. Out of the 730 entrepreneurs who responded to the survey, 352 respondents (48.2 per cent) were novice entrepreneurs and a further 378 respondents (51.8 per cent) were habitual entrepreneurs. Among the habitual entrepreneurs,

Table 3.12   Characteristics of respondents and surveyed businesses

Characteristics		Frequency/ mean	Percentage/ standard deviation
Respondents			
Gender	Male	628.0	14.0
	Female	102.0	86.0
Age		49.9	10.14
Parents immigrant?	Yes	46.0	6.3
	No	680.0	93.2
Highest level of education	Pre-UG degree	494.0	69.5
	UG degree	91.0	12.8
	PG degree	126.0	17.7
Surveyed businesses			
Path to ownership	Established	593.0	81.2
	Inherited[a]	26.0	3.6
	Purchased	111.0	15.2
Team-based ownership	Yes	261.0	35.8
	No	469.0	64.2
Age of business		18.8	18.2
Total employment[b]		26.1	371.7
Family business[c]	Yes	455.0	62.3
	No	275.0	37.7

Notes:
[a]   Only inheritors who had also established or purchased a business were considered.
[b]   Total employment includes full-time, part-time and casual employees, weighed at 1, 0.5 and 0.25, respectively.
[c]   More than 50% of voting shares are owned by a single family related by blood or marriage.

162 respondents (42.9 per cent) were serial entrepreneurs, while 216 respondents (57.1 per cent) were portfolio entrepreneurs. Table 3.13 provides a detailed breakdown of the type of ownership stake(s) held by the type of entrepreneur. The vast majority of novice entrepreneurs (84.7 per cent) held majority equity stakes in the business they owned. Further, 95.2 per cent of novice entrepreneurs had established the business they owned. Very few habitual entrepreneurs had just minority ownership stakes in businesses, with majority ownership, and minority and majority ownership being the more popular types of ownership (44.2 per cent and 51.9 per cent, respectively). Not surprisingly, a higher proportion of portfolio entrepreneurs (69.4 per cent) used a mixed strategy, while the

Table 3.13 Type of ownership held by novice and habitual (serial and portfolio) entrepreneurs

	Novice entrepreneurs (n = 352)		Habitual entrepreneurs (n=378)		Serial entrepreneurs (n = 162)		Portfolio entrepreneurs (n = 216)	
	No. (%)	% of total	No. (%)	% of total	No. (%)	% of total	No. (%)	% of total
Ownership stake:								
Minority ownership stake(s) only	54 (15.3)	7.4	15 (4.0)	2.1	10 (6.2)	1.3	5 (2.4)	0.7
Majority ownership stake(s) only	298 (84.7)	40.8	167 (44.2)	22.9	106 (65.4)	14.5	61 (28.2)	8.4
Majority and minority ownership stake(s)	N/A	N/A	196 (51.9)	26.8	46 (28.4)	6.2	150 (69.4)	20.6
Path to ownership:								
Start-up only	335 (95.2)	45.9	223 (59.0)	30.5	101 (62.3)	13.8	122 (56.5)	16.7
Purchase only	17 (4.8)	22.33	33 (8.7)	4.5	17 (10.5)	2.3	16 (7.4)	2.2
Mixed	N/A	N/A	122 (32.3)	16.7	44 (27.2)	6.0	78 (36.1)	10.7

majority of serial entrepreneurs (65.4 per cent) held majority stakes in the businesses they had owned. Both serial and portfolio entrepreneurs appeared to have a preference for start-up as a path to ownership (62.3 per cent and 56.5 per cent, respectively), though both groups also pursued a mixed strategy of start-up and purchase (27.2 per cent and 36.1 per cent, respectively).

CONCLUSION

This chapter has provided a discussion of the methodology utilized in this study. First, the research instrument and the sampling procedure were described. Second, the operationalization of the measures was discussed. Third, the issue of 'trustworthiness' was considered by emphasising the importance of generalizability of the results, and the validity and reliability of constructs used. Due to the relatively large sample size and the absence of non-response bias, the results from the study can be generalized to the wider population of independent business owners in Great Britain. The validity and reliability of the constructs/ measures to be used to test the presented hypotheses, were demonstrated. Where problems with validity and/or reliability were detected, steps were taken to ensure that the overall reliability and validity of the research would not be compromised. Most notably, components with low reliability and statements which did not exhibit convergent or discriminant validity were removed. Finally, the demographic characteristics of the responding entrepreneurs and their surveyed independent firms were briefly summarized.

A number of the respondents were also interviewed face-to-face. While useful, the quantitative nature of the study does not allow us to answer of number of 'how' and 'why' questions, in particular in relation to the entrepreneurial process. Therefore, the purpose of these interviews was to expand on a number of issues covered in the questionnaire. Where appropriate in the following chapters, evidence from these interviews is provided to supplement the quantitative evidence.

Overall, the analysis in this chapter suggests that it is reasonable to conclude that the dataset is of high quality in terms of the representativeness of the sample and the validity and reliability of the measures. The detailed investigation of the hypotheses developed in Chapter 2 follows in Chapters 4, 5 and 6, focusing on human capital, behavioural and performance-based differences between novice and habitual entrepreneurs, and then between serial and portfolio entrepreneurs respectively.

4. Human capital differences by type of entrepreneur

INTRODUCTION

This chapter examines differences in the human capital of different types of entrepreneur. The chapter commences with tests of the hypotheses developed in Chapter 2 using bivariate t-tests and Chi-square tests depending on the nature of the variable being explored. Hypotheses are tested that relate to general human capital (H_{1a} to H_{4b}), entrepreneurship-specific human capital (H_{5a} to H_{7d}) and venture-specific human capital (H_{8a} to H_{9b}). To ensure that inter-relationships among the independent variables are not overlooked, the bivariate analysis is followed by more robust multivariate analysis. In particular, given the dichotomous nature of the two dependent variables (whether the entrepreneur is a novice or a habitual entrepreneur, and whether the entrepreneur is a portfolio or serial entrepreneur), a logistic regression technique is utilized. This technique allows the identification of variables that are significantly associated with the selected dependent variables.

HUMAN CAPITAL BY TYPE OF ENTREPRENEUR: BIVARIATE ANALYSIS

This section provides a summary of the differences between novice and habitual entrepreneurs, and then serial and portfolio entrepreneurs with regard to their human capital. In turn, bivariate differences between the types of entrepreneurs are discussed in terms of general human capital, entrepreneurship-specific human capital and venture-specific human capital.

GENERAL HUMAN CAPITAL (GHK)

General human capital differences between the types of entrepreneurs are examined in relation to their highest level of education, managerial human capital, and technical and managerial capabilities.

Education

The entrepreneurs surveyed were asked to report their highest level of education. Table 4.1 shows that a statistically significant difference was not detected between novice and habitual entrepreneurs with regard to their highest level of education. These findings offer no support for hypothesis H_{1a}. We can conclude that habitual entrepreneurs do not report higher levels of education than novice entrepreneurs.

Table 4.1   Highest level of education reported by novice and habitual entrepreneurs

Variable	Novice		Habitual		χ^2 statistic	Sig. level (2-tailed)
	No.	%	No.	%		
Highest level of education					2.46	0.29
1. Below undergraduate 'first' degree[a]	271	72.8	256	68.3	1.89	0.17
2. Undergraduate 'first' degree[a]	45	12.1	47	12.5	0.03	0.91
3. Postgraduate degree[a]	56	15.1	72	19.2	2.26	0.15

Note: [a] Relates to respondents who answered 'yes' to this type of degree.

Table 4.2   Highest level of education reported by serial and portfolio entrepreneurs

Variable	Serial		Portfolio		χ^2 statistic	Sig. level (2-tailed)
	No.	%	No.	%		
Highest level of education					0.90	0.64
1. Below undergraduate 'first' degree[a]	112	70.4	144	66.7	0.60	0.50
2. Undergraduate 'first' degree[a]	20	12.6	27	12.5	0.01	1.00
3. Postgraduate degree[a]	27	17.0	45	20.8	0.88	0.43

Note: [a] Relates to respondents who answered 'yes' to this type of degree.

Table 4.2 shows that there was no significant difference between serial and portfolio entrepreneurs with respect to their highest level of education. Therefore, hypothesis H_{1b} cannot be supported.

Managerial Human Capital

To establish the nature of work experience acquired, respondents were asked to report on their job status immediately prior to starting, purchasing or inheriting their first business. Respondents selected from one of the following: 'managerial' (managerial experience), 'supervisory' (supervisory experience), 'self-employed' (self-employment experience) or 'supervised no one' (used as the reference category in further analysis). A statistically significant difference was established between novice and habitual entrepreneurs with regard to their level of attainment (Table 4.3). In particular, a significantly larger proportion of novice (29.2 per cent) rather than habitual entrepreneurs (21.7 per cent) indicated that they had 'supervised no one' ($p < 0.05$). Furthermore, a larger proportion of habitual rather than novice entrepreneurs reported managerial experience (34.8 per cent compared with 30.3 per cent), and self-employment experience (12 per cent compared with 9.2 per cent). These differences were not statistically significant.

Respondents were asked to indicate the number of full-time jobs they had held. Across all entrepreneurs surveyed, the mean number of full-time jobs held was 3.7. One entrepreneur had worked for 50 organizations, while under 4 per cent of entrepreneurs had not worked full-time in any organization. Table 4.3

Table 4.3   Level of attainment and number of full-time jobs held reported by novice and habitual entrepreneurs

Variable	Novice		Habitual		χ^2 statistic	Sig. level (2-tailed)
	No.	%	No.	%		
Level of attainment					6.72	0.08
1. Managerial experience	112	30.3	130	34.8	1.71	0.21
2. Supervisory experience	116	31.4	118	31.6	0.01	1.00
3. Self-employment experience	34	9.2	45	12.0	1.58	0.23
4. Supervised no one	**108**	**29.2**	**81**	**21.7**	**5.57**	**0.02**
Number of jobs					7.32	0.29
1. 0 previous FT jobs	15	4.2	12	3.3	0.41	0.56
2. 1 previous FT job	67	18.9	52	14.4	2.63	0.11
3. 2 previous FT jobs	59	16.6	69	19.1	0.73	0.44
4. 3 previous FT jobs	62	17.5	58	16.0	0.27	0.62
5. 4 previous FT jobs	62	17.5	60	16.6	0.10	0.77
6. 5 previous FT jobs	38	10.7	36	9.9	0.11	0.81
7. 6 or more previous FT jobs	**52**	**14.6**	**75**	**20.7**	**4.53**	**0.04**

shows that there was no significant difference between novice and habitual entrepreneurs with respect to the number of previous full-time jobs held. However, further analysis revealed that a significantly larger proportion of habitual entrepreneurs (20.7 per cent) had held six or more previous full-time jobs compared with novice entrepreneurs (14.6 per cent) ($p < 0.05$). Moreover, a significantly larger proportion of novice entrepreneurs (18.9 per cent) had held only one previous full-time job relative to their habitual counterparts (14.4 per cent) ($p < 0.10$). Taken together, the above evidence relating to the level of attainment and the number of previous jobs held suggests some support for hypothesis H_{2a}, that habitual entrepreneurs will report higher levels of managerial human capital.

For simplicity in later analysis, a new variable, 'managerial human capital' was created. This variable combined these two indicators. Details on how this measure was computed, was provided in Table 3.1. Table 4.4 shows that habitual entrepreneurs reported a significantly higher level of managerial human capital than their novice counterparts, lending support to hypothesis H_{2a}.

Table 4.4   Managerial human capital of novice and habitual entrepreneurs

Variable	Novice (n = 351)	Habitual (n = 358)	t-statistic	Df	Sig. level (2-tailed)
Managerial human capital	*9.06*	*10.23*	*−2.68*	*707*	*0.007*

To test hypothesis H_{2b}, differences between serial and portfolio entrepreneurs with respect to the level and nature of their managerial human capital were examined. Table 4.5 shows that there was a significant difference between serial and portfolio entrepreneurs in terms of their level of attainment ($p < 0.05$). A significantly larger proportion of portfolio entrepreneurs (40.7 per cent) reported they had managerial experience compared to their serial counterparts (26.9 per cent) ($p < 0.01$). Further, a significantly lower proportion of portfolio entrepreneurs (17.8 per cent) indicated that they had supervised no one, relative to serial entrepreneurs (26.9 per cent) ($p < 0.05$). There was no overall significant difference between serial and portfolio entrepreneurs in terms of the number of previous jobs held. Furthermore, Table 4.6 shows that there was no significant difference between the two types of entrepreneurs when the composite managerial human capital measure was utilized. Therefore, hypothesis H_{2b} is not supported.

Table 4.5   Level of attainment and number of full-time jobs held reported by serial and portfolio entrepreneurs

Variable	Serial		Portfolio		χ^2 statistic	Sig. level (2-tailed)
	No.	%	No.	%		
Level of attainment					*9.28*	*0.03*
Managerial experience	**43**	**26.9**	**87**	**40.7**	**7.67**	**0.01**
Supervisory experience	52	32.5	66	30.8	0.12	0.74
Self-employment experience	22	13.8	23	10.7	0.78	0.42
Supervised no one	**43**	**26.9**	**38**	**17.8**	**4.49**	**0.04**
Number of jobs					*6.72*	*0.35*
0 previous FT jobs	6	3.9	6	2.9	0.28	0.77
1 previous FT job	17	11.0	35	16.8	2.41	0.13
2 previous FT jobs	34	22.1	35	16.8	1.58	0.23
3 previous FT jobs	25	16.2	33	15.9	0.01	1.00
4 previous FT jobs	23	14.9	37	17.8	0.52	0.57
5 previous FT jobs	12	7.8	24	11.5	1.39	0.29
6 or more previous FT jobs	37	24.0	38	18.3	1.79	0.19

Table 4.6   Overall managerial human capital of serial and portfolio entrepreneurs

Variable	Serial (n = 154)	Portfolio (n = 204)	t-statistic	Df	Sig. level (2-tailed)
Managerial human capital	10.03	10.38	–0.56	356	0.58

Capabilities

As intimated in Table 2.1, entrepreneurial capabilities can be considered a component of human capital specific to entrepreneurship and are therefore explored later. Here, a distinction is made between a respondent's perceived level of managerial and technical capabilities. Table 4.7 shows that habitual entrepreneurs reported significantly higher levels of managerial capability than novice entrepreneurs ($p < 0.05$). Conversely, novice entrepreneurs reported significantly higher levels of technical capability ($p < 0.05$) than habitual entrepreneurs. These findings provide support for hypotheses H_{3a} and H_{4a}, respectively.

Among the habitual entrepreneurs, portfolio entrepreneurs reported a significantly higher level of managerial capability ($p < 0.05$) than serial entrepreneurs,

*Table 4.7   Perceived managerial and technical capabilities reported by
              novice and habitual entrepreneurs*

Variable (component scores)	Novice (n = 322)	Habitual (n = 361)	t-statistic	Df	Sig. level (2-tailed)
Managerial capability	**−0.09**	**0.08**	**−2.25**	**681**	**0.03**
Technical capability	**0.09**	**−0.08**	**2.10**	**681**	**0.04**

*Table 4.8   Perceived managerial and technical capabilities reported by
              serial and portfolio entrepreneurs*

Variable (component scores)	Serial (n = 157)	Portfolio (n = 204)	t-statistic	Df	Sig. level (2-tailed)
Managerial capability	**−0.04**	**0.18**	**−2.07**	**359**	**0.04**
Technical capability	−0.12	−0.04	−0.69	359	0.49

lending support for Hypothesis H_{3b} (Table 4.8). However, no significant difference was detected between serial and portfolio entrepreneurs with respect to their technical capability. Therefore, hypothesis H_{4b} could not be supported.

ENTREPRENEURSHIP-SPECIFIC HUMAN CAPITAL (SHK_E)

Entrepreneurial Capability

No significant differences were detected between novice and habitual entrepreneurs with regard to entrepreneurial capability (Table 4.9). Similarly, no significant difference was detected between serial and portfolio entrepreneurs (Table 4.10). Hypotheses H_{5a} and H_{5b}, therefore, cannot be supported.

Parental Background

Table 4.11 shows that a significantly higher proportion of habitual (27.9 per cent) rather than novice (19.7 per cent) entrepreneurs reported that they had parent(s) who were or are business owners. This finding lends support to hypothesis H_{6a}.

No significant difference was detected between serial and portfolio entrepreneurs with regard to parental business ownership (Table 4.12). Therefore hypothesis H_{6b} cannot be supported.

Table 4.9   Perceived entrepreneurial capability reported by novice and
*   habitual entrepreneurs*

Variable (component scores)	Novice (n = 322)	Habitual (n = 361)	t-statistic	Df	Sig. level (2-tailed)
Entrepreneurial capability	–0.01	0.01	–0.28	681	0.78

Table 4.10   Perceived entrepreneurial capability reported by serial and
*   portfolio entrepreneurs*

Variable (component scores)	Serial (n = 157)	Portfolio (n = 204)	t-statistic	Df	Sig. level (2-tailed)
Entrepreneurial Capability	–0.08	0.08	–1.41	359	0.16

Table 4.11   Parental business ownership reported by novice and habitual
*   entrepreneurs*

Variable	Novice		Habitual		χ^2 statistic	Sig. level (2-tailed)
	No.	%	No.	%		
Parent(s) business owner					6.90	0.01
Yes	73	19.7	105	27.9		
No	297	80.3	271	72.1		

Table 4.12   Parental business ownership reported by serial and portfolio
*   entrepreneurs*

Variable	Serial		Portfolio		χ^2 statistic	Sig. level (2-tailed)
	No.	%	No.	%		
Parent(s) business owner					0.39	0.56
Yes	42	26.3	63	29.2		
No	118	73.8	153	70.8		

Attitudes Toward Opportunity Identification

Table 4.13 shows that no significant differences between novice and habitual
entrepreneurs were detected with respect to statements relating to their attitudes

Table 4.13   Attitude towards opportunity identification reported by novice and habitual entrepreneurs [a]

Variable (mean scores)	Novice	Habitual	No. of respondents	t-statistic	Significance level (two-tailed)
Developmental Approach					
Identifying opportunities is really several steps over time[b]	3.76	3.81	682	−0.67	0.50
It is very important that the idea represents a concept which can be developed over time[b]	3.58	3.66	682	−1.05	0.29
The consideration of one opportunity often leads to other ones[b]	3.98	4.07	682	−1.49	0.14
New business opportunities often arise in connection to a specific problem[b]	3.69	3.77	682	−1.21	0.23
Alertness Approach					
The business opportunities I have identified over the years have been largely unrelated[c]	**2.84**	**2.86**	**682**	**−0.03**	**0.81**
Ideas for new business opportunities do not require specific market or technological knowledge[c]	2.97	3.12	682	−1.63	0.10

Notes:
[a]   The following scale was used: (1) strongly disagree, (2) disagree, (3) neutral, (4) agree, and (5) strongly agree.
[b]   Item belongs to the 'Developmental Approach' component identified in Table 3.7.
[c]   Item belongs to the 'Alertness Approach' component identified in Table 3.7.

Table 4.14 Attitude towards opportunity identification by serial and portfolio entrepreneurs[a]

Variable (mean scores)	Serial	Portfolio	No. of respondents	t-statistic	Significance level (two-tailed)
Developmental Approach					
Identifying opportunities is really several steps over time[b]	3.88	3.76	363	1.18	0.34
It is very important that the idea represents a concept which can be developed over time[b]	3.65	3.67	363	−0.19	0.85
The consideration of one opportunity often leads to other ones[b]	4.00	4.13	363	−1.49	0.14
New business opportunities often arise in connection to a specific problem[b]	3.72	3.81	363	−0.99	0.32
Alertness Approach					
The business opportunities I have identified over the years have been largely unrelated[c]	**2.69**	**3.00**	**363**	**−2.28**	**0.02**
Ideas for new business opportunities do not require specific market or technological knowledge[c]	3.09	3.15	363	−0.47	0.64

Notes:
[a] The following scale was used: (1) strongly disagree, (2) disagree, (3) neutral, (4) agree, and (5) strongly agree.
[b] Item belongs to the 'Developmental Approach' component identified in Table 3.7.
[c] Item belongs to the 'Alertness Approach' component identified in Table 3.7.

towards opportunity identification. Therefore, there is no support for hypotheses H_{7a} (relating to the alertness approach) or H_{7c} (relating to the developmental approach). It should be noted however, that hypothesis H_{7a} could not be rigorously tested because the statements relating to the alertness approach were associated with low construct reliability (see Chapter 3).

Additional analysis revealed no significant difference between serial and portfolio entrepreneurs with regard to the five developmental approach attitudes towards opportunity identification statements (Table 4.14). Consequently, hypothesis H_{7d} is not supported. With respect to the statements relating to alertness, as expected portfolio entrepreneurs held a more favourable attitude towards an alertness-based approach than serial entrepreneurs, lending some support for hypothesis H_{7b}. However, as intimated above hypothesis H_{7d} could not be rigorously tested.

VENTURE-SPECIFIC HUMAN CAPITAL (SHK$_V$)

As intimated earlier (Chapter 2, Table 2.1), motivations for establishing or purchasing a venture and the level of know-how relating to the task environment and the skills and abilities needed for the current venture can be viewed as elements of human capital specific to the venture. In this section, business similarity and motivations are discussed with regard to the entrepreneur types.

Domain Knowledge (Business and Task Similarity)

Respondents were asked to indicate how similar the surveyed business was, in various ways, to their previous main job or business. Nine statements relating to business similarity were explored within a PCA. Task environment similarity and skills similarity were identified (Table 3.9). Table 4.15 shows that habitual entrepreneurs report significantly higher task environment similarity scores. However, there was no significant difference between them with regard to skills/abilities similarity. Hence, H_{8a} is supported, whilst hypothesis H_{8c} cannot be supported.

Table 4.15   Business and task similarity reported by novice and habitual entrepreneurs

Variable (component scores)	Novice (n = 315)	Habitual (n = 345)	t-statistic	Df	Sig. level (2-tailed)
Business similarity	**−0.08**	**0.07**	**−1.90**	**658**	**0.06**
Task similarity	0.05	−0.04	1.14	658	0.26

Table 4.16   Business and task similarity reported by serial and portfolio entrepreneurs

Variable (component scores)	Serial (n = 145)	Portfolio (n = 199)	t-statistic	Df	Sig. level (2-tailed)
Business similarity	0.01	0.11	−0.97	343	0.33
Task similarity	−0.03	−0.05	0.25	343	0.80

No significant differences were detected between serial and portfolio entrepreneurs in terms of both dimensions of domain similarity (Table 4.16). Consequently, hypotheses H_{8b} and H_{8d} are not supported.

Motivations

Twenty-three statements relating to the motivations for starting or purchasing the surveyed business were explored within a PCA (Table 3.8). Six components were identified: 'personal development'; 'independence'; 'approval'; 'welfare'; 'tax'; and 'wealth'. Differences between novice and habitual entrepreneurs with regard to their various motivations are summarized in Table 4.17. A significant difference was found only with respect to one of the motivations. Habitual entrepreneurs were significantly more likely to highlight personal-development-related motives for starting or purchasing the surveyed business compared with novice entrepreneurs ($p < 0.01$). Personal development represents an intrinsic motivation. Consequently, there is some support for hypothesis H_{9a}.

Only one significant difference was detected between serial and portfolio entrepreneurs with regard to their motivations. Table 4.18 shows serial entre-

Table 4.17   Motivations reported by novice and habitual entrepreneurs

Variable (component scores)	Novice (n = 306)	Habitual (n = 344)	t-statistic	Df	Sig. level (2-tailed)
Intrinsic Motives					
Personal development	**−0.12**	**0.11**	**−2.92**	**648**	**0.00**
Independence	0.06	−0.06	1.53	648	0.13
Extrinsic Motives					
Approval	0.04	−0.03	0.87	648	0.38
Welfare	0.01	−0.01	0.11	648	0.91
Financial	0.01	−0.01	0.14	648	0.89
Reactive	0.04	−0.04	0.96	648	0.34

Table 4.18　Motivations reported by serial and portfolio entrepreneurs

Variable (component scores)	Serial (n = 147)	Portfolio (n = 197)	t-statistic	Df	Sig. level (2-tailed)
Intrinsic Motives					
Independence	0.05	0.15	−1.00	342	0.32
Personal development	0.02	−0.11	1.16	342	0.25
Extrinsic Motives					
Approval	**0.08**	**−0.12**	**1.79**	**342**	**0.07**
Welfare	0.02	−0.02	0.40	342	0.69
Financial	−0.37	0.02	−0.50	342	0.62
Reactive	−0.12	0.02	−1.22	342	0.23

preneurs found the extrinsic 'approval' motive to be more important than portfolio entrepreneurs. Hypothesis H_{9b} is, therefore, not supported.

The examples of respondents presented in the text box illustrate some of the differences between the motivations of the three types of entrepreneur. In particular, as Mary Fairburn developed her entrepreneurial experience, the personal confidence and development aspect became more important. For Norman Rough, the approval aspect in terms of using his reputation to help others with bodybuilding and keeping fit was evident.

HUMAN CAPITAL BY TYPE OF ENTREPRENEUR: MULTIVARIATE ANALYSIS

It was felt necessary to supplement the bivariate analysis with more sophisticated and robust multivariate analysis. Whilst investigations of a bivariate nature provide some guidance as to the underlying relationships present, complex interrelationships may be overlooked. As a result, maximum likelihood logistic estimation analysis is appropriate to test for the probability of an entrepreneur being a habitual entrepreneur (as opposed to a novice) and of being a portfolio entrepreneur among the habitual entrepreneur sample (as opposed to a serial entrepreneur). The first model explores the independent variables associated with the habitual entrepreneurs compared with novice entrepreneurs' dependent variable, whilst the second model explores the independent variables associated with portfolio entrepreneurs compared with serial entrepreneurs' dependent variable. Assumptions of logistic regression analysis are considered, particularly the issue of multicollinearity.

The significance of individual variables was established using the Wald statistic (Hair et al., 1995). The overall goodness of fit of each logistic regression

---

EXAMPLES OF MOTIVATIONS OF NOVICE, PORTFOLIO AND SERIAL ENTREPRENEURS

Novice: Graham Mather's main motivation to start a business was for independence and financial security. He believed that his industry-related experiences and his personal reputation as well as an extensive network of contacts would enable him to establish and run a successful business. In contrast, Lilias Cruickshank felt that, having been made redundant and not wishing to stay in the same sector, she had little alternative but to take up an offer to join her sister-in-law.

Portfolio: Mary Fairburn's motivation for the first two businesses was mainly a lifestyle choice, that is to become more independent and become involved in something that would be physically less demanding. Subsequently, having learnt how to deal with the problems of running a business and having acquired assets from previous business ownership, she has developed the confidence and ability to develop a portfolio of related businesses engaged in private cemeteries, memorial furniture and funeral direction.

Serial: For Norman Rough the main motivation for starting a business was to make use of the positive name he had developed in the world of weight training and bodybuilding to help others with bodybuilding and keeping fit. At the time, there was an absence of sports centres as gyms, as they have subsequently developed, and he wanted to run a business that was visually attractive and would provide a pleasant experience. The motive for subsequent businesses was to build on the client base in the health studio.

---

model was assessed in a number of ways. First, the overall significance of the model was ascertained with reference to the Chi-square statistic. Second, the percentage of cases predicted correctly was monitored. Finally, a pseudo r-square coefficient was assessed based on the Cox and Snell r-square coefficient and the Nagelkerke r-square figure coefficient.

The selection of independent variables was guided by the human capital framework discussed in Chapter 2. The two dependent variables were presumed to be associated with general human capital, entrepreneurship-specific human capital, and venture-specific human capital. Model 1 in the following discussion relates to HABITUAL as the binary dependent variable, which took a value of

'1' if the respondent was a habitual entrepreneur and '0' for a novice entrepreneur. In Model 1, the following relationships are assumed:

$$\text{HABITUAL} = f\ (\text{GHK, SHK}_E, \text{SHK}_V)$$

Where: GHK represents general human capital and is measured in terms of the age of the founder (*Age* and *Age*^{2} to account for possible non-linearities); *Gender*; the highest level of education (*Education*); the level of managerial human capital derived from both the number of previous experiences (jobs) and the level of attainment in previous jobs (*Managerial Human Capital*); and perceived capabilities (*Managerial capability* and *Technical capability*).

SHK$_E$ represents human capital specific to entrepreneurship and is measured in terms of the entrepreneur's perceived entrepreneurial capability (*Entrepreneurial capability*); parental business ownership experience (*Parent business owner*); and the entrepreneur's attitude towards opportunity identification in terms of the extent to which they considered a developmental approach to opportunity identification to be important (*Development*).

SHK$_V$ represents human capital specific to the venture and is measured in terms of the degree of business similarity (*Task environment similarity* and *Skills/abilities similarity*) and motivations for business ownership (*Approval, Welfare, Independence, Personal Development, Financial* and *Reactive* motives).

Model 2 relates to the PORTFOLIO binary dependent variable, which took a value of '1' if the respondent was a portfolio entrepreneur and '0' for a serial entrepreneur. In Model 2, the following relationships are assumed:

$$\text{PORTFOLIO} = f\ (\text{GHK, SHK}_E, \text{SHK}_V)$$

Several steps were taken to ensure that multicollinearity did not pose a problem in the models. First, several of the independent variables selected are based on orthogonal component scores derived from a PCA. Consequently, the correlation between the components is, by definition, close to zero. Second, a correlation matrix was calculated for the sample relating to habitual and novice entrepreneurs, as well as the subsample relating to portfolio and serial entrepreneurs. Here, the Variance Inflation Factor (VIF) scores were examined. These scores indicate the degree to which each independent variable is explained by the other independent variables. Independent variables with high VIF scores were removed from any further analysis, to minimize the problem of multicollinearity.

It was expected that there would be a strong correlation between *Age* and *Age*^{2}. To minimize any problems associated with multicollinearity between these two variables, *Age* was operationalized in terms of deviation from the mean (50 years) and *Age*^{2} as the square of the deviation from the mean age (Aiken and

West, 1991: 35). All independent variables were examined for multicollinearity. While there were some significant correlations between some of the independent variables, the VIF scores suggest that there are no serious problems with multi-collinearity (see Appendices 4.1 and 4.2 for the full sample and the habitual entrepreneurs' sub-sample, respectively). All VIF scores were well below the cut-off threshold of ten (Hair et al., 1995).

Model 1 in Table 4.19 is significant ($p < 0.0001$) and has a pseudo R^2 ranging between 0.09 and 0.11. A relatively low R^2 is not uncommon in cross-sectional studies. The percentage of respondents correctly classified was satisfactory at over 60 per cent. Five independent variables are individually significantly associated with the HABITUAL dependent variable. With respect to the GHK variables, two significant relationships were identified. Male entrepreneurs were significantly more likely to report that they were habitual entrepreneurs. Entre-preneurs reporting higher levels of perceived technical capability were less likely to be habitual entrepreneurs. This latter finding offers support for hypothesis H_{4a}, and is consistent with the bivariate evidence. Among the SHK_E variables, parental business ownership is significantly associated with HABITUAL. Con-sequently hypothesis H_{6a} is supported and is consistent with the bivariate evidence. As expected, respondents with parent(s) who were business owners were more likely to be habitual entrepreneurs. Two motivations associated with SHK_V were significantly related to HABITUAL. Respondents reporting high levels of welfare-based motivation were less likely to be a habitual entrepreneur. Conversely, those reporting personal development as an important motivation were more likely to be habitual entrepreneurs. These findings lend further sup-port for hypothesis H_{9a}, that habitual entrepreneurs will be more likely to be motivated by intrinsic motives, and less so by extrinsic motives. These findings are also consistent with the bivariate evidence. However, several significant re-lationships detected by the bivariate analysis were not supported by the multivariate logistic regression analysis. Most notably, independent variables relating to the highest level of education, managerial human capital, perceived managerial capability, and task environment similarity were not significantly associated with HABITUAL.

Model 2 in Table 4.19 focuses on the PORTFOLIO dependent variable. This model is significant ($p < 0.01$) and has a pseudo r-square ranging between 0.11 and 0.14. The percentage of respondents correctly classified is satisfactory at 64 per cent. Five independent variables are individually significantly associated with the PORTFOLIO dependent variable. Among the variables relating to GHK, the control variable relating to gender was significant. Male entrepre-neurs were more likely to be portfolio entrepreneurs. In addition, the perceived level of managerial capability was significantly and positively associated with PORTFOLIO, lending support to hypothesis H_{3b}. None of the variables relating to SHK_E were associated with PORTFOLIO. With respect to human capital

Table 4.19　　*Logistic regression of human capital variables associated with whether a respondent is a habitual or novice entrepreneur (Model 1) and whether a habitual entrepreneur is a portfolio or a serial entrepreneur (Model 2)*

Independent Variables	Model 1[a, b]		Model 2[c, d]	
	β	Significance	β	Significance
GHK				
Age	0.004		−0.007	
Age^2	−0.001		0.000	
Gender	**0.800**	**	**1.133**	*
Education	0.098		0.174	
Managerial Human Capital	0.012		−0.003	
Managerial capability	0.152		**0.408**	**
Technical capability	**−0.283**	**	0.134	
SHK$_E$				
Entrepreneurial capability	−0.094		0.194	
Parent business owners	**0.662**	***	−0.144	
Development	0.039		−0.102	
SHK$_V$				
Task environment similarity	0.141		**0.248**	†
Skills/abilities similarity	0.069		0.097	
Approval	−0.075		**−0.222**	†
Welfare	**−0.178**	†	−0.086	
Independence	−0.047		**−0.297**	*
Personal development	**0.210**	*	−0.004	
Financial	−0.040		0.048	
Reactive	−0.147		0.144	
Model χ^2	46.16	****	31.64	**
-2 log likelihood	668.20		354.03	
Overall predictive accuracy	60.2		64.1	
Cox and Snell R^2	0.085		0.106	
Nagelkerke R^2	0.114		0.143	
Number of entrepreneurs	518		281	

Notes:

† $p < 0.10$; * $p < 0.05$; ** $p < 0.01$; *** $p < 0.001$; **** $p < 0.0001$

Portfolio entrepreneurs were significantly more likely to be male ($p < 0.001$), report higher levels of managerial capability ($p < 0.01$) but lower levels of technical capability ($p < 0.10$) than their novice counterparts. Portfolio entrepreneurs were significantly more likely to have parent(s) who were business owners ($p < 0.05$), report higher levels of skills similarity between the surveyed business and their previous main activity ($p < 0.05$) and were more likely to be motivated by personal development ($p < 0.10$) than novice entrepreneurs.

Serial entrepreneurs reported significantly lower levels of technical ($p < 0.01$) and entrepreneurial capability ($p < 0.10$) than their novice counterparts. Furthermore, serial entrepreneurs were found to be more likely to have parent(s) who were business owners ($p < 0.01$) and were less likely to be motivated by reactive reasons for business ownership ($p < 0.10$) than novice entrepreneurs.

[a]　Reference category novice entrepreneurs.

[b]　VIF scores were well below the maximum appropriate level of 10 (maximum score of 1.33).

[c]　Reference category serial entrepreneurs.

[d]　VIF scores were well below the maximum appropriate level of 10 (maximum score of 1.33).

specific to the venture (SHK_V), intrinsic independence-based and extrinsic welfare-based motives were negatively and significantly associated with the likelihood of being a portfolio entrepreneur. These findings suggest that the intrinsic–extrinsic dichotomy may not be an appropriate means of categorizing motives for entrepreneurship. Supporting hypothesis H_{8d}, task environment similarity was positively and significantly associated with PORTFOLIO. We can infer that Model 2 has three significant relationships, which were not detected in the bivariate analysis (independence-based and approval-based motives and task environment similarity).

As an additional check for robustness, novice entrepreneurs were compared with portfolio and serial entrepreneurs with respect to their human capital profiles. A number of significant differences between novice and portfolio entrepreneurs were detected and are reported as footnotes to Table 4.19. However, as these differences do not relate specifically to the previously developed hypotheses they will not be discussed further.

CONCLUSION

Table 4.20 summarizes the findings of the bivariate and multivariate analyses. Hypotheses H_{7a} and H_{7b} could not be robustly tested within a multivariate framework due to low levels of reliability with the 'alertness' scale. Of the 20 remaining hypotheses, which were tested using both bivariate and multivariate analysis, the results were consistent between the two methods of analysis for 16 out of the 20. Three hypotheses were supported by the bivariate analysis, but not by the multivariate analysis (hypotheses H_{2a}, H_{3a}, and H_{8a}). Two hypotheses were supported by the multivariate analysis but not by the bivariate analysis (hypotheses H_{8d} and H_{9b}). Multivariate analysis is deemed to be more robust than bivariate analysis, largely on grounds of the ability of multivariate analysis to control for inter-relationships between the independent variables. Therefore, the results from the multivariate analysis should be given greater credence.

Four hypotheses were supported by both methods of analysis: hypothesis H_{3b} suggesting that portfolio entrepreneurs will report higher levels of managerial capability than serial entrepreneurs; hypothesis H_{4a} suggesting that habitual entrepreneurs will report lower levels of technical capability than novice entrepreneurs; hypothesis H_{6a} suggesting that habitual entrepreneurs are more likely to have parent(s) who owned a business or businesses; and hypothesis H_{9a} suggesting that habitual entrepreneurs would be more likely to be associated with intrinsic motives for business ownership than novice entrepreneurs.

Contrary to expectation there were a number of hypotheses for which there was no support (H_{1a}, H_{1b}, H_{2b}, H_{4b}, H_{5a}, H_{5b}, H_{6b}, H_{7c}, H_{7d}, H_{8b}, and H_{8c}). Details of these hypotheses are provided in Table 4.20.

Table 4.20 Summary of findings

Hypothesis number and description		Bivariate results	Multivariate results
H_{1a}	Education$_{habitual}$ > Education$_{novice}$	Not supported	Not supported
H_{1b}	Education$_{portfolio}$ > Education$_{serial}$	Not supported	Not supported
H_{2a}	Managerial HK$_{habitual}$ > Managerial HK$_{novice}$	Supported	Not supported
H_{2b}	Managerial HK$_{portfolio}$ > Managerial HK$_{serial}$	Not supported	Not supported
H_{3a}	Managerial capability$_{habitual}$ > Managerial capability$_{novice}$	Supported	Not supported
H_{3b}	Managerial capability$_{portfolio}$ > Managerial capability$_{serial}$	Supported	Supported
H_{4a}	Technical capability$_{habitual}$ < Technical capability$_{novice}$	Supported	Supported
H_{4b}	Technical capability$_{portfolio}$ < Technical capability$_{serial}$	Not supported	Not supported
H_{5a}	Entrepreneurial capability$_{habitual}$ > Entrepreneurial capability$_{novice}$	Not supported	Not supported
H_{5b}	Entrepreneurial capability$_{portfolio}$ > Entrepreneurial capability$_{serial}$	Not supported	Not supported
H_{6a}	Business owner parent$_{habitual}$ > Business owner parent$_{novice}$	Supported	Supported
H_{6b}	Business owner parent$_{portfolio}$ > Business owner parent$_{serial}$	Not supported	Not supported
H_{7a}	Alertness approach$_{habitual}$ > Alertness approach$_{novice}$	Not supported	–
H_{7b}	Alertness approach$_{portfolio}$ > Alertness approach$_{serial}$	Supported	–
H_{7c}	Developmental approach$_{habitual}$ > Developmental approach$_{novice}$	Not supported	Not supported
H_{7d}	Developmental approach$_{portfolio}$ < Developmental approach$_{serial}$	Not supported	Not supported
H_{8a}	Business similarity$_{habitual}$ > Business similarity$_{novice}$	Supported	Not supported
H_{8b}	Business similarity$_{portfolio}$ > Business similarity$_{serial}$	Not supported	Not supported
H_{8c}	Task similarity$_{habitual}$ > Task similarity$_{novice}$	Not supported	Not supported
H_{8d}	Task similarity$_{portfolio}$ > Task similarity$_{serial}$	Not supported	Not supported
H_{9a}	Intrinsic motivation$_{habitual}$ > Intrinsic motivation$_{novice}$	Some support	Supported
H_{9b}	Intrinsic motivation$_{portfolio}$ < Intrinsic motivation$_{serial}$	Not supported	Supported

Overall, the findings suggest that a number of human capital-based characteristics other than the level and nature of business ownership experience distinguish habitual entrepreneurs from novice entrepreneurs. Further, these variables can distinguish portfolio entrepreneurs from serial entrepreneurs. Habitual entrepreneurs are more likely to be motivated by intrinsic factors (especially personal development) and less by extrinsic factors (such as welfare-based motives) than novice entrepreneurs. Moreover habitual entrepreneurs report lower levels of perceived technical capability and are more likely to come from a background of business ownership through parent(s) who owned a business or businesses. Among the habitual entrepreneurs, the findings suggest that portfolio entrepreneurs can be distinguished from serial entrepreneurs in terms of a number of human capital-based characteristics. In particular, portfolio entrepreneurs are more likely to report higher levels of perceived managerial capability, task similarity between the current business and the previous main business/job, and are less likely to report intrinsic motives for business ownership (such as approval and independence-based motives) than serial entrepreneurs.

The following chapter explores the relationship between business ownership experience and entrepreneurial behaviour (that is, opportunity identification and exploitation). Differences between novice and habitual entrepreneurs and then between serial and portfolio entrepreneurs are examined.

Table 4A.1 Correlation matrix relating to model 1 (n= 518)

Variable	Mean	S.D.	VIF	1	2	3	4	5	6	7
1. Age	0.85	9.60	1.18							
2. Age²	-0.96	124.02	1.13	-0.17						
3. Gender	92.83	0.33	1.15	0.15	-0.10					
4. Education	0.52	0.81	1.08	-0.05	-0.08	-0.03				
5. Managerial human capital	10.04	5.70	1.16	0.19	-0.20	0.06	0.06			
6. Managerial capability	-0.05	1.02	1.23	-0.05	0.06	0.03	-0.04	0.06		
7. Technical capability	0.01	1.02	1.20	0.02	0.01	0.17	0.04	-0.02	0.00	
8. Entrepreneurial capability	0.01	1.00	1.18	-0.03	-0.02	-0.09	-0.09	0.14	-0.03	-0.02
9. Parent business owners	0.36	0.48	1.09	-0.03	0.08	0.01	0.05	-0.10	0.07	-0.06
10. Development	-0.01	0.97	1.33	-0.16	-0.02	-0.04	-0.02	0.04	0.27	0.25
11. Approval	-0.01	1.00	1.08	-0.16	0.13	-0.11	-0.12	-0.06	0.09	-0.03
12. Welfare	-0.05	0.97	1.10	0.08	0.08	-0.02	-0.01	-0.09	0.04	-0.05
13. Personal development	-0.01	0.99	1.24	-0.05	0.03	-0.01	0.08	0.12	0.28	0.17
14. Independence	-0.01	0.99	1.10	-0.10	-0.09	-0.15	0.07	0.03	0.05	0.04
15. Financial	-0.01	1.00	1.07	-0.03	-0.09	0.12	-0.02	0.07	0.14	0.03
16. Reactive	0.01	1.00	1.06	-0.07	0.00	0.00	-0.01	-0.09	0.06	0.01
17. Business similarity	0.01	0.99	1.12	0.05	-0.09	-0.16	0.09	0.03	0.00	-0.11
18. Task similarity	0.00	0.99	1.05	-0.05	-0.03	-0.02	-0.07	-0.09	0.01	-0.04

Variable	8	9	10	11	12	13	14	15	16	17
9. Parent business owners	0.02									
10. Development	0.18	0.03								
11. Approval	0.05	0.01	0.07							
12. Welfare	0.08	0.20	0.04	-0.02						
13. Personal development	0.17	0.07	0.24	-0.01	-0.05					
14. Independence	0.10	-0.07	0.17	0.02	0.02	-0.02				
15. Financial	0.08	-0.05	0.10	-0.01	-0.01	0.00	-0.04			
16. Reactive	0.11	0.04	0.04	-0.03	0.01	0.01	-0.01	-0.04		
17. Business similarity	-0.04	0.04	0.09	-0.05	-0.06	0.07	-0.03	-0.02	-0.13	
18. Task similarity	-0.08	-0.06	0.05	-0.01	0.03	0.02	0.04	-0.04	0.01	-0.01

Note: *r* has to be 0.09 or higher to be significant at p < 0.05 and has to be 0.12 or higher to be significant at p < 0.01 (two-tailed).

APPENDIX 4.2

Table 4A.2 Correlation matrix relating to model 2 (n= 281)

Variable	Mean	S.D.	VIF	1	2	3	4	5	6	7
1. Age	-0.59	9.27	1.23							
2. Age^2	86.02	115.41	1.17	-0.28						
3. Gender	0.90	0.30	1.15	0.12	-0.07					
4. Education	0.56	0.83	1.13	-0.06	-0.04	-0.02				
5. Managerial human capital	10.43	5.91	1.16	0.18	-0.19	0.05	0.09			
6. Managerial capability	-0.07	1.05	1.25	-0.10	0.04	0.06	-0.02	0.05		
7. Technical capability	-0.09	1.06	1.22	0.04	-0.03	0.22	0.05	0.01	0.00	
8. Entrepreneurial capability	0.07	1.03	1.14	-0.02	-0.03	-0.05	-0.15	0.07	-0.03	-0.07
9. Parent business owners	0.42	0.49	1.15	-0.03	0.11	-0.03	0.06	-0.14	0.00	-0.03
10. Development	-0.01	0.97	1.30	-0.12	-0.03	-0.01	-0.08	0.00	0.27	0.23
11. Approval	-0.06	1.00	1.09	-0.05	0.04	-0.09	-0.15	-0.04	0.07	-0.08
12. Welfare	-0.10	1.00	1.21	0.11	0.07	0.02	0.02	-0.10	0.06	0.02
13. Personal development	0.10	1.00	1.33	-0.10	0.08	0.08	0.08	0.11	0.32	0.23
14. Independence	-0.05	1.01	1.14	-0.07	-0.10	0.00	0.00	0.03	0.04	0.05
15. Financial	-0.01	1.03	1.09	-0.06	-0.08	-0.08	-0.08	0.04	0.12	0.02
16. Reactive	-0.05	1.04	1.04	-0.05	0.00	0.01	0.03	-0.13	0.04	-0.01
17. Business similarity	0.10	0.97	1.13	0.07	-0.08	-0.14	0.08	0.07	0.04	-0.04
18. Task similarity	0.01	0.97	1.07	-0.02	0.01	-0.08	-0.12	-0.09	0.00	-0.01

Variable	8	9	10	11	12	13	14	15	16	17
9. Parent business owners	-0.02									
10. Development	0.09	0.00								
11. Approval	0.04	0.02	0.03							
12. Welfare	0.09	0.26	0.10	-0.09						
13. Personal development	0.12	0.08	0.23	0.02	-0.03					
14. Independence	0.15	-0.10	0.20	-0.02	0.11	-0.05				
15. Financial	0.07	-0.06	0.09	-0.09	0.00	-0.04	0.03			
16. Reactive	0.08	0.01	0.01	-0.07	0.00	0.01	0.00	-0.01		
17. Business similarity	-0.10	0.04	0.10	-0.07	-0.11	0.04	-0.12	-0.02	-0.06	
18. Task similarity	-0.04	-0.06	0.11	-0.06	0.07	-0.02	0.06	-0.06	0.02	-0.06

Note: r has to be 0.12 or higher to be significant at $p < 0.05$ and r has to be 0.15 or higher to be significant at $p < 0.01$ (two-tailed).

5. Information search and opportunity identification, pursuit, and exploitation by type of entrepreneur

INTRODUCTION

This chapter adopts a human capital framework to explore differences between the types of entrepreneurs with regards to information search and opportunity identification, pursuit, and exploitation. Presented hypotheses will be tested with a bivariate statistical framework and then a multivariate statistical framework. Tests will compare habitual and novice entrepreneurs, and then serial and portfolio entrepreneurs will be compared. Finally, some conclusions are presented.

INFORMATION SEARCH AND OPPORTUNITY IDENTIFICATION, PURSUIT, AND EXPLOITATION: BIVARIATE ANALYSIS

Information Search

Respondents were presented with 14 sources of information. They were asked to indicate if they had used any of them. Table 5.1 shows that habitual entrepreneurs used weakly significantly ($p < 0.09$) more information sources (8.94) than novice entrepreneurs (8.37). Table 5.2 shows that while portfolio entrepreneurs used more information sources than serial entrepreneurs, this difference was not statistically significant. Overall, these findings do not provide support for hypotheses H_{10a} and H_{10b}. Contrary to expectations, habitual entrepreneurs used more information sources than their novice counterparts.

Tables 5.3 and 5.4 report individual sources of information used by types of entrepreneur. Table 5.3 shows that a significantly larger proportion of habitual rather than novice entrepreneurs utilized employees, consultants, financiers, and national government sources.

Table 5.4 reports differences between serial and portfolio entrepreneurs with respect to the information sources used; only two significant differences were

Table 5.1   Number of information sources utilized by novice and habitual entrepreneurs

Variable	Novice	Habitual	n	t-statistic	Sig. level (2-tailed)
Number of information sources used	8.37	8.94	730	−1.71	0.09

Table 5.2   Number of information sources utilized by serial and portfolio entrepreneurs

Variable (mean scores)	Serial	Portfolio	n	t-statistic	Sig. level (2-tailed)
Number of information sources used	8.57	9.22	378	−1.43	0.15

Table 5.3   Information sources utilized by novice and habitual entrepreneurs

Variable	Novice[a] No.	%	Habitual[a] No.	%	χ^2 statistic	Sig. level
Suppliers	250	71.0	266	70.4	0.04	0.87
Employees	**208**	**59.1**	**267**	**70.6**	**10.69**	**0.00**
Customers	292	83.0	327	86.5	1.79	0.22
Other business owners	271	77.0	305	80.7	1.50	0.34
Consultants	**167**	**47.4**	**207**	**54.8**	**3.91**	**0.05**
Financiers	**183**	**52.0**	**225**	**59.5**	**4.20**	**0.04**
Personal friends	250	71.0	282	74.6	1.18	0.28
Family	250	71.0	277	73.3	0.46	0.51
Magazines/newspapers	224	63.6	244	64.6	0.07	0.82
Trade publications	240	68.2	259	68.5	0.01	0.94
Patent filings	102	29.0	120	31.7	0.66	0.42
Technical literature	184	52.3	208	55.0	0.56	0.46
National government sources	**137**	**38.9**	**170**	**45.0**	**2.74**	**0.10**
Local enterprise/development agencies	174	49.4	200	52.9	0.88	0.37

Note: [a] Number and proportion of entrepreneurs who indicated that they had used the source of information in question.

Table 5.4　Information sources utilized by serial and portfolio entrepreneurs

Variable	Serial[a]		Portfolio[a]		χ^2 statistic	Sig. level
	No.	%	No.	%		
Suppliers	114	70.4	152	70.4	0.00	1.00
Employees	107	66.0	160	74.1	2.87	0.11
Customers	140	86.4	187	86.6	0.00	1.00
Other business owners	129	79.6	176	81.5	0.20	0.69
Consultants	**77**	**47.5**	**130**	**60.2**	**5.98**	**0.02**
Financiers	93	57.4	132	61.1	0.53	0.53
Personal friends	118	72.8	164	75.9	0.47	0.55
Family	114	70.4	163	75.5	1.23	0.29
Magazines/newspapers	100	61.7	144	66.7	0.99	0.33
Trade publications	106	65.4	153	70.8	1.25	0.27
Patent filings	48	29.6	72	33.3	0.59	0.50
Technical literature	**80**	**49.4**	**128**	**59.3**	**3.65**	**0.06**
National government sources	69	42.6	101	46.8	0.65	0.47
Local enterprise/development agencies	83	51.2	117	54.2	0.32	0.60

Note:　[a] Number and proportion of entrepreneurs who indicated that they had used the source of information in question.

detected. Significantly larger proportions of portfolio rather than serial entrepreneurs had used consultants as a source of information, and had used technical literature. The latter difference was only weakly significant.

The examples presented in the text box illustrate some of the similarities and differences between the information search processes of the three types of entrepreneur. (For example, Mary Fairburn made greater use of technical information in later ventures.)

EXAMPLES OF INFORMATION SEARCH BY NOVICE, PORTFOLIO AND SERIAL ENTREPRENEURS

Novice: James Drummond set up a civil engineering consultancy after working all over the world on various projects. After deciding to stop his worldwide travel, he was headhunted into an engineering and construction business located in the area of the country where he wanted to settle down. The intention was to follow this by setting up his own business when he was ready. When he was ready, he set up a small office and began to look for work, some of which was obtained from the consultancy firm for which he had worked, through family contacts and by exploiting the desire of local customers for a locally based firm. He has subsequently considered a number of related opportunities but none have been pursued, partly because of the risk and a lack of financial resources.

Portfolio: Mike Kosic used his personal reputation and resources to act as a 'hub' in business opportunity networks. Kosic reports to be always on the lookout for something that might make good returns without too much capital investment. The businesses he owns have been brought to him by family and friends who had either been involved in the businesses or who had expressed an interest in starting a business in a particular area. In contrast, Mary Fairburn's search process seems to have become more sophisticated as the number of businesses increased. From initially searching for a venture that would enable a lifestyle shift and discovering opportunities almost by 'accident', as an entrepreneur she has become more systematic. First, she consciously looked to expand into a related business area in her third business, although even here the precise venture was identified by 'accident'. Second, she took a deliberate decision to move into the funeral director business and invested considerable effort into looking at how funerals were managed in the UK and Europe, as well as attending an exhibition on funeral directing in Paris.

Serial: After extensive experience working in his father's haulage business, Wilson Smith decided at the age of 29 to move into the licensed trade. His father's haulage business faced difficulties and the funds from the business sale were used to purchase a poorly performing public house. He has subsequently owned several public houses and restaurants as well as a nightclub, but currently owns one hotel. Although a serial entrepreneur, Smith only became involved in the search process once he had decided to move on from the business he was in. He always used the same process which was to look around for an area that should be good but wasn't. This included looking at the trade press for what was for sale and developing contacts in the trade.

Entrepreneurs were also asked to indicate whether the sources of information used have been useful. Table 5.5 shows that novice rather than habitual entrepreneurs found customers and financiers were more useful. Further, Table 5.6

Table 5.5   Usefulness of information sources utilized by novice and habitual entrepreneurs[a]

Variable (mean scores)	Novice	Habitual	No. of respondents	t-statistic	Sig. level (2-tailed)
Suppliers	3.82	3.88	516	–0.68	0.50
Employees	3.69	3.66	619	0.39	0.70
Customers	**4.29**	**4.14**	**619**	**2.69**	**0.01**
Other business owners	3.72	3.82	576	–1.33	0.18
Consultants	2.88	2.88	374	–0.03	0.97
Financiers	**2.98**	**2.78**	**408**	**1.65**	**0.10**
Personal friends	3.47	3.38	532	0.97	0.33
Family	3.50	3.41	527	0.92	0.36
Magazines/newspapers	3.24	3.22	468	0.20	0.84
Trade publications	3.46	3.46	499	–0.01	0.99
Patent filings	2.54	2.57	222	–0.20	0.85
Technical literature	3.32	3.27	392	0.43	0.67
National government sources	2.62	2.74	307	–0.87	0.38
Local enterprise/development agencies	2.98	2.78	374	1.51	0.13

Note: [a] The following scale was used: (1) not at all useful, (2) not useful, (3) neither not useful nor useful, (4) useful, and (5) very useful.

shows that serial entrepreneurs rather than portfolio entrepreneurs suggested that trade publications were significantly more useful.

Respondents' views relating to the usefulness of cited information sources were used to create an information search intensity measure. As proposed by Cooper et al. (1995) (Table 3.3), this measure relates to those information sources cited by 60 per cent of respondents. Of the 14 information sources, only eight had been used by 60 per cent of the respondents. The information search intensity measure was computed by summing the ('usefulness') ratings for all eight information sources. Table 5.7 shows no significant differences were detected between novice and habitual entrepreneurs with regard to the information search intensity measure. Moreover, Table 5.8 shows no significant differences were detected between serial and portfolio entrepreneurs. Consequently, hypotheses H_{10a} and H_{10b} cannot be supported.

Opportunity Identification, Pursuit and Exploitation

Though the results relating to the amount of information sought suggests that there are no significant differences between the different types of entrepreneur, the extent to which this information is 'converted' into opportunities is worth

Table 5.6   Usefulness of information sources utilized by serial and portfolio entrepreneurs[a]

Variable (mean scores)	Serial	Portfolio	No. of respondents	t-statistic	Sig. level (2-tailed)
Suppliers	3.96	3.81	266	1.55	0.12
Employees	3.66	3.66	267	0.06	0.95
Customers	4.13	4.14	327	–0.19	0.85
Other business owners	3.77	3.85	305	–0.91	0.37
Consultants	2.81	2.93	207	–0.74	0.46
Financiers	2.80	2.77	225	0.18	0.85
Personal friends	3.36	3.40	282	–0.26	0.79
Family	3.49	3.36	277	1.03	0.31
Magazines/newspapers	3.26	3.19	244	0.54	0.59
Trade publications	**3.67**	**3.31**	**259**	**2.86**	**0.01**
Patent filings	2.54	2.58	120	–0.23	0.82
Technical literature	3.29	3.27	208	0.14	0.89
National government sources	2.78	2.70	170	0.45	0.66
Local enterprise/development agencies	2.80	2.77	200	0.15	0.88

Note: [a] The following scale was used: (1) not at all useful, (2) not useful, (3) neither not useful nor useful, (4) useful, and (5) very useful.

Table 5.7   Information search intensity of novice and habitual entrepreneurs

Variable (mean scores)	Novice	Habitual	No. of respondents	t-statistic	Sig. level (2-tailed)
Information search intensity	20.69	21.44	730	–1.06	0.29

Table 5.8   Information search intensity of serial and portfolio entrepreneurs

Variable (mean scores)	Serial	Portfolio	No. of respondents	t-statistic	Sig. level (2-tailed)
Information search intensity	21.10	21.70	378	–0.63	0.53

exploring. In this section the extent and nature of opportunity identification reported by the types of entrepreneurs is explored. Respondents were asked to indicate the number of opportunities for creating or purchasing a business they had (a) identified and (b) pursued (such as by committing time and financial resources) within the last five years. Table 5.9 illustrates that a significantly

Table 5.9 Number of opportunities identified and pursued reported by novice and habitual entrepreneurs

Variable	Novice		Habitual		χ^2 statistic	Sig. level
	No.	%	No.	%		
Opportunities identified					**62.19**	**0.00**
0	**218**	**65.5**	**134**	**36.1**	**60.46**	**0.00**
1	32	9.6	50	13.5	2.55	0.13
2 or more	**83**	**24.9**	**187**	**50.4**	**48.19**	**0.00**
Opportunities pursued					**22.80**	**0.00**
0	**32**	**27.8**	**26**	**11.0**	**15.99**	**0.00**
1	48	41.7	85	35.9	1.14	0.29
2 or more	**35**	**30.4**	**126**	**53.2**	**16.12**	**0.00**
Opportunities considered to be successes					**11.97**	**0.00**
0	**15**	**18.5**	**37**	**17.8**	**3.99**	**0.06**
1	**51**	**63.0**	**90**	**43.3**	**3.13**	**0.09**
2 or more	**15**	**18.5**	**81**	**38.9**	**15.01**	**0.00**

Table 5.10 Number of opportunities identified and pursued reported by serial and portfolio entrepreneurs

Variable	Serial		Portfolio		χ^2 statistic	Sig. level
	No.	%	No.	%		
Opportunities identified					**10.65**	**0.01**
0	**71**	**44.9**	**63**	**29.6**	**9.28**	**0.00**
1	22	13.9	28	13.1	0.05	0.88
2 or more	**65**	**41.1**	**122**	**57.3**	**9.45**	**0.00**
Opportunities pursued					**20.23**	**0.00**
0	**17**	**19.5**	**9**	**6.0**	**10.34**	**0.00**
1	**39**	**44.8**	**46**	**30.7**	**4.80**	**0.04**
2 or more	**31**	**35.6**	**95**	**63.3**	**16.97**	**0.00**
Opportunities considered to be successes					**22.16**	**0.00**
0	**24**	**34.3**	**13**	**9.4**	**28.02**	**0.00**
1	30	42.9	60	43.5	0.63	0.48
2 or more	**16**	**22.9**	**65**	**47.1**	**15.22**	**0.00**

larger proportion of habitual entrepreneurs had identified a greater number of opportunities over the past five years than novice entrepreneurs. Hypothesis H_{11a} is, therefore, supported. In addition, Table 5.9 shows that a significantly larger proportion of habitual entrepreneurs compared to novice entrepreneurs had pursued two or more opportunities. Furthermore, a significantly larger proportion of habitual rather than novice entrepreneurs considered two or more of the pursued opportunities to be successes.

Table 5.10 shows that a significantly larger proportion of portfolio rather than serial entrepreneurs had identified and pursued a greater number of opportunities for creating or purchasing a business. Hypothesis H_{11b} is, therefore, supported. A significantly larger proportion of portfolio rather than serial entrepreneurs considered two or more of the pursued opportunities to be successes. Conversely, a significantly larger proportion of serial rather than portfolio entrepreneurs considered none of the pursued opportunities to be successes.

The proportion of identified opportunities that are actually exploited was also monitored. While an individual may be very good at identifying opportunities, these opportunities may remain no more than an idea that has not been evaluated. Table 5.11 shows a significant difference between novice and habitual entrepreneur in terms of the proportion of identified opportunities they had pursued. A significantly larger proportion of novice entrepreneur reported that they had not pursued any of the opportunities for creating or purchasing a business they had identified. Furthermore, a significantly larger proportion of habitual rather than novice entrepreneurs indicated that they had pursued all the opportunities they had identified over the past five years. These findings lend support for hypothesis H_{12a}.

Table 5.11 Proportion of identified opportunities pursued by novice and habitual entrepreneurs

Variable	Novice		Habitual		χ^2 statistic	Sig. level
	No.	%	No.	%		
Proportion of identified opportunities pursued					**16.26**	**0.00**
No identified opportunities pursued	**32**	**27.8**	**26**	**11.2**	**15.40**	**0.00**
Less that 50% of identified opportunities pursued	20	17.4	41	17.6	0.00	1.00
50% or more identified opportunities were pursued	24	20.9	57	24.5	0.56	0.50
All identified opportunities were pursued	**39**	**33.9**	**109**	**46.8**	**5.22**	**0.03**

Table 5.12   Proportion of identified opportunities pursued by serial and portfolio entrepreneurs

Variable	Serial		Portfolio		χ^2 statistic	Sig. level
	No.	%	No.	%		
Proportion of identified opportunities pursued					**11.22**	**0.01**
No identified opportunities pursued[a]	**17**	**19.8**	**9**	**6.1**	**10.09**	**0.00**
Less that 50% of identified opportunities pursued	11	12.8	30	20.4	2.17	0.16
50% or more identified opportunities were pursued	19	22.1	38	25.9	0.42	0.64
All identified opportunities were pursued	39	45.3	70	47.9	0.11	0.79

Table 5.13   Mode of exploitation for the surveyed business reported by novice and habitual entrepreneurs

Variable	Novice		Habitual		χ^2 statistic	Sig. level
	No.	%	No.	%		
Mode of exploitation					**25.37**	**0.00**
Start-up	**299**	**84.9**	**294**	**77.8**	**6.14**	**0.01**
Purchase	53	15.1	58	15.3	0.01	0.92
Inheritance	–	–	26	6.9	n/a	n/a

A significant difference was detected between serial and portfolio entrepreneurs in terms of the proportion of identified opportunities pursued. Table 5.12 shows that a significantly higher proportion of serial rather than portfolio entrepreneurs reported that they had not pursued any of the opportunities for creating or purchasing a business they had identified over the past five years. This finding offers some support for hypothesis H_{12b}.

A significant difference was detected between novice and habitual entrepreneurs with respect to the selected mode of exploitation. Table 5.13 shows that a significantly larger proportion of novice rather than habitual entrepreneurs had exploited the opportunity associated with the surveyed business through a start-up. Hypothesis H_{13a} is, therefore, supported.

Table 5.14 shows that a larger proportion of portfolio entrepreneurs compared with their serial counterparts had exploited the opportunity through a start-up mode. Conversely, a larger proportion of serial entrepreneurs used a purchase

Table 5.14   *Mode of exploitation for the surveyed business reported by serial and portfolio entrepreneurs*

Variable	Serial		Portfolio		χ^2 statistic	Sig. level
	No.	%	No.	%		
Mode of exploitation					*3.90*	*0.14*
Start-up	126	81.3	168	85.3	0.00	1.00
Purchase	29	18.7	29	14.7	1.43	0.25
Inheritance	–	–	19	8.8	n/a	n/a

mode of exploitation. Both of these differences were not statistically significant. Consequently, there is no support for hypothesis H_{13b}.

The examples presented in the text box illustrate some of the differences between the opportunity recognition approaches of the three types of entrepreneur. While Lilias Cruickshank and Norman Rough, novice and serial entrepreneurs respectively, started their businesses, Mary Fairburn effected her ventures via the acquisition route.

EXAMPLES OF OPPORTUNITY RECOGNITION BY NOVICE, PORTFOLIO AND SERIAL ENTREPRENEURS

Novice: Lilias Cruickshank was made redundant and did not wish to continue in the area of management recruitment. Having been employed in this sector for over 20 years, she sought something different but was unclear what this was. The opportunity was brought to her by her sister-in-law, a qualified nursery nurse, who wanted to try and run her own nursery in an area that did not have a nursery nearby. Although neither had started a business before, they had complementary skills in terms of nursery nurse experience and profit-centred managerial experience.

Portfolio: Mary Fairburn's first two business opportunities arose because of lifestyle choices without her having any experience in running either kind of venture. The first opportunity, to go into antiques retailing, was recognized as a way of enabling a move from an existing location and occupation. The second, the acquisition of a private cemetery business, arose because of a relocation decision and a search for something different from the first business that would not be seasonal. The third opportunity was recognized as a result of a search to expand by doing something connected to the cemetery, and materialized when the memorials business with whom she had traded went into liquidation and the entrepreneur took the view that she could run it better than the previous owner. The fourth opportunity, a funeral service business, was recognized as an opportunity to move into a related business where she felt she could offer a better service. The business forms essentially selected themselves based on their situation.

Serial: Norman Rough identified his first business opportunity, a health and fitness club, out of his professional interests. People asked him how they could do bodybuilding in an organized way so he decided to make use of this level of interest and his reputation from competing nationally in the sport to start up in business. The subsequent opportunity for a cosmetic salon presented itself as an extension of the customer base in the health and fitness club. However, the third business emerged from an active decision to start a design consultancy. Having trained in architectural design, Rough identified an opportunity to provide for clients small specialized design work with a complete service that met their needs (in terms of being able to undertake both design and architectural work).

INFORMATION SEARCH AND OPPORTUNITY IDENTIFICATION, PURSUIT, AND EXPLOITATION: MULTIVARIATE ANALYSIS

The hypotheses developed in Chapter 2 were also tested within a multivariate statistical framework. Ordinary Least Squares (OLS) regression analysis was used[1]. A confirmatory forced-entry OLS regression approach was utilized. While forced-entry regression tends to produce lower overall model fit (R^2), it is often deemed more robust by identifying a more parsimonious model (Hair et al., 1995). Furthermore, it minimizes the risk from other methods that theoretically important variables may be deemed statistically inconsequential and excluded from the final model.

Appendices 5.1 and 5.2 provide the means and standard deviations for the independent and control variables as well as the correlation coefficients between the independent and control variables, and the VIF scores for the full sample and the habitual entrepreneurs subsample, respectively. The correlation matrix and the VIF scores suggest that the models will not be seriously distorted by multicollinearity. The reader will note the slight variation in the sample size across various models which is due to a number of respondents who filed missing information for some of the selected dependent and independent variables. For example, for the models relating to information search (that is, number of information sources used and search intensity) 612 respondents were used, while 599 respondents were used for the opportunity identification models. Sample sensitivity tests were conducted. The information search models were, for example, run on the sample of 599 respondents. The difference between the two models was negligible. Models relating to the samples containing most respondents are now discussed.

Two OLS regression models are presented. The first model explores the contribution made by the control variables (Models 1a, 1b, 4a, 3b, 7a, 5b, 10a and 7b). The independent variables relating to business ownership experience were not included within the first model. Variables relating to general human capital and human capital specific to entrepreneurship other than business ownership experience were included in the control model. For the models relating to the full sample (both novice and habitual entrepreneurs) two additional regression models are presented. In the first additional model, habitual entrepreneur dummy variable (HABITUAL) is included (Models 2a, 5a, 8a and 11a). By comparing this model against the control model, the contribution of including business ownership experience could be ascertained with reference to the change in the adjusted R^2 between the two models. To test for definitional sensitivities, a second additional model was computed. Instead of the habitual entrepreneur dummy variable, a continuous variable representing the number of previous minority and/or majority businesses owned was included (Models 3a, 6a, 9a and 12a).

A similar set of models was computed for the subsample of habitual entrepreneurs. The first model included the control variables only (Models 1b, 3b, 5b and 7b). The second model introduced the PORTFOLIO dummy variable representing whether the entrepreneur was a portfolio entrepreneur or not (Models 2b, 4b, 6b and 8b).

In addition to the analysis carried out to test the hypotheses developed in Chapter 2, it was also deemed appropriate to check for the possibility of similarities and differences between novice and serial entrepreneurs, and between novice and portfolio entrepreneurs. Significant differences between the two pairs are also reported in the notes following each model reported in this chapter. The following discussion, however, focuses on the full models used to test the relevant hypotheses.

Number of Information Sources Used

In the following discussion, the dependent variable relates to the number of information sources used (NUMBER OF INFORMATION SOURCES). The first model (Model 1a) explores the association between the control variables and the dependent variable. The following relationship is assumed (see discussion of multivariate analysis in Chapter 4 for a description of the control variables):

Model 1a:

NUMBER OF INFORMATION SOURCES $= f\,(\text{GHK, SHK}_E)$

The next models (Models 2a and 3a) explore the association between the control variables, independent business ownership experience variables and the dependent variable. In Model 2a, the independent variable relates to the binary HABITUAL variable. In Model 3a, the independent variable relates to the continuous TOTAL variable. The following relationships were assumed:

Model 2a:

NUMBER OF INFORMATION SOURCES $= f\,(\text{GHK, SHK}_E\text{, HABITUAL})$

Model 3a:

NUMBER OF INFORMATION SOURCES $= f\,(\text{GHK, SHK}_E\text{, TOTAL})$

With respect to the habitual entrepreneur subsample, the following relationship was assumed for the control Model 1b:

NUMBER OF INFORMATION SOURCES $= f\,(\text{GHK, SHK}_E)$

The PORTFOLIO represents the binary independent that was then introduced. The following relationship was assumed in Model 2b:

NUMBER OF INFORMATION SOURCES $= f\,(\text{GHK, SHK}_E\text{, PORTFOLIO})$

All models relating to the full sample of habitual and novice entrepreneurs (Models 1a, 2a and 3a) were significant at the 0.001 level (Table 5.15). Relative to the control model (Model 1a), the introduction of the business ownership experience variables (HABITUAL in Model 2a and TOTAL in Model 3a) had no significant effect on the model fit (R^2). Consistent with the bivariate analysis reported earlier, Models 2a and 3a indicate that neither of the ownership experience

Table 5.15 *OLS regression models of variables associated with the number of information sources used by novice and habitual entrepreneurs*

Independent variables	Model 1a[a] β		Model 2a[a] β		Model 3a[a] β	
GHK						
Age	–0.03		–0.03		–0.03	
Age^2	–0.02		–0.02		–0.02	
Gender	0.06		0.06		0.06	
Education	0.04		0.04		0.04	
Managerial human capital	0.03		0.03		0.03	
Managerial capability	**0.11**	**	**0.10**	**	**0.11**	**
Technical capability	–0.01		–0.01		–0.01	
SHK$_E$						
Entrepreneurial capability	**0.07**	†	**0.07**	†	**0.07**	†
Parent business owners	0.05		0.05		0.05	
Development	**0.14**	**	**0.14**	**	**0.14**	**
HABITUAL	–		0.00		–	
TOTAL	–		–		–0.01	
F-value	3.50	****	3.17	***	3.17	****
R^2	0.06		0.06		0.06	
Adjusted R^2	0.04		0.04		0.04	
Change in R^2	–		0.00		0.00	
N	612		612		612	

Notes:
† $p < 0.10$; * $p < 0.05$; ** $p < 0.01$; *** $p < 0.001$; **** $p < 0.0001$.
[a] VIF scores for all the models were well below the maximum level of 10 (maximum score of 2.09).

variables were related to the number of information sources used. Consequently, there is no support for hypothesis H$_{10a}$.

Two control variables relating to GHK (gender and perceived managerial capability) were weakly significantly related to the number of information sources used in all three models. Male entrepreneurs and those reporting higher levels of perceived managerial capability used more information sources in both Models 2a and 3a. Among the variables relating to SHK$_E$, those respondents reporting higher levels of entrepreneurial capability and those indicating the

Table 5.16   OLS regression models of variables associated with the number
of information sources used by serial and portfolio
entrepreneurs

Independent variables	Model 1b[a] β		Model 2b[a] β	
GHK				
Age	0.02		0.02	
Age^2	–0.04		–0.04	
Gender	**0.10**	†	0.09	
Education	0.05		0.04	
Managerial human capital	0.03		0.03	
Managerial capability	**0.13**	*	**0.12**	*
Technical capability	0.05		0.05	
SHK$_E$				
Entrepreneurial capability	**0.10**	†	**0.10**	†
Parent business owners	–0.03		–0.03	
Development	**0.12**	*	**0.13**	*
PORTFOLIO[b]	–		0.03	
F-value	2.40	**	2.20	**
R^2	0.07		0.07	
Adjusted R^2	0.04		0.04	
Change in R^2	–		0.00	
N	323		323	

Notes:
† $p < 0.10$; * $p < 0.05$; ** $p < 0.01$; *** $p < 0.001$; **** $p < 0.0001$.
No significant differences were detected between novice and serial entrepreneurs or novice and portfolio entrepreneurs.
[a]   VIF scores for both models were well below the maximum appropriate level of 10 (maximum score of 2.68).
[b]   Reference category: serial entrepreneurs.

importance of a developmental approach to opportunity identification used more information sources.

Models 1b and 2b in Table 5.16 relate to the sample of habitual entrepreneurs alone. Both models were significant at the 0.01 level. The inclusion of the portfolio entrepreneur dummy variable had no effect on the R^2 when compared with the control model (Model 1b). Among habitual entrepreneurs, there was no significant association between being a portfolio entrepreneur and the number of information sources used. Hypothesis H_{10b} is, therefore, not supported. In line with the full sample models (incorporating both novice and habitual entrepreneurs) the habitual-entrepreneur-only models suggest that gender, managerial capability, entrepreneurial capability and emphasis on a developmental approach to opportunity identification were all significantly related to the number of information sources used.

Information Search Intensity

The information search intensity variable was also selected as a dependent variable. It takes into account the particular information source and its importance. The method of analysis follows the logic presented to explore the dependent variable in the previous section (number of information sources used). Consequently, the first model (Model 4a) explores the association between the control variables and the dependent variable. The following relationship is assumed:

Model 4a:

$$\text{INFORMATION SEARCH INTENSITY} = f\,(\text{GHK, SHK}_E)$$

The next models (Models 5a and 6a) explore the association between the control variables, independent business ownership experience variables and the information search intensity dependent variable. In Model 5a, the independent variable relates to the binary HABITUAL variable. In Model 6a, the independent variable relates to the continuous TOTAL variable. The following relationships were assumed:

Model 5a:

$$\text{INFORMATION SEARCH INTENSITY} = f\,(\text{GHK, SHK}_E, \text{HABITUAL})$$

Model 6a:

$$\text{INFORMATION SEARCH INTENSITY} = f\,(\text{GHK, SHK}_E, \text{TOTAL})$$

With respect to the habitual entrepreneur subsample, the following relationship was assumed for the control Model 3b:

$$\text{INFORMATION SEARCH INTENSITY} = f\,(\text{GHK, SHK}_E)$$

The PORTFOLIO variable was then introduced. The following relationship was assumed in Model 4b:

INFORMATION SEARCH INTENSITY $= f$ (GHK, SHK_E, PORTFOLIO)

Table 5.17 shows that both the control Model 4a and the full Models 5a and 6a were highly significant with an R^2 of 0.10. The inclusion of the business ownership variables had no impact on the overall model fit. Hypothesis H_{10a} is, therefore, not supported. The finding is in line with the bivariate evidence.

Among the control variables positively related to information search intensity were managerial capability; entrepreneurial capability; having at least one parent who was a business owner; and a favourable attitude towards a developmental

Table 5.17   OLS regression models of variables associated with information search intensity of novice and habitual entrepreneurs

Independent variables	Model 4a[a] β		Model 5a[a] β		Model 6a[a] β	
GHK						
Age	−0.06		−0.06		−0.06	
Age^2	0.04		0.04		0.04	
Gender	−0.01		−0.01		−0.01	
Education	0.02		0.02		0.02	
Managerial human capital	0.03		0.03		0.03	
Managerial capability	**0.09**	*	**0.09**	*	**0.09**	*
Technical capability	**−0.09**	*	**−0.09**	*	**−0.09**	*
SHK$_E$						
Entrepreneurial capability	**0.10**	*	**0.10**	*	**0.10**	*
Parent business owners	**0.07**	†	**0.07**	†	**0.07**	†
Development	**0.22**	****	**0.22**	****	**0.22**	****
HABITUAL	−		−0.02			
TOTAL	−		−		−0.02	
F-value	6.62	****	6.04	****	6.03	****
R^2	0.10		0.10		0.10	
Adjusted R^2	0.08		0.08		0.08	
Change in R^2	−		0.00		0.00	
N	612		612		612	

Notes:
† $p < 0.10$; * $p < 0.05$; ** $p < 0.01$; *** $p < 0.001$; **** $p < 0.0001$.
[a]   VIF scores for all the models were well below the maximum level of 10 (maximum score of 2.09).

Table 5.18 OLS regression models of variables associated with information search intensity of serial and portfolio entrepreneurs

Independent Variables	Model 3b[a] β		Model 4b[a] β	
GHK				
Age	−0.06		−0.06	
Age^2	0.04		0.04	
Gender	0.04		0.04	
Education	0.02		0.02	
Managerial human capital	−0.01		−0.01	
Managerial capability	**0.12**	**	**0.12**	**
Technical capability	−0.06		−0.06	
SHK$_E$				
Entrepreneurial capability	**0.12**	*	**0.12**	*
Parent business owners	−0.02		−0.02	
Development	**0.22**	****	**0.22**	****
PORTFOLIO[b]			−0.01	
F-value	3.45	****	3.13	****
R^2	0.10		0.10	
Adjusted R^2	0.07		0.07	
Change in R^2	−		0.00	
N	323		323	

Notes:
† $p < 0.10$; * $p < 0.05$; ** $p < 0.01$; *** $p < 0.001$; **** $p < 0.0001$.
No significant differences were detected between novice and serial entrepreneurs or novice and portfolio entrepreneurs.
[a] VIF scores for both models were well below the maximum appropriate level of 10 (maximum score of 2.68).
[b] Reference category: serial entrepreneurs.

approach to opportunity identification. Entrepreneurs reporting a high perceived level of technical capability, however, reported significantly lower levels of information search intensity.

Table 5.18 shows the relationship between information search intensity and the nature of business ownership experience (that is, being a portfolio or a serial entrepreneur). Both the control Model 3a and full Model 4b were highly significant and they both have an adjusted R^2 of 0.07. The inclusion of the PORTFOLIO variable in Model 4b had no significant impact on the overall model fit. More-over, PORTFOLIO is not individually significantly associated with information search intensity. Hypothesis H_{10b} is, therefore, not supported.

As found in Models 5a and 6a with regard to the full sample, high information search intensity was positively associated with managerial capability, entrepreneurial capability, and a favourable attitude towards a developmental approach to opportunity identification.

Opportunity Identification

Here the dependent variable is the number of opportunities identified in a given period (NUMBER OF OPPORTUNITIES IDENTIFIED). The logic in the previous two sections is followed. For the full sample, the control model (Model 7a) was specified as:

$$\text{NUMBER OF OPPORTUNITIES IDENTIFIED} = f(\text{GHK, SHK}_E, \\ \text{INFORMATION SEARCH INTENSITY})$$

As before, the two business ownership variables, HABITUAL and TOTAL, were then included. Models 8a and 9a, were specified as follows, respectively:

$$\text{NUMBER OF OPPORTUNITIES IDENTIFIED} = f(\text{GHK, SHK}_E, \\ \text{INFORMATION SEARCH INTENSITY, HABITUAL})$$

$$\text{NUMBER OF OPPORTUNITIES IDENTIFIED} = f(\text{GHK, SHK}_E, \\ \text{INFORMATION SEARCH INTENSITY, TOTAL})$$

With respect to the habitual entrepreneur subsample, the following relationship was assumed for the control Model 5b:

$$\text{NUMBER OF OPPORTUNITIES IDENTIFIED} = f(\text{GHK, SHK}_E, \\ \text{INFORMATION SEARCH INTENSITY})$$

The binary PORTFOLIO variable was then introduced. The following relationship was assumed in Model 6b:

$$\text{NUMBER OF OPPORTUNITIES IDENTIFIED} = f(\text{GHK, SHK}_E, \\ \text{INFORMATION SEARCH INTENSITY, PORTFOLIO})$$

With regard to the full sample (both novice and habitual entrepreneurs) the control Model 7a is highly significant, with an adjusted R^2 of 0.11 (see Table 5.19). The full Models 8a and 9a were also highly significant, with adjusted

Table 5.19 OLS regression models of variables associated with the number of opportunities for creating/purchasing an opportunity identified by novice and habitual entrepreneurs

Independent variables	Model 7a[a] β		Model 8a[a] β		Model 9a[a] β	
GHK						
Age	**−0.20**	****	**−0.22**	****	**−0.23**	****
Age^2	0.00		0.01		0.01	
Gender	**0.18**	****	**0.15**	****	**0.14**	****
Education	**0.10**	**	**0.09**	*	**0.09**	*
Managerial human capital	**0.07**	†	0.06		**0.07**	†
Managerial capability	**0.09**	*	**0.08**	*	0.06	
Technical capability	−0.03		−0.01		−0.01	
SHK$_E$						
Entrepreneurial capability	**0.12**	**	**0.13**	**	**0.10**	**
Parent business owners	0.02		−0.01		−0.04	
Development	0.07		0.06		**0.08**	†
Search intensity	**0.09**	*	**0.10**	*	**0.10**	**
HABITUAL	–		**0.23**	****	–	
TOTAL	–		–		**0.33**	****
F-value	7.83	****	10.53	****	14.68	****
R^2	0.13		0.18		0.23	
Adjusted R^2	0.11		0.16		0.22	
Change in R^2	–		0.05	****	0.10	****
N	599		599		599	

Notes:
† $p < 0.10$; * $p < 0.05$; ** $p < 0.01$; *** $p < 0.001$; **** $p < 0.0001$.
Serial entrepreneurs identified significantly more opportunities than novice entrepreneurs ($p < 0.01$).
Portfolio entrepreneurs identified significantly more opportunities than novice entrepreneurs ($p < 0.0001$).
[a] VIF scores for all models were well below the maximum level of 10 (maximum score of 2.09).

R^2 0.16 and 0.2, respectively. An examination of the R^2 in each model suggests that the inclusion of both business ownership experience variables (HABITU-AL and TOTAL) resulted in a significant improvement in the model fit. Furthermore, both HABITUAL and TOTAL were highly significant. Consequently hypothesis H_{11a} is supported. These findings are in line with the bivariate evidence.

Models 8a and 9a also show that younger entrepreneurs and males identified more opportunities. Entrepreneurs reporting higher levels of education, managerial human capital, managerial capability, entrepreneurial capability and information search intensity also reported the identification of more opportunities.

Table 5.20   *OLS regression models of variables associated with the number*
of opportunities for creating/purchasing an opportunity
identified by serial and portfolio entrepreneurs

Independent variables	Model 5b[a] β		Model 6b[a] β	
GHK				
Age	**–0.20**	****	**–0.19**	****
Age^2	–0.02		–0.02	
Gender	**0.11**	**	0.09	
Education	0.06		0.05	
Managerial human capital	0.06		0.06	
Managerial capability	**0.14**	**	**0.12**	*
Technical capability	0.00		0.00	
SHK$_E$				
Entrepreneurial capability	**0.20**	****	**0.19**	***
Parent business owners	–0.04		–0.04	
Development	0.00		0.01	
Search intensity	0.08		0.08	
PORTFOLIO[b]	–		**0.15**	**
F-value	3.45	****	3.76	****
R^2	0.14		0.16	
Adjusted R^2	0.10		0.12	
Change in R^2	–		0.02	**
N	319		319	

Notes:
† $p < 0.10$; * $p < 0.05$; ** $p < 0.01$; *** $p < 0.001$; **** $p < 0.0001$.
[a]   VIF scores for both models were well below the maximum appropriate level of 10 (maximum score of 2.68).
[b]   Reference category: serial entrepreneurs.

Among the habitual entrepreneurs, Table 5.20 shows that although the control Model 5b and the full Model 6b were highly significant ($p < 0.0001$), the inclusion of the PORTFOLIO dummy variable resulted in a significant ($p < 0.01$) improvement in the model fit. The PORTFOLIO variable was significantly ($p < 0.01$) and positively associated with the number of opportunities identified. This finding lends support to hypothesis H_{11b} that portfolio entrepreneurs will identify more opportunities in a given period than their serial counterparts.

Opportunity Pursuit

In this section the dependent variable explored relates to the proportion of opportunities identified that were pursued (PROPORTION OF OPPORTUNITIES PURSUED). As before, the control model computed on the full sample (novice and habitual entrepreneurs) was specified as follows:

Model 10a:

PROPORTION OF OPPORTUNITIES PURSUED $= f$ (GHK, SHK$_E$, INFORMATION SEARCH INTENSITY)

In Models 11a and 12a, the two business ownership experience independent variables (HABITUAL and TOTAL) were included, respectively. The following relationships were assumed:

Model 11a:
PROPORTION OF OPPORTUNITIES PURSUED $= f$ (GHK, SHK$_E$, INFORMATION SEARCH INTENSITY, HABITUAL)

Model 12a:

PROPORTION OF OPPORTUNITIES PURSUED $= f$ (GHK, SHK$_E$, INFORMATION SEARCH INTENSITY, TOTAL)

With regard to the subsample of habitual entrepreneurs, the control model (Model 7b) was specified as follows:

PROPORTION OF OPPORTUNITIES PURSUED $= f$ (GHK, SHK$_E$, INFORMATION SEARCH INTENSITY)

The PORTFOLIO independent variable was then added in Model 8b. Model 8b was specified as follows:

PROPORTION OF OPPORTUNITIES PURSUED = f(GHK, SHK$_E$, INFORMATION SEARCH INTENSITY, PORTFOLIO)

Table 5.21 shows that the control Model 10a and Model 12a are not significant. However, Model 11a was significant at $p < 0.05$, with an adjusted R^2 of 0.04. Compared to the control model, the inclusion of the HABITUAL variable

Table 5.21 *OLS regression models of variables associated with the proportion of identified opportunities that were pursued by novice and habitual entrepreneurs*

Independent variables	Model 10a[a] β	Model 11a[a] β	Model 12a[a] β
GHK			
Age	**0.12** †	0.09	**0.12** †
Age^2	0.09	0.09	0.09
Gender	–0.02	–0.03	–0.02
Education	–0.03	–0.02	–0.03
Managerial human capital	–0.02	–0.02	–0.02
Managerial capability	0.08	0.07	0.08
Technical capability	0.08	0.09	0.08
SHK$_E$			
Entrepreneurial capability	0.07	0.06	0.07
Parent business owners	–0.01	–0.02	–0.01
Development	0.06	0.06	0.06
Search Intensity	**–0.14** *	**–0.12** *	**–0.14** *
HABITUAL	–	**0.17** **	–
TOTAL	–	–	0.02
F-value	1.37 n/s[b]	1.67 *	1.26 n/s[b]
R^2	0.05	0.08	0.05
Adjusted R^2	0.01	0.04	0.01
Change in R^2	–	0.03 **	0.00
N	299	299	299

Notes:
† $p < 0.10$; * $p < 0.05$; ** $p < 0.01$; *** $p < 0.001$; **** $p < 0.0001$.
[a] Variance Inflation Factor (VIF) scores for all models were well below the maximum level of 10 (maximum score of 2.84).
[b] Not significant.

resulted in a significant improvement in the model fit. Consequently, hypothesis H$_{12a}$ is supported.

Table 5.22 shows that both the control Model 7b and full Model 8b are significant, with a minimum adjusted R^2 of 0.05. The inclusion of the PORTFOLIO

Table 5.22 *OLS regression models of variables associated with the proportion of identified opportunities that were pursued by serial and portfolio entrepreneurs*

Independent variables	Model 7b[a] β	Model 8b[a] β
GHK		
Age	0.07	0.07
Age^2	**0.16** *	**0.17** *
Gender	0.01	−0.02
Education	−0.06	−0.07
Managerial human capital	−0.05	−0.04
Managerial capability	0.08	0.07
Technical capability	**0.13** †	**0.13** †
SHK$_E$		
Entrepreneurial capability	0.09	0.07
Parent business owners	0.01	0.02
Development	**0.17** *	**0.18** *
Search Intensity	**−0.19** *	**−0.19** **
PORTFOLIO[b]	–	**0.13** †
F-value	1.85 *	2.01 *
R^2	0.10	0.11
Adjusted R^2	0.05	0.06
Change in R^2	–	0.02 †
N	202	202

Notes:
† $p < 0.10$; * $p < 0.05$; ** $p < 0.01$; *** $p < 0.001$; **** $p < 0.0001$.
Portfolio entrepreneurs pursued a significantly larger proportion of identified opportunities than novice entrepreneurs ($p < 0.0001$). No significant difference between serial and novice entrepreneurs was detected.
[a]   VIF scores for both models were well below the maximum appropriate level of 10 (maximum score of 3.46).
[b]   Reference category: serial entrepreneurs.

variable resulted in a significant improvement in the model fit and the variable itself was significant. Hypothesis H_{12b} is, therefore, supported.

Opportunity Exploitation

In this section, the dependent variable explored relates to the mode of exploitation. In particular, the LIKELIHOOD OF PURCHASE dependent variable is a binary variable which takes a value of '1' if the respondent had purchased the surveyed business and '0' if otherwise. Given the binary nature of this dependent variable, a logistic regression was computed. The control model (Model 13a) for the full sample was based on the following assumed relationship:

$$\text{LIKELIHOOD OF PURCHASE} = f(\text{GHK, SHK}_E, \text{INFORMATION SEARCH INTENSITY})$$

The full models (Model 14a and 15a) included the two business ownership independent variables and were specified as follows:

Model 14a:

$$\text{LIKELIHOOD OF PURCHASE} = f(\text{GHK, SHK}_E, \text{INFORMATION SEARCH INTENSITY, HABITUAL})$$

Model 15a:

$$\text{LIKELIHOOD OF PURCHASE} = f(\text{GHK, SHK}_E, \text{INFORMATION SEARCH INTENSITY, TOTAL})$$

The control model (Model 9b) for the subsample of habitual entrepreneurs assumed the following relationship:

$$\text{LIKELIHOOD OF PURCHASE} = f(\text{GHK, SHK}_E, \text{INFORMATION SEARCH INTENSITY})$$

In Model 10b, the PORTFOLIO independent variable was introduced. The following relationship is assumed:

$$\text{LIKELIHOOD OF PURCHASE} = f(\text{GHK, SHK}_E, \text{INFORMATION SEARCH INTENSITY, PORTFOLIO})$$

Table 5.23 reports findings relating to the full sample and shows that the control Model 13a and full Models 14a and 15a are significant, with an R^2 ranging between 0.06 and 0.10 depending on the R^2 indicator used. The inclusion

Table 5.23   Logistic regression models of variables associated with the purchase of a business as the mode of exploitation for the surveyed business by novice and habitual entrepreneurs

Independent variables	Model 10a[a] β		Model 11a[a] β		Model 12a[a] β	
GHK						
Age	0.01		0.01		0.01	
Age^2	**–0.01**	*	**–0.01**	*	**–0.01**	*
Gender	–0.29		–0.28		–0.30	
Education	0.16		0.16		0.16	
Managerial human capital	**–0.06**	**	**–0.06**	**	**–0.06**	**
Managerial capability	0.04		0.05		0.04	
Technical capability	**–0.36**	**	**–0.36**	**	**–0.36**	**
SHK$_E$						
Entrepreneurial capability	**–0.29**	*	**–0.29**	*	**–0.29**	*
Parent business owners	0.41		**0.42**	†	**0.40**	†
Development	–0.04		–0.04		–0.05	
Search Intensity	0.01		0.01		0.01	
HABITUAL	–		–0.06		–	
TOTAL	–		–		0.02	
Model χ^2	35.97	***	36.03	***	36.04	***
-2 log likelihood	485.5		485.5		485.5	
Overall predictive accuracy	84.12		84.12		84.29	
Cox and Snell R^2	0.06		0.06		0.06	
Nagelkerke R^2	0.10		0.10		0.10	
n	592		592		592	

Notes:
† $p < 0.10$; * $p < 0.05$; ** $p < 0.01$; *** $p < 0.001$; **** $p < 0.0001$.
[a]   VIF scores for all models were well below the maximum level of 10 (maximum score of 2.84).

of both business ownership experience variables (HABITUAL and TOTAL) did not significantly improve the model fit. Further, these independent variables were not individually significant. Consequently, hypothesis H$_{13a}$ cannot be supported.

Entrepreneurs reporting higher levels of managerial human capital, technical capability, and entrepreneurial capability were less likely to have purchased their

*Table 5.24   Logistic regression models of variables associated with the
             purchase of a business as the mode of exploitation for the
             surveyed business by serial and portfolio entrepreneurs*

Independent variables	Model 7b[a] β	Model 8b[a] β
GHK		
Age	**0.04** †	**0.04** †
Age^2	**−0.01** *	**−0.01** *
Gender	−0.66	−0.61
Education	0.11	0.11
Managerial human capital	**−0.05** †	**−0.05** †
Managerial capability	0.11	0.12
Technical capability	**−0.50** **	**−0.50** **
SHK$_E$		
Entrepreneurial capability	−0.24	−0.23
Parent business owners	0.36	0.35
Development	−0.01	−0.01
Search Intensity	0.00	0.00
PORTFOLIO [b]	−	−0.25
Model χ^2	27.93 **	28.50 **
-2 log likelihood	240.2	239.7
Overall predictive accuracy (%)	84.49	84.49
Cox & Snell R^2	0.09	0.09
Nagelkerke R^2	0.15	0.15
n	303	303

Notes:
† $p < 0.10$; * $p < 0.05$; ** $p < 0.01$; *** $p < 0.001$; **** $p < 0.0001$.
No significant differences between novice and serial or novice and portfolio entrepreneurs were detected.
[a] VIF scores for both models were well below the maximum appropriate level of 10 (maximum score of 3.46).
[b] Reference category: serial entrepreneurs.

surveyed business. Entrepreneurs who had at least one parent who was or is a business owner were more likely to have purchased the surveyed business.

With respect to the subsample of habitual entrepreneurs, Table 5.24 shows that while the control Model 9b and the full Model 10b were significant, the inclusion of PORTFOLIO had no significant effect on the model fit. Furthermore, PORTFOLIO itself was not significant. Hence, there is no support for hypothesis H_{13b}. As highlighted in Models 11a and 12a, managerial human capital and technical capability were negatively associated with the likelihood of having purchased the surveyed business. Finally, while there appeared to be a significant and positive relationship between the age of the entrepreneur and the likelihood of having purchased the surveyed business, this relationship was not linear. This is evident from the significance of the Age^2 variable. Hence, while older entrepreneurs appear to be more likely to purchase a business, beyond a certain age this relationship is reversed.

CONCLUSION

Table 5.25 summarizes the findings of the bivariate and multivariate analyses relating to information search as well as opportunity identification, pursuit and exploitation. Many of the relationships detected by the bivariate analyses were supported by the multivariate analyses. Table 5.25 shows that there is no support for hypotheses H_{10a} and H_{10b} that, respectively, habitual and portfolio entrepreneur would search for less information than their novice and serial counterparts. Despite these findings supporting hypotheses H_{11a} and H_{11b} however, both habitual and portfolio entrepreneurs were able to identify significantly more opportunities in the five years prior to the study when compared with novice and serial entrepreneurs respectively. Furthermore, supporting hypotheses H_{12a} and H_{12b}, it was found that habitual entrepreneurs, particularly portfolio entrepreneurs, were more likely to pursue an identified opportunity than their novice or serial counterparts. Finally, in contrast to the bivariate evidence, there was no support for the hypothesis that habitual entrepreneurs would be more likely

Table 5.25   Summary of findings relating to information search and opportunity identification, pursuit and exploitation

Hypothesis number and description		Bivariate results	Multivariate results
H_{10a}	Info. Search$_{habitual}$ < Info. Search$_{novice}$	Not supported	Not supported
H_{10b}	Info. Search$_{portfolio}$ < Info. Search$_{serial}$	Not supported	Not supported
H_{11a}	Opp. Identification$_{habitual}$ > Opp. Identification$_{novice}$	Supported	Supported
H_{11b}	Opp. Identification$_{portfolio}$ > Opp. Identification$_{serial}$	Supported	Supported
H_{12a}	Opp. Pursuit$_{habitual}$ > Opp. Pursuit$_{novice}$	Supported	Supported
H_{12b}	Opp. Pursuit$_{portfolio}$ > Opp. Pursuit$_{serial}$	Supported	Supported
H_{13a}	Purchase$_{habitual}$ > Purchase$_{novice}$	Some support	Not supported
H_{13b}	Purchase$_{portfolio}$ < Purchase$_{serial}$	Not supported	Not supported

to opt for the purchase of a business as a mode of opportunity exploitation (hypothesis H_{13a}). There was also no support for hypothesis H_{13b}.

Overall the above findings suggest that there is a relationship between the extent and nature of business ownership experience and information search as well as opportunity identification, pursuit and exploitation. Habitual entrepreneurs, particularly portfolio entrepreneurs, appear to be able to identify more opportunities for creating or purchasing a business in a given period than novice or serial entrepreneurs. Furthermore, habitual and portfolio entrepreneurs were more likely to pursue identified opportunities (that is, commit time and resources to evaluating the opportunity). The following chapter explores differences between the types of entrepreneur with regard to the performance of the entrepreneurs and their surveyed businesses.

NOTE

1. For a number of the dependent variables (for example, the number of opportunities identified and number of opportunities pursued) an ordered probit or ordered logit approach is deemed superior to OLS. To test our hypotheses we used both OLS regression and ordered probit modelling. There were no differences in the results. For consistency, we report only the OLS regression results in this chapter.

APPENDIX 5.1

Table 5A.1 Correlation Matrix Relating to Models 1a–15a (n= 612) [a]

Variables	Mean	S.D.	VIF	1	2	3	4	5	6	7	8	9	10	11
1. Age[b]	-0.23	10.00	1.10	1.00										
2. Age²	99.84	136.03	1.04	0.00	1.00									
3. Gender	0.87	0.34	1.10	0.18	-0.01	1.00								
4. Education	0.49	0.79	1.04	-0.03	-0.06	-0.02	1.00							
5. Managerial human capital	9.75	5.76	1.11	0.18	-0.15	0.07	0.08	1.00						
6. Managerial capability	-0.01	1.00	1.09	-0.03	-0.02	-0.09	-0.10	0.10	1.00					
7. Technical capability	0.00	1.01	1.14	0.02	0.01	0.15	0.03	-0.01	-0.02	1.00				
8. Entrepreneurial capability	-0.01	1.00	1.12	0.01	0.05	0.03	-0.07	0.05	-0.01	0.00	1.00			
9. Development	-0.02	0.99	1.27	-0.12	-0.03	-0.03	-0.04	0.07	0.19	0.26	0.28	1.00		
10. Parent business owners	0.36	0.48	1.05	-0.02	0.09	-0.02	0.02	-0.11	0.01	-0.06	0.07	0.04	1.00	
11. Habitual [c]	0.53	0.50	1.07	0.08	-0.02	0.10	0.05	0.07	0.08	-0.09	0.00	0.03	0.14	1.00
12. Total [c]	2.18	2.05	1.07	0.10	-0.01	0.11	0.03	0.03	0.09	-0.06	0.07	-0.01	0.17	0.54
13. Serial [c]	0.24	0.42	1.19	0.05	0.00	-0.03	0.00	0.02	-0.03	-0.06	-0.05	0.01	0.09	1.00
14. Portfolio [c]	0.29	0.46	1.23	0.04	-0.02	0.15	0.05	0.06	0.11	-0.04	0.05	0.02	0.07	-0.36

Notes:

r has to be 0.08 or higher to be significant at $p < 0.05$ (two-tailed) and r has to be 0.11 or higher to be significant at $p < 0.01$ (two-tailed).

[a] While there was some variation in the sample sizes for each model, a comparison of the correlation matrices for each model revealed no major discrepancies. For simplicity, the model containing the highest number of respondents is reported.

[b] The reader is reminded that age was measured in terms of deviation from the mean age of the group of respondents.

[c] As these variables are introduced separately into the regression models, the correlations between them are not required.

APPENDIX 5.2

Table 5A.2   Correlation matrix relating to models 1b–15b (n= 323)[a]

Variables	Mean	S.D.	VIF	1	2	3	4	5	6	7	8	9	10
1. Age[b]	0.52	9.84	1.06	1.00									
2. Age^2	96.78	137.85	1.04	-0.27	1.00								
3. Gender	0.90	0.30	1.10	0.09	-0.11	1.00							
4. Education	0.53	0.81	1.06	-0.06	0.01	0.02	1.00						
5. Managerial human capital	1.012	5.93	1.09	0.18	-0.17	0.03	0.17	1.00					
6. Managerial capability	0.01	1.01	1.08	-0.04	0.02	-0.14	-0.14	0.00	1.00				
7. Technical capability	-0.01	1.04	1.12	0.02	-0.09	0.21	0.09	0.00	-0.14	1.00			
8. Entrepreneurial capability	-0.01	1.02	1.10	-0.06	0.07	0.06	0.04	0.04	0.00	-0.03	1.00		
9. Parent business owners	0.42	0.49	1.03	0.00	0.06	-0.07	-0.03	-0.22	0.08	-0.04	0.02	1.00	
10. Development	0.01	0.99	1.19	-0.02	-0.13	0.04	0.02	-0.01	0.13	0.18	0.20	0.04	1.00
11. Portfolio	0.55	0.50	1.05	-0.01	-0.01	0.17	0.07	0.01	0.04	-0.03	0.13	-0.08	-0.08

Notes:

r has to be 0.12 or higher to be significant at p < 0.05 (two-tailed) and r has to be 0.15 or higher to be significant at p < 0.01 (two-tailed).

a   While there was some variation in the sample sizes for each model, a comparison of the correlation matrices for each model revealed no major discrepancies. For simplicity, the model containing the highest number of respondents is reported.

b   The reader is reminded that age was measured in terms of deviation from the mean age of the group of respondents.

6. Firm and entrepreneur performance by type of entrepreneur

INTRODUCTION

The performance of surveyed firms owned by novice and habitual as well as serial and portfolio entrepreneurs are examined with regard to several financial and non-financial performance indicators. In addition, a number of indicators relating to the entrepreneurs' performance are discussed. The structure of the chapter is as follows. First, surveyed firm performance differences between novice and habitual entrepreneurs, and then serial and portfolio entrepreneurs, are examined within a bivariate statistical framework. Firm performance is monitored with regard to the surveyed business in terms of two weighted performance measures, sales and employment growth, as well as profitability relative to competitors. This is followed by a discussion of entrepreneur performance with regard to the standard of living in relation to when the surveyed business was first started or purchased and money taken out of the business(es) owned. In the penultimate section, firm and then entrepreneur performance differences are examined within a multivariate statistical framework. Finally, conclusions are provided.

FIRM AND ENTREPRENEUR PERFORMANCE: BIVARIATE ANALYSIS

This section presents the findings relating to differences reported by novice and habitual and then serial and portfolio entrepreneurs in terms of various dimensions of performance within a bivariate framework.

Firm Performance

Table 6.1 shows that no significant differences were detected between novice and habitual entrepreneurs with respect to the two weighted performance measures, and profit relative to competitors.

The employment contribution made by each type of entrepreneur between 1996 and 2001 is summarized in Table 6.2. In total, firms owned by habitual

Table 6.1   Performance of the surveyed businesses reported by novice and habitual entrepreneurs

Variable	Novice (n = 294)	Habitual (n = 348)	t-statistic	Df	Sig. level (2-tailed)
Weighted performance (I)[a]	11.95	11.55	1.24	640	0.22
Weighted performance (II)[b]	12.97	12.96	0.30	640	0.98
Profit relative to competitors[c]	3.42	3.39	0.51	640	0.61

Notes:
[a]   Weighted performance (I) relates to the original Naman and Slevin (1993) measure.
[b]   Weighted performance (II) relates to the extended measure.
[c]   The following scale was used: (1) very poor; (2) poor; (3) about average; (4) good; and (5) very good.

Table 6.2   Total employment contribution of surveyed businesses 1996–2001 by type of entrepreneur[a]

Variable	Novice (n = 274)	Habitual (n = 313)	Serial (n = 132)	Portfolio (n = 181)
Gross absolute total employment loss in firms reporting total employment losses	88.50	299.75	86.5	213.25
Gross absolute total employment growth in total employment growing firms	679.25	2 106.00	1 031.25	1 074.75
Gross absolute total employment growth reported by the 4% fastest total employment growing firms[c]	376.50	802.25	822.00[b]	500.50
Proportion of total employment growth reported by the 4% fastest total employment growing firms	55.43	38.03	79.71[b]	46.57

Notes:
[a]   Full-time, part-time and casual employees were taken into account in the measure of total employment by scoring full-time, part-time and casual employees as 1, 0.5 and 0.25, respectively.
[b]   One serial entrepreneur reported a growth of 640 jobs (62% of all employment growth in the serial entrepreneurs subsample).
[c]   Among the fastest growing 4% of firms, firms owned by habitual entrepreneurs reported a significantly higher number of jobs created (101 jobs) than novice entrepreneurs (31 jobs) ($p < 0.01$). There was no significant difference between the 4% fastest employment growing firms owned by serial and portfolio entrepreneurs in terms of the average number of jobs created (137 and 63 jobs, respectively). These differences were tested using non-parametric Mann-Whitney U tests due to the small number of cases involved.

entrepreneurs had lost just under 300 jobs. In comparison, firms owned by novice entrepreneurs had lost 88.5 jobs. Among those firms that had created jobs during the period in question, those owned by the habitual entrepreneurs had created just under 2110 jobs compared with just under 670 jobs by firms owned by novice entrepreneurs. Reflecting evidence from elsewhere about the skewed growth performance of SMEs, the top 4 per cent fastest growing businesses that were owned by habitual entrepreneurs had created 802.25 (38.03 per cent) of all jobs created. In comparison, among these firms, those

Table 6.3   *Employment and sales growth of the surveyed businesses reported by novice and habitual entrepreneurs*

Variable	Novice (n = 232)	Habitual (n = 292)	t-statistic	Df	Sig. level (2-tailed)
Employment growth (1996–2001)[a]					
Absolute total employment change	2.29	6.09	–1.44	522	0.15
Absolute total employment change standardized by business age	0.19	0.49	–1.37	522	0.17
Percentage change in total employment	37	80	–1.12	522	0.26
Number of jobs lost by firms reporting total employment losses	**1.51**	**3.75**	**3.09**	**136**	**0.00**
Number of jobs created by firms reporting total employment growth	**5.19**	**12.66**	**–1.63**	**296**	**0.10**
Sales growth (1996–1999)					
Absolute change in sales	**149 518**	**367 724**	**–1.97**	**463**	**0.05**
Absolute change in sales standardized by business age	**13 067**	**28 971**	**–1.97**	**463**	**0.05**
Absolute change in sales standardized by employment in 1996	33 731	67 519	–1.45	463	0.15
Absolute change in sales standardized by employment in 1996 then by business age	**3 141**	**7 106**	**–1.68**	**463**	**0.09**
Percentage change in sales	110	128	–0.43	463	0.67

Note: [a] Full-time, part-time and casual employees were taken into account in the measure of total employment by scoring full-time, part-time and casual employees as 1, 0.5 and 0.25, respectively.

owned by novice entrepreneurs had created 376.5 (55.43 per cent) of all jobs.

Finer-level employment and sales change reported by novice and habitual entrepreneur firms are reported in Table 6.3. No significant differences were detected between the two groups in terms of absolute total employment change, absolute total employment change standardized by business age, or the percentage change in total employment. Firms owned by habitual entrepreneurs that had reported job losses lost significantly more jobs that their novice counterparts (3.75 jobs lost compared with 1.51 jobs lost). However, job-creating firms owned by habitual entrepreneurs reported that they had created more jobs (12.66) than their novice counterparts (5.19). This difference was only weakly significant. Table 6.4 reports the number of firms that reported job losses, no

Table 6.4   Total employment contribution of surveyed businesses owned by novice and habitual entrepreneurs over the 1996–2001 period

Variable	Novice		Habitual		χ^2 statistic	Sig. level (2-tailed)
	No.	%	No.	%		
					7.69	***0.021***
Number of firms reporting total employment losses	58	21.2	80	25.6	1.57	0.242
Number of firms reporting no change in total employment size	**85**	**31.0**	**66**	**21.1**	**7.55**	**0.008**
Number of firms reporting total employment growth	131	47.8	167	53.4	1.80	0.186

Table 6.5   Performance of the surveyed businesses reported by serial and portfolio entrepreneurs

Variable	Serial (n = 151)	Portfolio (n = 197)	t-statistic	Df	Sig. level (2-tailed)
Weighted performance (I)[a]	11.45	11.62	−0.38	346	0.71
Weighted performance (II)[b]	**12.60**	**13.24**	**−1.71**	**346**	**0.09**
Profit relative to competitors[c]	3.36	3.41	−0.45	346	0.66

Notes:

[a] Weighted performance (I) relates to the original Naman and Slevin (1993) measure.

[b] Weighted performance (II) relates to the extended measure.

[c] The following scale was used: (1) very poor; (2) poor; (3) about average; (4) good; and (5) very good.

Table 6.6　Employment and sales change of the surveyed businesses reported by serial and portfolio entrepreneurs

Variable	Serial (n = 124)	Portfolio (n = 168)	t-statistic	Df	Sig. level (2-tailed)
Employment growth (1996–2001)[a]					
Absolute total employment change 1996–2001	7.60	4.97	0.56	290	0.58
Absolute total employment change 1996–2001 standardized by business age	0.66	0.36	0.78	290	0.44
Percentage change in total employment 1996–2001	50	102	–0.78	290	0.44
Number of jobs lost by firms reporting total employment losses	2.62	4.54	1.60	78	0.12
Number of jobs created by firms reporting total employment growth	14.91	11.07	0.47	165	0.64
Sales growth (1996–1999)					
Absolute change in sales 1996–2001	233 733	465 091	–1.24	257	0.22
Absolute change in sales 1996–2001 standardized by business age	22 218	33 879	–0.89	257	0.37
Absolute change in sales 1996–2001 standardized by employment in 1996	53 250	77 889	–0.60	257	0.55
Absolute change in sales 1996–2001 standardized by employment in 1996 then by business age	7 795	6 605	0.29	257	0.77
Percentage change in sales 1996–2001	147	114	0.65	257	0.52

Note:　[a] Full-time, part-time and casual employees were taken into account in the measure of total employment by scoring full-time, part-time and causal employees as 1, 0.5 and 0.25, respectively.

change in employment and job creation. While there was an overall significant difference between novice and habitual entrepreneurs, this difference was largely attributable to the larger proportion of firms owned by novice entrepreneurs that had reported no change in total employment over the period 1996 to 2001. With respect to sales growth (Table 6.3), no significant differences between the two groups were detected in terms of the absolute change in sales standardized by employment, or the percentage change in sales over the period 1996 to 1999. Habitual entrepreneurs did, however, report significantly higher rates of growth in terms of the absolute change in sales (£367 724 compared with £149 518 for novice entrepreneurs); absolute change in sales standardized by business age (£28 971 compared with £13 067); and absolute change in sales standardized by both employment at the start of the period and business age (£7 106 compared with £3 141).

Table 6.5 shows that significant differences were detected between serial and portfolio entrepreneurs in terms of weighted performance (I) and profit relative to competitors. However portfolio entrepreneurs reported a significantly higher weighted performance II than serial entrepreneurs.

Table 6.6 shows that no significant differences between serial and portfolio entrepreneurs with regard to employment and change in sales of the surveyed firms were detected. Further, Table 6.7 shows that there was no significant difference in the proportion of firms owned by serial and portfolio entrepreneurs who had reported either job losses, no change in employment size or job creation.

Table 6.7   Total employment contribution of surveyed businesses owned by serial and portfolio entrepreneurs over the 1996–2001 period

Variable	Serial		Portfolio		χ^2 statistic	Sig. level (2-tailed)
	No.	%	No.	%		
					0.37	*0.831*
Number of firms reporting total employment losses	33	25.0	47	26.0	0.04	0.896
Number of firms reporting no change in total employment size	30	22.7	36	19.9	0.37	0.576
Number of firms reporting total employment growth	69	52.3	98	54.1	0.11	0.819

Entrepreneur Performance

No significant differences were detected between novice and habitual entrepreneurs with regard to standard of living relative to when the respondent first started or purchased the surveyed business. Habitual entrepreneurs, however, had taken significantly greater amounts of money out of the business(es) they currently owned compared to novice entrepreneurs (£36 660 to £28 036, respectively). This finding is not particularly surprising, as portfolio entrepreneurs among the habitual entrepreneurs group by definition own multiple businesses.

To control for this effect, the amount of money taken out was standardized by the number of businesses currently owned. Table 6.8 shows that when standardized for the number of businesses currently owned, habitual entrepreneurs had taken significantly smaller amounts of money out of their business(es) than their novice counterparts (£21 462 and £28 036, respectively). Unfortunately in this study it was not possible to identify the size of each of the businesses owned by portfolio entrepreneurs. It may be the case that portfolio entrepreneurs own

Table 6.8 Entrepreneur performance reported by novice and habitual entrepreneurs

Variable	Novice (n = 294)	Habitual (n = 348)	t-statistic	Df	Sig. level (2-tailed)
Standard of living relative to when first started/ purchased this business[a]	3.78	3.82	−0.67	640	0.50
Money taken out (I)[b]	**28 036**	**36 660**	**−3.42**	**640**	**0.00**
Money taken out (II)[c]	**28 036**	**21 462**	**3.31**	**640**	**0.00**

Notes:
[a] The following scale was used: (1) very poor; (2) poor; (3) about average; (4) good; and (5) very good.
[b] Money taken out (I) relates to the amount of money taken out of all businesses currently owned over the past 12 months.
[c] Money taken out (II) relates to the Money taken out (I) measure standardized by the number of businesses currently owned.

Table 6.9 Entrepreneur performance reported by serial and portfolio entrepreneurs

Variable (factor scores)	Serial (n = 151)	Portfolio (n = 197)	t-statistic	Df	Sig. level (2-tailed)
Standard of living relative to when first started/ purchased this business[a]	**3.70**	**3.92**	**−2.08**	**346**	**0.04**
Money taken out (I)[b]	**25 944**	**44 873**	**−5.32**	**346**	**0.00**
Money taken out (II)[c]	**25 944**	**18 028**	**3.48**	**346**	**0.00**

Notes:
[a] The following scale was used: (1) very poor; (2) poor; (3) about average; (4) good; and (5) very good.
[b] Money taken out (I) relates to the amount of money taken out of all businesses currently owned over the past 12 months.
[c] Money taken out (II) relates to the Money taken out (I) measure standardized by the number of businesses currently owned.

several smaller businesses. Consequently, measures of money taken out standardized by the number of businesses owned should be interpreted with caution.

Table 6.9 shows that portfolio entrepreneurs reported a significantly higher standard of living relative to their serial counterparts. Before controlling for the number of businesses currently owned, portfolio entrepreneurs reported that they had taken significantly more money out of the business(es) they owned in the previous 12 months than serial entrepreneurs (£44873 compared with £25944). When the amount of money taken out was standardized by the number of business currently owned, however, portfolio entrepreneurs reported significantly smaller amounts of money taken out over the previous 12 months than serial entrepreneurs (£18028 compared with £25944).

Summary

Consistent with previous studies (Birley and Westhead, 1993b; Kolvereid and Bullvåg, 1993; Westhead and Wright, 1998a, b) the bivariate analysis provides mixed evidence. Habitual entrepreneurs did not outperform novice entrepreneurs in terms of the surveyed business, but they did report higher levels of sales growth during the given period. Furthermore, habitual entrepreneurs were able to take out more money in the given period relative to their novice counterparts. However, when this amount was standardized by the number of businesses currently owned, habitual entrepreneurs took out significantly less money than novice entrepreneurs.

There were few significant differences between serial and portfolio entrepreneurs. Portfolio entrepreneurs did report a significantly higher standard of living compared to when they first started or established the surveyed business than serial entrepreneurs. The results relating to the amount of money taken out of business(es) owned mirrored earlier findings relating to habitual entrepreneurs. Portfolio entrepreneurs did take out a significantly larger amount of money than their serial counterparts. When this amount was standardized by the number of businesses currently owned, portfolio entrepreneurs actually took out less money per business than serial entrepreneurs.

FIRM AND ENTREPRENEUR PERFORMANCE: MULTIVARIATE ANALYSIS

The bivariate results discussed above provide an initial indication of the extent and nature of performance-based differences between novice and habitual entrepreneurs and serial and portfolio entrepreneurs. Consistent with previous chapters where results have been presented, it was deemed necessary to supplement this initial analysis with multivariate analysis, allowing the researcher to control for other factors that are expected to influence performance based on theory and previous empirical studies. As in the previous chapter, a confirmatory forced-entry OLS regression approach was utilized.

Appendices 6.1 and 6.2 provide the means and standard deviations for the independent and control variables as well as the correlation coefficients between the independent and control variables and VIF scores for the full sample and the habitual entrepreneurs subsample respectively. This evidence suggests that the multivariate OLS models will not be seriously distorted by multicollinearity.

Firm performance is often deemed sensitive by respondents, which can result in a reluctance to answer performance questions: this problem was encountered in this study. Performance measures relating to satisfaction appear to have been seen as involving less sensitive information by the respondents than those relating to sales and profitability. If the analysis relates to the respondents that answered all performance questions, there would be a considerable reduction in the working sample size. A valid sample for each performance-dependent variable was selected. Consequently, the valid sample of respondents varies between the selected performance models. A correlation matrix and VIF scores were computed for each sample. Though not reported here, a comparison of each of the correlation matrices and VIF scores revealed that there were no major inconsistencies resulting from varying sample sizes.

To determine the extent to which the business ownership experience variables (that is, habitual versus novice entrepreneur and portfolio versus serial entrepreneur) 'explained' performance, as in the previous chapter two OLS regression models were conducted. The first models represent the control models (Models 1i to 8i), where the independent variables relating to business ownership experience were excluded. Variables relating to general and specific human capital (other than business ownership experience): the environment, firm characteristics and strategy were included in these control models. The following relationships were assumed in each control model:

Control Model:

PERFORMANCE = f (GHK, SHK$_E$, SHK$_V$, INFORMATION SEARCH INTENSITY, ENVIRONMENT, STRATEGY, FIRM-SPECIFIC)

Where: ENVIRONMENT is measured in terms of: the respondents' expectation of what will happen to the number of competitors in the next five years (*Expectation of competition*); the extent to which the respondent felt the business was changing rapidly (*Business change*); and three industry dummy variables (*Agriculture, Manufacturing* and *Construction,* with the reference category selected being services).

STRATEGY was measured in terms of three broad strategies (*Differentiation, Innovation* and *Cost-based*) (see Table 3.10).

FIRM-SPECIFIC characteristics were measured in terms of: employment size (*10–49 employees, 50 or more employees* with 1–9 employees as the reference category); business age (*1–5 years* old, *6–10 years* old with 11 years or older as the reference category); mode of opportunity exploitation (*Purchased* or not); and the number of initial equity partners (*Number of equity partners*).

Details of GHK, SHK_E and SHK_V and INFORMATION SEARCH INTENSITY were provided in the previous chapter and Tables 3.1–3.3.

In Chapter 4, the data were explored to establish if novice and habitual entrepreneurs could be distinguished in terms of elements of general and specific human capital other than business ownership experience. Business ownership experience may, therefore, be endogenous in the performance equations. To formally check for endogeneity, a Hausman test was conducted (Hausman, 1978, 1983). For all performance equations, the null hypothesis of no endogeneity could not be rejected at standard significance levels.

In the full models, in addition to the control variables discussed above, the business ownership experience independent variables were introduced sequentially. Three sets of independent variables relating to business ownership experience were considered. The first two of these relate to HABITUAL and TOTAL (as discussed in Chapters 4 and 5). The third set of independent variable was operationalized to capture the learning effects from failure and success discussed in Chapter 2. Four independent dummy variables were considered: $HABITUAL_{failed}$, $HABITUAL_{successful}$, $HABITUAL_{Mixed\ (no\ exit)}$, and $HABITUAL_{Mixed\ (with\ exit)}$. $HABITUAL_{failed}$ represents a dummy variable which took a value of '1' if the habitual entrepreneur reported that the proportion of business that had failed (closed or been sold because the performance was too low in relation to the entrepreneur's expectations, or had faced bankruptcy, liquidation or receivership) was greater than those that had been sold or closed because there was an opportunity to realize a capital gain or a better opportunity presented itself; and '0' otherwise. $HABITUAL_{successful}$ took a value of '1' if the habitual entrepreneur reported that the proportion of business which had failed (closed or been sold because the performance was too low in relation to the entrepreneur's expectations, or had faced bankruptcy, liquidation or receivership) was less than those which had been sold or closed because there was an opportunity to realize a capital gain or a better opportunity presented itself; and '0' otherwise. $HABITUAL_{Mixed\ (no\ exit)}$ took a value of '1' if the habitual entrepreneur had not closed or sold any businesses (a pure portfolio entrepreneur). And $HABITUAL_{Mixed\ (with\ exit)}$ took a value of '1' if the habitual entrepreneur has closed or sold the same number of businesses due to failure and success. The reference category for all four dummy variables was the novice entrepreneur group.

Based on the above definitions of the control and independent variables, the following relationships were assumed and tested for each performance-dependent variable in turn:

PERFORMANCE = f (GHK, SHK$_E$, SHK$_V$, INFORMATION SEARCH INTENSITY, ENVIRONMENT, STRATEGY, FIRM-SPECIFIC, HABITUAL)

PERFORMANCE = f (GHK, SHK$_E$, SHK$_V$, INFORMATION SEARCH INTENSITY, ENVIRONMENT, STRATEGY, FIRM-SPECIFIC, TOTAL)

PERFORMANCE = f (GHK, SHK$_E$, SHK$_V$, INFORMATION SEARCH INTENSITY, ENVIRONMENT, STRATEGY, FIRM-SPECIFIC, HABITUAL$_{\text{failed}}$, HABITUAL$_{\text{successful}}$, HABITUAL$_{\text{Mixed (No exit)}}$, HABITUAL$_{\text{Mixed (With exit)}}$)

For the models carried out on the habitual entrepreneur subsample one set of control models as described above and one set of models containing the PORTFOLIO independent variable are presented. The full set of models was specified as follows:

PERFORMANCE = f (GHK, SHK$_E$, SHK$_V$, ENVIRONMENT, STRATEGY, FIRM-SPECIFIC, PORTFOLIO)

In addition to the analysis carried out to test the hypotheses developed in Chapter 2, it was also deemed appropriate to check for the possibility of similarities and differences between novice and serial entrepreneurs and between novice and portfolio entrepreneurs. Significant differences between the two pairs are also reported in the notes following each model reported in this chapter. The following discussion, however, focuses on the models that allow for the direct testing of the hypotheses.

Before doing so, however, it was deemed necessary to examine the relationship between the various performance measures used. As intimated earlier, there is considerable heterogeneity in the selection of performance measures across studies. The correlation matrix in Table 6.10 illustrates the extent to which the performance measures used in this study were related to each other. This table shows that there is a strong correlation particularly between: weighted performance (I); weighted performance (II); profit relative to competitors; standard of living; money taken out (I) and money taken out (II). The measures relating to growth (absolute change in employment, absolute change in sales, percentage change in employment and percentage change in sales) appear to be less strongly correlated with the other performance measures. This suggests a need to distin-

Table 6.10 Correlation matrix relating to the performance variables

Variable	Mean	S.D.	1	2	3	4	5	6	7	8	9
1. Weighted performance (I) [a]	13.06	0.86	1.00								
2. Weighted performance (II) [b]	11.74	3.50	0.86****	1.00							
3. Profit relative to competitors	3.44	0.94	0.47****	0.45****	1.00						
4. Absolute total employment change (log of)	1.59	0.11	0.10*	0.07†	0.06	1.00					
5. Percentage change in total employment	71.15	470.47	0.10*	0.06†	0.06	0.19****	1.00				
6. Absolute change in sales (log of)	6.32	0.32	0.19****	0.15***	0.10*	0.32****	0.07†	1.00			
7. Percentage change in sales	133.05	472.53	0.14***	0.14***	0.11*	0.06	0.11*	0.11*	1.00		
8. Standard of living	3.84	2.38	0.35****	0.38****	0.42****	0.04	0.03	0.13**	0.11*	1.00	
9. Money taken out (I) [c]	35 718	32 957	0.35****	0.32****	0.33****	0.29****	0.14**	0.09*	0.16****	0.40****	1.00
10. Money taken out (II) [d]	26 853	26 844	0.33****	0.28****	0.31****	0.17****	0.08*	0.15****	0.18****	0.35****	0.83****

Notes:
† $p < 0.10$; * $p < 0.05$; ** $p < 0.01$; *** $p < 0.001$; **** $p < 0.0001$
n = 435.
[a] Weighted performance (I) relates to the original Naman and Slevin (1993) measure.
[b] Weighted performance (II) relates to the extended measure.
[c] Money taken out (I) relates to the amount of money taken out of all businesses currently owned over the past 12 months.
[d] Money taken out (II) relates to the Money taken out (I) measure standardized by the number of businesses currently owned.

guish between growth and operating performance (in term of the firm and/or the entrepreneur). Despite the significant correlation among some of the performance measures, the discussion below is based on regression models run for each performance measure. This allows the reader to determine the extent to which the independent variable (that is, ownership experience) and the control variables are consistently related to the performance measures.

Firm Performance

Weighted performance index (I)

Table 6.11 reports regression models relating to the dependent variable corresponding to Naman and Slevin's (1993) weighted performance index. As explained above, Control Model 1i relates to the model where all variables except the business ownership experience variables are included. This is followed by Models 1a, 1b and 1c, which relate to those models where the HABITUAL, TOTAL and then the $HABITUAL_{failed}$, $HABITUAL_{successful}$, $HABITUAL_{Mixed (No exit)}$ and $HABITUAL_{Mixed (With exit)}$ variables are included, respectively. Both the Control Model 1i and Models 1a, 1b and 1c were found to be significant and had an adjusted R^2 of 0.15 (the adjusted R^2 was 0.15 for Model 1b). By examining the change in R^2 for Models 1b and 1c (in relation to the control model), it is evident that the inclusion of the TOTAL and $HABITUAL_{failed}$, $HABITUAL_{successful}$, $HABITUAL_{Mixed (No exit)}$ and $HABITUAL_{Mixed (With exit)}$ business ownership experience variables did not result in a significant improvement in the models, despite $HABITUAL_{failed}$ being significantly and negatively associated with performance. There was, however, a significant increase in the model R^2 resulting from the addition of the HABITUAL variable. Based on the significance of the coefficient for this variable, it appears that habitual entrepreneurs are significantly and negatively associated with firm performance. Consistent with the bivariate evidence, hypothesis H_{14a} cannot be supported. Further, neither habitual entrepreneurs who had been successful nor those who had failed outperformed their novice counterparts. Consequently, there is no support for H_{14c} or H_{14d}.

Several control variables were significantly associated with the dependent variable. Lower levels of performance were reported by older and female entrepreneurs and those reporting high levels of technical capability. Conversely, high levels of performance were associated with entrepreneurs highlighting managerial and entrepreneurial capabilities, a firm size between 10 and 49 employees (as opposed to between 0 and 9 employees), and being motivated by financial reasons. These results were consistent across all models (Model 1a, 1b and 1c).

Differences between serial and portfolio entrepreneurs are reported in Table 6.12 with regard to weighted firm performance. Both the Control Model 1ii and Model 1d were significant, with an adjusted R^2 of 0.14. By comparing Control

Table 6.11 OLS regression relating to the weighted performance index (I) (total sample)

Independent variables	Control Model 1i		Model 1a		Model 1b		Model 1c	
	β	Sig	β	Sig	β	Sig	β	Sig
GHK								
Age	-0.12	*	-0.12	*	-0.12	*	-0.11	*
Age²	0.02		0.02		0.02		0.02	
Gender	0.09	†	0.10	†	0.09	†	0.09	
Education	-0.05		-0.04		-0.04		-0.04	
Managerial human capital	-0.03		-0.03		-0.03		-0.03	
Managerial capability	0.20	****	0.20	****	0.21	****	0.21	****
Technical capability	-0.10	†	-0.12	*	-0.10	†	-0.12	*
SHK_E								
Entrepreneurial capability	0.22	****	0.21	****	0.22	****	0.21	****
Development	-0.04		-0.04		-0.05		-0.03	
Parent business owners	-0.09	†	-0.08		-0.08		-0.08	
SHK_V								
Business similarity	-0.04		-0.04		-0.04		-0.05	
Task similarity	-0.06		-0.06		-0.06		-0.06	
Approval	-0.01		-0.02		-0.01		-0.02	
Welfare	-0.01		-0.01		-0.01		-0.01	
Personal development	0.06		0.07		0.06		0.06	
Independence	-0.03		-0.03		-0.03		-0.03	
Financial motives	0.12	*	0.12	*	0.12	*	0.12	*
Reactive motives	0.07		0.07		0.07		0.06	
Environment								
Expectation of competition	-0.03		-0.03		-0.03		-0.04	

	(1)	(2)	(3)	(4)
Business change	−0.07	−0.07	−0.07	−0.06
Agriculture	−0.06	−0.06	−0.06	−0.06
Manufacturing	0.02	0.01	0.01	0.01
Construction	−0.08	−0.08	−0.08	−0.07
Strategy				
Differentiation strategy	0.07	0.07	0.07	0.07
Innovation strategy	0.04	0.05	0.04	0.04
Cost-based strategy	−0.01	−0.01	−0.01	−0.02
Firm-specific				
10–49 employees	0.09 †	0.10 †	0.10 †	0.10 †
50 or more employees	−0.02	−0.02	−0.02	−0.01
Business 1–5yrs old	−0.02	−0.02	−0.02	−0.03
Business 6–10 yrs old	0.01	0.02	0.01	0.02
Purchased business	−0.04	−0.04	−0.04	−0.04
No. of equity partners	−0.04	−0.05	−0.05	−0.05
HABITUAL	–	−0.08 †	–	–
TOTAL	–	–	−0.04	–
HABITUAL$_{FAILED}$	–	–	–	−0.10
HABITUAL$_{SUCCESSFUL}$	–	–	–	−0.06
HABITUAL$_{MIXED (NO EXIT)}$	–	–	–	−0.06
HABITUAL$_{MIXED (WITH EXIT)}$	–	–	–	0.04 †
F-value	3.16 ****	3.16 ****	3.08 ****	2.97 ****
R^2	0.23	0.23	0.23	0.24
Adjusted R^2	0.16	0.16	0.15	0.16
Change in R^2		0.01 †	0.00	0.01
N	378	378	378	378

Note: † $p < 0.10$; * $p < 0.05$; ** $p < 0.01$; *** $p < 0.001$; **** $p < 0.0001$.

143

Table 6.12 *OLS regression relating to the weighted performance index (I) and the extended weighted performance index (habitual entrepreneurs subsample)*

Independent variables	Control Model 1ii		Model 1d		Control Model 2ii		Model 2d	
	β	Sig	β	Sig	β	Sig	β	Sig
GHK								
Age	-0.14	†	-0.14	†	-0.06		-0.06	
Age²	0.03		0.03		0.11		0.10	
Gender	0.13	†	0.14	†	0.11		0.09	
Education	0.04		0.04		-0.03		-0.04	
Managerial human capital	-0.01		-0.01		0.07		0.07	
Managerial capability	0.25	***	0.26	***	0.29	****	0.27	****
Technical capability	-0.15	*	-0.15	*	-0.02		-0.03	
SHK$_E$								
Entrepreneurial capability	0.23	**	0.23	**	0.25	**	0.24	**
Development	-0.04		-0.04		0.05		0.05	
Parent business owners	-0.12	†	-0.12	†	-0.13	†	-0.13	†
SHK$_V$								
Business similarity	-0.02		-0.02		0.02		0.01	
Task similarity	-0.04		-0.04		0.00		0.00	
Approval	0.00		0.00		-0.04		-0.04	
Welfare	0.02		0.02		0.08		0.08	
Personal development	0.08		0.08		-0.01		-0.01	
Independence	-0.03		-0.03		-0.04		-0.03	
Financial motives	0.12	†	0.12	†	0.13	†	0.12	†
Reactive motives	0.05		0.05		0.00		-0.01	

	Model 1	Model 2	Model 3	Model 4
Environment				
Expectation of competition	-0.01	-0.01	-0.01	-0.01
Business change	-0.01	-0.01	-0.01	-0.01
Agriculture	-0.04	-0.04	-0.08	-0.08
Manufacturing	0.00	0.00	-0.02	-0.01
Construction	-0.08	-0.08	-0.05	-0.04
Strategy				
Differentiation strategy	0.09	0.09	0.16 *	0.17 *
Innovation strategy	-0.04	-0.04	-0.06	-0.06
Cost-based strategy	-0.04	-0.04	-0.10	-0.10
Firm-specific				
10–49 employees	0.06	0.07	0.09	0.08
50 or more employees	-0.04	-0.04	-0.05	-0.06
Business 1–5yrs old	-0.06	-0.06	0.00	0.00
Business 6–10 yrs old	-0.04	-0.04	0.06	0.07
Purchased business	-0.02	-0.02	-0.05	-0.05
No. of equity partners	-0.10	-0.10	-0.09	-0.09
PORTFOLIO	–	-0.01	–	0.07
F-value	2.16 ***	2.08 ***	2.61 ****	2.57 ****
R^2	0.27	0.27	0.31	0.31
Adjusted R^2	0.14	0.14	0.19	0.19
Change in R^2	–	0.00	–	0.00
N	221	221	221	221

Notes:
† $p < 0.10$; * $p < 0.05$; ** $p < 0.01$; *** $p < 0.001$; **** $p < 0.0001$.
No significant differences between novice and serial or novice and portfolio entrepreneurs were detected.

Model 1ii with Model 1d, one can see that the inclusion of the PORTFOLIO variable has no impact on the model. This finding is mirrored by the non-sig-nificance of the PORTFOLIO variable in Model 1d. This finding is consistent with the bivariate analysis presented earlier. Consequently, hypothesis H_{14b} is not supported. In line with the findings relating to the full sample (see Table 6.11), those entrepreneurs who were younger, were female, and reported high levels of technical capability reported lower levels of performance. Entrepre-neurs reporting high levels of managerial and entrepreneurial capabilities, and financial motives reported higher performance. One additional variable was significantly related to performance in the habitual-only sample, which did not come through in the full sample. Entrepreneurs who had a parent or parents who were business owners reported lower levels of performance ($p < 0.10$). While having at least one parent who was or is a business owner may provide the en-trepreneur indirect access to knowledge relating to entrepreneurship, it may also induce overconfidence. Entrepreneurs may repeat patterns of behaviour that have been subconsciously learnt but which are not necessarily best practice.

Extended weighted performance index (II)
The Naman and Slevin (1993) weighted performance index was extended. Several items were added to the original weighted performance index to reflect what was perceived to be a more complete view of performance (see Table 3.4). Table 6.13 reports findings relating to OLS models where the dependent variable was the extended weighted performance index (weighted performance (II)). Both Control Model 2i and Models 2a, 2b and 2c were highly significant, with an adjusted R^2 of 0.19. The inclusion of none of the business ownership experience variables had a significant impact on the model fit. Further, the non-significance of the HABITUAL and TOTAL variables suggests that there was no support for hypothesis H_{14a}. These findings are consistent with the re-sults from the bivariate analysis. As habitual entrepreneurs who had failed (HABITUAL$_{failed}$) and those who had been successful (HABITUAL$_{successful}$) reported lower levels of performance than novice entrepreneurs, there is no support for hypotheses H_{14c} and H_{14d}. Several of the control variables were found to be consistently and significantly related to the extended performance measure. Once again, the perception of high entrepreneurial capability, man-agerial capability and being financially motivated to start or purchase the surveyed business were associated with higher performance. In addition, the firm size being between 10 and 49 employees (as opposed to being smaller) was found to be associated with higher performance. Rapid business change and operating in the agricultural sector (as opposed to services) were associated with lower performance.

Table 6.12 reports models relating to the habitual entrepreneur subsample. Both the Control Model 2ii and Model 2d were highly significant with an adjusted R^2 of 0.19. The inclusion of the PORTFOLIO variable did not result in an improvement in the model, and the variable was insignificant. Consequently, there is no support for hypothesis H_{14b}. This finding contrasts with the results from the bivariate analysis, where portfolio entrepreneurs reported significantly higher levels of extended weighted performance (II). Among the control variables managerial capability, entrepreneurial capability, financial motives, and the adoption of a differentiation strategy were associated with higher performance. Having at least one parent who was or is a business owner was associated with lower extended weighted performance.

Profit relative to competitors
Profit relative to competitors was selected as the dependent variable with regard to the full sample. Table 6.14 shows that the Control Model 3i and Models 3a, 3b and 3c were all significant with a minimum adjusted R^2 of 0.08. By comparing Control Model 3i with Model 3a, it is evident that the inclusion of the business ownership experience HABITUAL resulted in a significant improvement in the model R^2. Being a habitual entrepreneur (Model 3a) was significantly though negatively associated with profit relative to competitors. This contrasts with the results from the bivariate analysis, which detected no significant differences between novice and habitual entrepreneurs. Consequently, hypothesis H_{14a} cannot be supported.

The inclusion of the HABITUAL$_{failed}$, HABITUAL$_{successful}$, HABITUAL$_{Mixed}$ $_{(No\ exit)}$ and HABITUAL$_{Mixed\ (With\ exit)}$ business ownership experience variables had no impact on the overall model. None of these variables were significantly associated with profit relative to performance with the exception of those habitual entrepreneurs who reported that they had not exited from any of the businesses they owned, although they were a mixture of successes and failure. These habitual entrepreneurs were associated with poorer profit relative to competitors ($p < 0.10$). Consequently, there is no support for hypotheses H_{14c} or H_{14d}.

Among the control variables an entrepreneurial capability, the adoption of an innovation strategy and the adoption of a cost-based strategy were all associated with superior profit relative to competitors. In contrast, younger entrepreneurs and those reporting a developmental attitude towards opportunity identification reported poorer profit relative to competitors. These relationships between the control variables and the dependent variable held across all models.

Table 6.15 reports findings relating to habitual entrepreneurs alone. Both the Control Model 3ii and Model 3d were significant, with a minimum adjusted R^2 of 0.09. The inclusion of the PORTFOLIO variable had no impact on the model. Consistent with the bivariate evidence, the PORTFOLIO variable was not significantly related to profit relative to competitors. Therefore, there is no support for hypothesis H_{14b}.

Table 6.13   OLS regression relating to the extended weighted performance index (II) (total sample)

Independent variables	Control Model 2i β	Sig	Model 2a β	Sig	Model 2b β	Sig	Model 2c β	Sig
GHK								
Age	-0.08		-0.08		-0.08		-0.08	
Age²	0.06		0.06		0.06		0.06	
Gender	0.05		0.05		0.05		0.04	
Education	-0.07		-0.07		-0.07		-0.07	
Managerial human capital	0.01		0.01		0.01		0.01	
Managerial capability	0.26	****	0.26	****	0.26	****	0.27	****
Technical capability	0.02		0.02		0.02		0.02	
SHK$_E$								
Entrepreneurial capability	0.21	****	0.21	****	0.21	****	0.21	****
Development	0.01		0.01		0.01		0.01	
Parent business owners	-0.07		-0.07		-0.07		-0.07	
SHK$_V$								
Business similarity	-0.01		-0.01		-0.01		-0.02	
Task similarity	-0.01		-0.01		-0.01		-0.02	
Approval	-0.01		-0.01		-0.01		-0.01	
Welfare	0.03		0.03		0.03		0.03	
Personal development	0.00		0.00		0.00		-0.01	
Independence	0.00		0.00		0.00		0.00	
Financial motives	0.14	**	0.14	**	0.14	**	0.15	**
Reactive motives	0.05		0.05		0.05		0.05	
Environment								
Expectation of competition	-0.04		-0.04		-0.04		-0.05	

	Model 1	Model 2	Model 3	Model 4
Business change	−0.14 **	−0.14 **	−0.14 **	−0.13 *
Agriculture	−0.12 *	−0.12 *	−0.12 *	−0.11 *
Manufacturing	0.01	0.01	0.01	0.02
Construction	−0.04	−0.04	−0.04	−0.03
Strategy				
Differentiation strategy	0.08	0.08	0.08	0.08
Innovation strategy	0.06	0.06	0.06	0.04
Cost-based strategy	−0.06	−0.06	−0.06	−0.07
Firm-specific				
10–49 employees	0.10 †	0.11 *	0.11 †	0.10 †
50 or more employees	−0.01	0.00	−0.01	0.00
Business 1–5yrs old	0.03	0.02	0.03	0.02
Business 6–10 yrs old	0.08	0.08	0.08	0.08
Purchased business	−0.03	−0.03	−0.03	−0.03
No. of equity partners	−0.02	−0.02	−0.02	−0.01
HABITUAL	–	−0.02	–	–
TOTAL	–	–	−0.02	–
HABITUAL$_{\text{FAILED}}$	–	–	–	−0.09 †
HABITUAL$_{\text{SUCCESSFUL}}$	–	–	–	−0.03
HABITUAL$_{\text{MIXED (NO EXIT)}}$	–	–	–	0.02
HABITUAL$_{\text{MIXED (WITH EXIT)}}$	–	–	–	0.05
F-value	3.77 ****	3.66 ****	3.65 ****	3.52 ****
R^2	0.26	0.26	0.26	0.27
Adjusted R^2	0.19	0.19	0.19	0.19
Change in R^2	–	0.00	0.00	0.01
N	378	378	378	378

Note: † $p < 0.10$; * $p < 0.05$; ** $p < 0.01$; *** $p < 0.001$; **** $p < 0.0001$.

Table 6.14 OLS regression relating to profit relative to competitors (total sample)

Independent variables	Control Model 3i		Model 3a		Model 3b		Model 3c	
	β	Sig	β	Sig	β	Sig	β	Sig
GHK								
Age	-0.14	*	-0.14	*	-0.14	*	-0.13	*
Age²	0.00		0.00		0.01		0.01	
Gender	0.08		0.08		0.08		0.08	
Education	0.01		0.02		0.01		0.01	
Managerial human capital	0.01		0.01		0.01		0.02	
Managerial capability	0.09		0.09		0.10		0.09	
Technical capability	0.06		0.05		0.06		0.05	
SHK$_E$								
Entrepreneurial capability	0.20	**	0.19	**	0.20	**	0.19	**
Development	-0.12	*	-0.12	*	-0.13	*	-0.11	†
Parent business owners	-0.04		-0.03		-0.03		-0.03	
SHK$_V$								
Business similarity	0.02		0.03		0.03		0.03	
Task similarity	0.00		0.00		0.00		0.00	
Approval	0.06		0.05		0.06		0.04	
Welfare	0.01		0.00		0.01		0.01	
Personal development	0.02		0.03		0.02		0.03	
Independence	0.02		0.02		0.02		0.02	
Financial motives	0.07		0.06		0.07		0.07	
Reactive motives	0.02		0.02		0.02		0.02	
Environment								
Expectation of competition	-0.03		-0.03		-0.03		-0.03	

	Model 1	Model 2	Model 3	Model 4
Business change	-0.06	-0.06	-0.06	-0.06
Agriculture	-0.07	-0.07	-0.07	-0.07
Manufacturing	0.03	0.03	0.03	0.02
Construction	-0.03	-0.02	-0.03	-0.02
Strategy				
Differentiation strategy	0.08	0.09	0.08	0.08
Innovation strategy	0.10 †	0.11 †	0.11 †	0.11 †
Cost-based strategy	0.10 †	0.10 †	0.10 †	0.10 †
Firm-specific				
10–49 employees	0.08	0.09	0.09	0.10
50 or more employees	0.01	0.02	0.01	0.02
Business 1–5yrs old	-0.01	-0.02	-0.01	-0.02
Business 6–10 yrs old	0.03	0.04	0.03	0.03
Purchased business	0.02	0.02	0.02	0.02
No. of equity partners	-0.08	-0.08	-0.08	-0.09
HABITUAL	–	-0.10 †	–	–
TOTAL	–	–	-0.04	–
HABITUAL$_{FAILED}$	–	–	–	-0.08
HABITUAL$_{SUCCESSFUL}$	–	–	–	-0.05
HABITUAL$_{MIXED\ (NO\ EXIT)}$				-0.10 †
HABITUAL$_{MIXED\ (WITH\ EXIT)}$				0.03
F-value	2.01 ***	2.06 ***	1.96 **	1.92 **
R^2	0.16	0.17	0.16	0.17
Adjusted R^2	0.08	0.09	0.08	0.08
Change in R^2	–	0.01	0.00	0.01
N	373	373	373	373

Note: † $p < 0.10$; * $p < 0.05$; ** $p < 0.01$; *** $p < 0.001$; **** $p < 0.0001$.

151

Table 6.15   OLS regression relating to profit relative to competitors (habitual entrepreneurs subsample)

Independent variables	Control Model 3ii		Model 3d	
	β	Sig	β	Sig
GHK				
Age	-0.16	*	-0.16	*
Age²	0.06		0.07	
Gender	0.10		0.12	
Education	0.07		0.08	
Managerial human capital	0.01		0.01	
Managerial capability	0.07		0.09	
Technical capability	-0.05		-0.04	
SHK$_E$				
Entrepreneurial capability	0.15	†	0.16	†
Development	-0.17	*	-0.17	*
Parent business owners	-0.01		-0.02	
SHK$_V$				
Business similarity	0.03		0.04	
Task similarity	0.08		0.08	
Approval	0.09		0.09	
Welfare	-0.03		-0.03	
Personal development	0.11		0.11	
Independence	-0.02		-0.03	
Financial motives	0.04		0.05	
Reactive motives	-0.01		-0.01	
Environment				
Expectation of competition	-0.03		-0.03	

Business change	0.01	0.01
Agriculture	−0.08	−0.08
Manufacturing	0.09	0.08
Construction	−0.07	−0.08
Strategy		
Differentiation strategy	0.20 *	0.20 *
Innovation strategy	0.13	0.13
Cost-based strategy	0.08	0.09
Firm-specific		
10–49 employees	0.02	0.03
50 or more employees	−0.02	−0.02
Business 1–5yrs old	−0.03	−0.04
Business 6–10 yrs old	−0.04	−0.04
Purchased business	−0.05	−0.06
No. of equity partners	−0.05	−0.05
PORTFOLIO	–	−0.09
F-value	1.66 *	1.65 *
R^2	0.22	0.23
Adjusted R^2	0.09	0.09
Change in R^2	–	0.01
N	218	218

Notes:
† $p < 0.10$; * $p < 0.05$; ** $p < 0.01$; *** $p < 0.001$; **** $p < 0.0001$.
Portfolio entrepreneurs were negatively associated with profit relative to competitors in comparison to novice entrepreneurs ($p < 0.005$). No significant differences between novice and serial entrepreneurs were detected.

Table 6.16 OLS regression relating to the absolute change in total employment (log) during 1996–2001 (total sample)

Independent variables	Control Model 7i β	Sig	Model 7a β	Sig	Model 7b β	Sig	Model 7c β	Sig
GHK								
Age	-0.04		-0.04		-0.03		-0.03	
Age²	-0.03		-0.03		-0.03		-0.03	
Gender	0.01		0.01		0.01		0.01	
Education	-0.01		-0.01		-0.01		-0.02	
Managerial human capital	0.02		0.02		0.02		0.01	
Managerial capability	0.02		0.02		0.02		0.03	
Technical capability	-0.12	*	-0.12	*	-0.12	*	-0.12	*
SHK$_E$								
Entrepreneurial capability	0.09		0.08		0.09		0.10	
Development	-0.04		-0.04		-0.05		-0.04	
Parent business owners	-0.08		-0.08		-0.07		-0.08	
SHK$_V$								
Business similarity	-0.02		-0.02		-0.02		-0.01	
Task similarity	-0.07		-0.07		-0.07		-0.06	
Approval	-0.09	†	-0.09	†	-0.09	†	-0.10	†
Welfare	0.14	**	0.14	**	0.14	**	0.15	**
Personal Development	0.15	**	0.15	**	0.15	**	0.14	*
Independence	-0.04		-0.04		-0.04		-0.05	
Financial motives	-0.02		-0.02		-0.02		-0.01	
Reactive motives	0.07		0.07		0.07		0.06	
Environment								
Expectation of competition	-0.07		-0.07		-0.07		-0.06	

	Model 1	Model 2	Model 3	Model 4
Business change	0.05	0.05	0.05	0.04
Agriculture	-0.10 †	-0.10 †	-0.10 †	-0.10 †
Manufacturing	-0.01	-0.01	-0.02	-0.02
Construction	0.03	0.03	0.03	0.02
Strategy				
Differentiation strategy	0.05	0.05	0.05	0.04
Innovation strategy	0.05	0.05	0.05	0.05
Cost-based strategy	-0.08	-0.07	-0.08	-0.08
Firm-specific				
10–49 employees	0.12 *	0.13 *	0.13 *	0.13 *
50 or more employees	0.29 ****	0.29 ****	0.29 ****	0.28 ****
Business 1–5yrs old	0.04	0.03	0.03	0.04
Business 6–10 yrs old	0.03	0.03	0.03	0.04
Purchased business	-0.02	-0.03	-0.02	-0.02
No. of equity partners	-0.06	-0.06	-0.06	-0.06
HABITUAL	–	-0.01	–	–
TOTAL	–		-0.02	–
HABITUAL_FAILED	–	–	–	0.03
HABITUAL_SUCCESSFUL	–	–	–	-0.06
HABITUAL_MIXED (NO EXIT)				-0.02
HABITUAL_MIXED (WITH EXIT)				0.06
F-value	2.71 ****	2.62 ****	2.63 ****	2.51 ****
R^2	0.20	0.20	0.20	0.21
Adjusted R^2	0.13	0.13	0.13	0.13
Change in R^2	–	0.00	0.00	0.01
N	375	375	375	375

Notes:
† $p < 0.10$; * $p < 0.05$; ** $p < 0.01$; *** $p < 0.001$; **** $p < 0.0001$.
A constant value was added to negative employment change values to ensure that a logarithm could be taken.

Among the control variables similar relationships held between the dependent variable and the age of the entrepreneur, entrepreneurial capability and a developmental attitude towards opportunity identification. In direct contrast to the findings relating to the full sample, the adoption of an innovation and/or cost-based strategy were found to be associated with superior profit performance. In the only sample of habitual entrepreneurs, the adoption of a differentiation strategy was associated with superior firm performance relative to competitors.

Employment change
Employment change was examined over the period 1996 to 2001. The log of the absolute change in employment and the percentage of change were considered. Ideally a regression model for each of these employment measures would have been run. However, for the full sample, where the percentage change in employment was the dependent variable, the resulting model was not significant. Therefore, the log of absolute change in employment is the dependent variable in Table 6.16.

With respect to this dependent variable, the Control Model 7i and Models 7a, 7b and 7c were all highly significant, with a minimum R^2 of 0.13. The inclusion of the business ownership experience variables had no significant effect on the overall model fit relative to the control model and none of the business ownership experience variables were individually significant. Consequently, there is no support for hypotheses H_{14a}, H_{14c} or H_{14d}. Several control variables, however, were significantly related to growth. Technical capability, approval-based motives and operating in the agricultural sector (as opposed to the services sector) were negatively related to the absolute change in employment between 1996 and 2001. In contrast, motives based on welfare and personal development and firm size, were positively associated with employment growth.

Table 6.18 reports findings relating to the habitual entrepreneur subsample. The models reported relate to the absolute change in employment Control Model 7ii and Model 7d relates to the absolute change in employment dependent variable. Both models were significant, with an adjusted R^2 of 0.09. The addition of the PORTFOLIO variable to the control model had no significant effect and the variable itself was not significant (consistent with the bivariate results), lending no support to hypothesis H_{14b}. The absolute change in employment was positively and significantly related to motives based on welfare and personal development, and a firm size of 50 or more employees (as opposed to less than 10 employees). Technical capability and operating in the agricultural sector were negatively related to absolute employment change.

Change in sales

Change in sales was examined for the period between 1996 and 1999. For the full sample, where the absolute change in sales was the dependent variable, the resulting model was not significant. Therefore, the percentage change in sales was the dependent variable reported in Table 6.17.

The overall significance of the models was weaker when the dependent variable was changed to the percentage change in sales, as illustrated in Table 6.17. As with the previous dependent variable, none of the business ownership variables were significantly related to the percentage change in sales (consistent with the bivariate results), nor did they have a significant effect on the overall model fit when compared to Control Model 8i. Therefore, there is no support for hypotheses H_{14a}, H_{14c} or H_{14d}. Among the control variables, entrepreneurial capability and a business aged between six and ten years was positively associated with the percentage sales growth. The age of the entrepreneur, independence-based motives, and an employment size of 10 to 49 employees (in comparison to fewer employees) were negatively associated with the percentage sales growth.

Table 6.18 reports the regression models where the dependent variable related to the absolute change in sales (Control Model 8ii and Model 8d). Both these models were more highly significant than models 7ii and 7d ($p < 0.001$) and also had a higher R^2 (0.28 with an adjusted R^2 of 0.13). The PORTFOLIO variable had no significant effect on the model fit, nor was it significantly related to the absolute change in sales. Six control variables were related to sales change: technical capability (negatively associated); operating in the agricultural sector (negatively associated); employing 50 or more employees (positively associated); education (negatively associated); a developmental attitude towards opportunity identification (negatively associated); and the adoption of an innovation-based business strategy (positively associated).

Entrepreneur Performance

Current standard of living

An entrepreneur's reported current standard of living in relation to when he or she first started or purchased the surveyed business is the dependent variable in Table 6.19. Relating to the full sample, Table 6.19 shows that the Control Model 4i and Models 4a, 4b and 4c were all significant, and had a minimum adjusted R^2 of 0.10. While the inclusion of the HABITUAL and TOTAL variables resulted in no significant improvement, the inclusion of the HABITUAL$_{failed}$, HABITUAL$_{successful}$, HABITUAL$_{Mixed (No exit)}$ and HABITUAL$_{Mixed (With exit)}$ variables resulted in a significant improvement in the relevant models. Among these latter variables, only HABITUAL$_{failed}$ was significantly (though negatively) related to the dependent variable. Overall, there is no support for hypotheses H_{14a},

Table 6.17   OLS regression relating to the percentage change in sales 1996–1999 (total sample)

Independent variables	Control Model 8i		Model 8a		Model 8b		Model 8c	
	β	Sig	β	Sig	β	Sig	β	Sig
GHK								
Age	-0.16	**	-0.16	**	-0.16	*	-0.16	**
Age^2	0.04		0.04		0.04		0.04	†
Gender	-0.09		-0.09		-0.09		-0.11	
Education	0.02		0.01		0.02		0.02	
Managerial human capital	0.08		0.08		0.08		0.08	
Managerial capability	0.09		0.09		0.10		0.09	
Technical capability	0.09		0.09		0.09		0.09	
SHK$_E$								
Entrepreneurial capability	0.19	**	0.19	**	0.19	**	0.19	**
Development	-0.08		-0.08		-0.08		-0.07	
Parent business owners	-0.08		-0.08		-0.07		-0.08	
SHK$_V$								
Business similarity	0.02		0.02		0.03		0.01	
Task similarity	0.00		0.00		0.00		-0.01	
Approval	0.08		0.08		0.08		0.08	
Welfare	0.01		0.01		0.01		0.01	
Personal development	0.06		0.06		0.06		0.06	
Independence	-0.10	†	-0.10	†	-0.11	†	-0.10	†
Financial motives	0.04		0.04		0.04		0.05	
Reactive motives	0.03		0.03		0.02		0.03	
Environment								
Expectation of competition	-0.09		-0.09		-0.09		-0.09	

	Model 1	Model 2	Model 3	Model 4
Business change	0.06	0.06	0.07	0.07
Agriculture	-0.03	-0.03	-0.03	-0.03
Manufacturing	0.10	0.10	0.09	0.11†
Construction	0.02	0.02	0.02	0.03
Strategy				
Differentiation strategy	-0.02	-0.02	-0.02	-0.02
Innovation strategy	-0.01	-0.01	-0.00	-0.01
Cost-based strategy	-0.09	-0.09	-0.10	-0.10
Firm-specific				
10–49 employees	-0.11†	-0.12†	-0.11†	-0.12†
50 or more employees	-0.06	-0.06	-0.06	-0.05
Business 1–5yrs old	-0.01	-0.01	-0.01	-0.02
Business 6–10 yrs old	0.11†	0.11†	0.11†	0.11†
Purchased business	-0.02	-0.02	-0.02	-0.03
No. of equity partners	0.06	0.06	0.06	0.06
HABITUAL	–	0.01		–
TOTAL	–	–	-0.04	–
HABITUAL_{FAILED}	–	–	–	-0.05
HABITUAL_{SUCCESSFUL}	–	–	–	0.01
HABITUAL_{MIXED (NO EXIT)}				0.04
HABITUAL_{MIXED (WITH EXIT)}				-0.01
F-value	1.96**	1.89**	1.91**	1.78**
R^2	0.18	0.18	0.18	0.18
Adjusted R^2	0.09	0.08	0.09	0.08
Change in R^2	–	0.00	0.00	0.01
N	322	322	322	322

Note: † $p < 0.10$; * $p < 0.05$; ** $p < 0.01$; *** $p < 0.001$; **** $p < 0.0001$.

Table 6.18   OLS regression relating to the change in absolute employment and sales (log) (habitual entrepreneurs subsample)

Independent variables	Control Model 7ii		Model 7d		Control Model 8ii		Model 8d	
	β	Sig	β	Sig	β	Sig	β	Sig
GHK								
Age	-0.04		-0.04		-0.11		-0.11	
Age²	-0.06		-0.06		-0.03		-0.04	
Gender	0.04		0.05		0.10		0.09	
Education	-0.03		-0.02		-0.12		-0.13	†
Managerial human capital	0.04		0.03		0.04		0.04	
Managerial capability	-0.04		-0.02		-0.03		-0.04	
Technical capability	-0.19	*	-0.18	*	-0.17	*	-0.17	*
SHK$_E$								
Entrepreneurial capability	0.05		0.05		0.07		0.07	
Development	-0.07		-0.08		-0.14	†	-0.14	†
Parent business owners	-0.05		-0.06		0.01		0.01	
SHK$_V$								
Business similarity	0.01		0.01		0.02		0.02	
Task similarity	-0.07		-0.07		-0.08		-0.08	
Approval	-0.08		-0.09		-0.03		-0.03	
Welfare	0.21	**	0.21	**	-0.03		-0.03	
Personal development	0.21	**	0.21	**	0.05		0.05	
Independence	-0.05		-0.06		-0.04		-0.03	
Financial motives	0.01		0.01		-0.05		-0.05	
Reactive motives	0.04		0.04		0.01		0.01	

160

	Model 1	Model 2	Model 3	Model 4
Environment				
Expectation of competition	-0.07	-0.08	-0.04	-0.03
Business change	0.00	0.00	-0.11	-0.11
Agriculture	-0.16*	-0.15*	-0.15†	-0.15*
Manufacturing	-0.01	-0.02	-0.12	-0.12
Construction	0.02	0.01	-0.06	-0.06
Strategy				
Differentiation strategy	0.11	0.10	0.10	0.10
Innovation strategy	0.09	0.09	0.23**	0.23**
Cost-based strategy	-0.07	-0.06	0.10	0.10
Firm-specific				
10–49 employees	0.07	0.09	0.01	0.00
50 or more employees	0.28****	0.28****	0.35****	0.35****
Business 1–5yrs old	0.04	0.04	-0.01	-0.01
Business 6–10 yrs old	0.02	0.01	-0.03	-0.03
Purchased business	-0.03	-0.03	-0.04	-0.03
No. of equity partners	-0.08	-0.08	0.03	0.03
PORTFOLIO	–	-0.08	–	0.05
F-value	1.65*	1.64*	1.95***	1.89***
R^2	0.22	0.23	0.28	0.28
Adjusted R^2	0.09	0.09	0.14	0.13
Change in R^2	–	0.01	–	0.00
N	218	218	194	194

Notes:
† $p < 0.10$; * $p < 0.05$; ** $p < 0.01$; *** $p < 0.001$; **** $p < 0.0001$.
No significant differences were detected between novice and serial or novice and portfolio entrepreneurs with respect to both dependent variables.
A constant value was added to negative employment/sales change values to ensure that a logarithm could be taken.

Table 6.19 OLS regression relating to the current standard of living relative to when the entrepreneur first established or purchased the surveyed business (total sample)

Independent Variables	Control Model 4i		Model 4a		Model 4b		Model 4c	
	β	Sig	β	Sig	β	Sig	β	Sig
GHK								
Age	-0.19	***	-0.19	***	-0.19	***	-0.19	***
Age^2	0.05		0.05		0.05		0.05	
Gender	0.03		0.03		0.03		0.02	
Education	0.03		0.03		0.03		0.04	
Managerial human capital	-0.03		-0.03		-0.03		-0.02	
Managerial capability	0.09		0.09		0.09		0.09	
Technical capability	-0.04		-0.05		-0.04		-0.06	
SHK$_E$								
Entrepreneurial capability	0.15	*	0.14	*	0.15	*	0.13	*
Development	-0.05		-0.05		-0.05		-0.05	
Parent business owners	-0.02		-0.02		-0.02		-0.01	
SHK$_V$								
Business similarity	-0.06		-0.06		-0.06		-0.07	
Task similarity	-0.03		-0.03		-0.03		-0.04	
Approval	-0.01		-0.01		-0.01		-0.01	
Welfare	-0.04		-0.05		-0.04		-0.05	
Personal development	-0.02		-0.01		-0.02		-0.01	
Independence	-0.01		-0.01		-0.01		-0.01	
Financial motives	0.14	**	0.14	**	0.14	**	0.14	**
Reactive motives	0.01		0.01		0.01		0.01	
Environment								
Expectation of competition	-0.07		-0.07		-0.07		-0.08	

	Model 1	Model 2	Model 3	Model 4
Business change	-0.17 **	-0.17 **	-0.17 **	-0.15 **
Agriculture	0.01	0.01	0.01	0.02
Manufacturing	0.06	0.06	0.06	0.07
Construction	-0.08	-0.07	-0.08	-0.05
Strategy				
Differentiation strategy	0.05	0.05	0.05	0.06
Innovation strategy	0.05	0.06	0.05	0.06
Cost-based strategy	-0.08	-0.07	-0.08	-0.07
Firm-specific				
10–49 employees	0.17 **	0.17 **	0.17 **	0.17 **
50 or more employees	0.11 *	0.11 *	0.11 *	0.12 *
Business 1–5yrs old	-0.04	-0.05	-0.04	-0.06
Business 6–10 yrs old	-0.05	-0.05	-0.05	-0.05
Purchased business	-0.03	-0.03	-0.03	-0.03
No. of equity partners	-0.01	-0.01	-0.01	-0.01
HABITUAL	–	-0.07	–	–
TOTAL	–	–	-0.01	–
HABITUAL$_{\text{FAILED}}$	–	–	–	-0.15 *
HABITUAL$_{\text{SUCCESSFUL}}$	–	–	–	0.02
HABITUAL$_{\text{MIXED (NO EXIT)}}$				-0.04
HABITUAL$_{\text{MIXED (WITH EXIT)}}$				-0.06
F-value	2.34 ****	2.34 ****	2.26 ****	2.35 ****
R^2	0.18	0.18	0.18	0.20
Adjusted R^2	0.10	0.11	0.10	0.11
Change in R^2	–	0.01	0.00	0.02 †
N	378	378	378	378

Note: † $p < 0.10$; * $p < 0.05$; ** $p < 0.01$; *** $p < 0.001$; **** $p < 0.0001$.

Table 6.20 OLS regression relating to standard of living (habitual entrepreneurs subsample)

Independent variables	Control Model 4ii		Model 4d	
	β	Sig	β	Sig
GHK				
Age	-0.21	**	-0.21	**
Age²	0.05		0.04	
Gender	0.04		0.03	
Education	0.07		0.07	
Managerial human capital	-0.06		-0.05	
Managerial capability	0.07		0.07	
Technical capability	-0.07		-0.08	
SHK_E				
Entrepreneurial capability	0.12		0.12	
Development	-0.11		-0.10	
Parent business owners	-0.07		-0.07	
SHK_V				
Business similarity	-0.06		-0.06	
Task similarity	0.05		0.05	
Approval	0.01		0.01	
Welfare	-0.02		-0.02	
Personal development	0.08		0.08	
Independence	-0.03		-0.02	
Financial motives	0.10		0.10	
Reactive motives	-0.05		-0.05	

		PORTFOLIO
Environment		
Expectation of competition	-0.09	-0.09
Business change	-0.19 *	-0.19 *
Agriculture	-0.02	-0.02
Manufacturing	0.05	0.06
Construction	-0.09	-0.08
Strategy		
Differentiation strategy	0.14 †	0.14 †
Innovation strategy	0.11	0.10
Cost-based strategy	0.02	0.03
Firm-specific		
10–49 employees	0.19 *	0.18 *
50 or more employees	0.12 †	0.12
Business 1–5yrs old	0.00	0.00
Business 6–10 yrs old	-0.06	-0.05
Purchased business	-0.02	-0.01
No. of equity partners	-0.07	-0.06
PORTFOLIO	–	0.05
F-value	1.75 *	1.70 *
R^2	0.23	0.23
Adjusted R^2	0.10	0.10
Change in R^2	–	–
N	221	221

Notes:
† $p < 0.10$; * $p < 0.05$; ** $p < 0.01$; *** $p < 0.001$; **** $p < 0.0001$.
No significant differences were detected between novice and serial entrepreneurs or novice and portfolio entrepreneurs.

165

Table 6.21   OLS regression relating to money taken out of business(es) owned

Independent variables	Control Model 5i β	Sig	Model 5a β	Sig	Model 5b β	Sig	Model 5c β	Sig
GHK								
Age	-0.10	*	-0.10	*	-0.10	*	-0.10	*
Age^2	-0.03		-0.03		-0.04		-0.03	
Gender	0.09	†	0.10	†	0.09	†	0.08	†
Education	0.20	****	0.20	****	0.20	****	0.20	****
Managerial human capital	0.02		0.02		0.02		0.03	
Managerial capability	0.09	†	0.09	†	0.08		0.09	†
Technical capability	0.00		0.00		0.00		0.00	
SHK$_E$								
Entrepreneurial capability	0.14	**	0.14	**	0.14	**	0.14	**
Development	-0.14	**	-0.14	**	-0.14	**	-0.14	**
Parent business owners	-0.05		-0.05		-0.05		-0.05	
SHK$_V$								
Business similarity	-0.11	*	-0.11	*	-0.11	*	-0.13	*
Task similarity	-0.02		-0.02		-0.02		-0.03	
Approval	-0.07		-0.07	†	-0.07	†	-0.07	
Welfare	-0.04		-0.04		-0.04		-0.04	
Personal Development	0.06		0.06		0.06		0.05	
Independence	0.01		0.01		0.01		0.01	
Financial motives	0.14	**	0.14	**	0.14	**	0.15	**
Reactive motives	0.13	**	0.13	**	0.13	**	0.12	**
Environment								
Expectation of competition	-0.04		-0.04		-0.04		-0.05	

166

Business change	0.07	0.07	0.07	0.08
Agriculture	-0.09 †	-0.09 †	-0.09 †	-0.09 †
Manufacturing	-0.05	-0.05	-0.05	-0.04
Construction	-0.04	-0.03	-0.04	-0.02
Strategy				
Differentiation strategy	-0.05	-0.05	-0.05	-0.05
Innovation strategy	-0.07	-0.07	-0.08	-0.09
Cost-based strategy	-0.01	-0.01	-0.02	0.00
Firm-specific				
10–49 employees	0.32 ****	0.32 ****	0.32 ****	0.32 ****
50 or more employees	0.19 ****	0.19 ****	0.19 ****	0.20 ****
Business 1–5yrs old	-0.11 *	-0.11 *	-0.11 *	-0.12 *
Business 6–10 yrs old	-0.01	-0.01	-0.01	-0.01
Purchased business	-0.07	-0.07	-0.07	-0.07
No. of equity partners	0.03	0.03	0.02	0.04
HABITUAL	–	0.00	–	–
TOTAL	–		0.02	–
HABITUAL$_{FAILED}$	–		–	-0.07
HABITUAL$_{SUCCESSFUL}$	–		–	-0.01
HABITUAL$_{MIXED (NO EXIT)}$				0.04
HABITUAL$_{MIXED (WITH EXIT)}$				0.05
F-value	5.81 ****	5.62 ****	5.56 ****	5.33 ****
R^2	0.36	0.36	0.36	0.37
Adjusted R^2	0.30	0.30	0.29	0.30
Change in R^2	–	0.00	0.00	0.01
N	364	364	364	364

Note: † $p < 0.10$; * $p < 0.05$; ** $p < 0.01$; *** $p < 0.001$; **** $p < 0.0001$.

H_{14c} or H_{14d}. Among the control variables entrepreneurial capability, financial motives, and a firm size greater than nine, were positively and significantly related to the current standard of living.

Table 6.20 reports findings relating to the subsample of habitual entrepreneurs. Both the Control Model 4ii and Model 4d were found to be significant, with an adjusted R^2 of 0.10. The PORTFOLIO variable was not significantly related to the current standard of living of the entrepreneur. This is in contrast to the bivariate evidence where portfolio entrepreneurs reported a higher standard of living relative to serial entrepreneurs. The control model did not result in a significant improvement to the model fit. Five control variables were significantly related to the dependent variable. The age of the entrepreneur and the level of business change were negatively related to the entrepreneur's current standard of living. The adoption of a differentiation strategy and firm size, however, were positively related to the dependent variable.

Amount of money taken out of the business(es) owned

The total amount of money taken out of the business(es) owned over the 12 months prior to the survey by the entrepreneurs is the dependent variable in Table 6.21. All models reported in Table 6.21 are significant and had a minimum adjusted R^2 of 0.29. When the Control Model 5i was compared with Models 5a, 5b and 5c the inclusion of business ownership experience variables had no significant impact on the overall model. In fact, none of the business ownership variables were significantly related to the amount of money taken out. Conversely, the bivariate evidence detected that habitual entrepreneurs took out significantly more money from the business(es) they owned than their novice counterparts. Multivariate evidence, however, fails to support hypotheses H_{14a}, H_{14c} and H_{14d}.

A number of significant relationships were detected between the dependent and control variables. Younger entrepreneurs, female entrepreneurs, entrepreneurs reporting a developmental attitude towards opportunity identification, the degree of business similarity, being involved in the agricultural sector and the surveyed business being between one and five years of age ($p < 0.05$) related to lower amounts of money taken out. In contrast, the education level of the entrepreneur, managerial capability, entrepreneurial capability, financial and reactive motives for starting or purchasing the surveyed business, and firm size were positively related to the amount of money taken out of the business(es) currently owned.

With respect to the habitual entrepreneur subsample, Table 6.22 shows that both the Control Model 5ii and Model 5d were highly significant, and had a minimum adjusted R^2 of 0.29. The addition of the PORTFOLIO variable resulted in a significant improvement in the model fit, and the variable was significantly and positively related to the amount of money taken out. This finding lends support to hypothesis H_{14b} and is consistent with the finding from the bivariate analysis.

Several significant relationships were detected between the control variables and the dependent variable. There was some variation between the control model and Model 5d in relation to the control variables found to be significant. The results relating to the full model (Model 5d) alone will be highlighted. While education, entrepreneurial capability, personal development and financial motives, and firm size were positively related to the amount of money taken out, a developmental attitude towards opportunity identification and business similarity were negatively related to the amount of money taken out.

The finding that being a portfolio entrepreneur is significantly related to higher amounts of money taken out is not particularly surprising since portfolio entrepreneurs by definition owned at least two businesses at the time of the survey. Given the higher number of businesses owned, portfolio entrepreneurs will on average be able to take out more total money than their serial (or novice) counterparts. It is interesting, therefore, to examine if different types of entrepreneurs take out more or less money *per business owned* over the period of study. Accordingly, the original 'money taken out' variable (money taken out (I)) was standardized by the number of businesses currently owned (money taken out (II)). Tables 6.22 and 6.23 report findings relating to this standardized dependent variable, with regard to the habitual subsample and the full sample respectively.

Table 6.23 shows that the Control Model 6i and Models 6a, 6b and 6c were highly significant and had a minimum adjusted R^2 of 0.17. The inclusion of each of the business ownership experience variables resulted in a significant improvement in the model fit. Each business ownership experience variable was significantly, but negatively, associated with the dependent variable. That is, being a habitual entrepreneur (HABITUAL), having owned more businesses (TOTAL), having been a failing habitual entrepreneur ($HABITUAL_{failed}$) or having been a successful habitual entrepreneur ($HABITUAL_{successful}$) were all negatively related to the amount of money taken out per business. One interpretation of this finding could be that habitual entrepreneurs may be more motivated by growth and less so by immediate financial rewards and therefore they re-invest funds into their businesses, taking a longer-term view of business performance. Alternatively habitual entrepreneurs, particularly portfolio entrepreneurs, may hold lower ownership stakes in the businesses that they own, resulting in lower amounts of money being taken out of each business.

Table 6.22 reports findings relating to the subsample of habitual entrepreneurs. Both the Control Model 6ii and Model 6d were significant with a minimum R^2 of 0.31 (and a minimum adjusted R^2 of 0.19). Once again the inclusion of the PORTFOLIO variable resulted in a significant improvement in the model fit. However in direct contrast to the earlier finding that portfolio

Table 6.22 OLS regression relating to money taken out of business(es) owned and money taken out of business(es) owned standardized by the number of businesses currently owned

Independent variables	Control Model 5ii		Model 5d		Control Model 6ii		Model 6d	
	β	Sig	β	Sig	β	Sig	β	Sig
GHK								
Age	-0.11	†	-0.10		-0.11		-0.11	
Age²	-0.02		-0.03		-0.11		-0.1	
Gender	0.13	†	0.09		0.02		0.07	
Education	0.20	**	0.18	**	0.15	*	0.17	*
Managerial human capital	0.07		0.08		0.14	*	0.12	†
Managerial capability	0.12	*	0.08		0.05		0.10	
Technical capability	-0.09		-0.10		-0.08		-0.06	
SHK_E								
Entrepreneurial capability	0.13	*	0.12	†	0.16	*	0.17	*
Development	-0.18	*	-0.16	*	-0.08		-0.11	
Parent business owners	-0.07		-0.05		0.02		0.00	
SHK_V								
Business similarity	-0.15	*	-0.16	**	-0.21	**	-0.18	**
Task similarity	0.05		0.04		0.10		0.11	†
Approval	-0.10	*	-0.10		-0.13	†	-0.14	*
Welfare	0.03		0.03		0.03		0.03	
Personal development	0.12		0.12	†	0.14	†	0.14	†
Independence	-0.04		-0.03		-0.04		-0.07	
Financial motives	0.13		0.12	†	0.08		0.08	
Reactive motives	0.11		0.10	†	0.06		0.08	
Environment								
Expectation of competition	-0.05		-0.04		0.01		-0.01	

	Model 1		Model 2		Model 3		Model 4	
Business change	0.08		0.08		0.13	†	0.13	†
Agriculture	-0.05		-0.06		-0.03		-0.03	
Manufacturing	0.01		0.04		0.06		0.03	
Construction	0.01		0.03		-0.02		-0.04	
Strategy								
Differentiation strategy	0.02		0.02		0.06		0.05	
Innovation strategy	-0.11	†	-0.12		-0.16	*	-0.15	†
Cost-based strategy	-0.04		-0.06		-0.12	†	-0.10	
Firm-specific								
10–49 employees	0.32	****	0.29	****	0.20	**	0.23	**
50 or more employees	0.22	†	0.21	***	0.20	**	0.20	**
Business 1–5yrs old	-0.07		-0.06		-0.07		-0.07	
Business 6–10 yrs old	0.00		0.02		0.05		0.03	
Purchased business	-0.09		-0.08		-0.05		-0.07	
No. of equity partners	-0.03		-0.02		0.01		0.00	
PORTFOLIO	–		0.19	**	–		-0.24	****
F-value	3.77	****	4.08	****	2.59	****	3.10	****
R^2	0.40		0.43		0.31		0.36	
Adjusted R^2	0.29		0.32		0.19		0.24	
Change in R^2	–		0.03	***	–		0.05	****
N	216		216		216		216	

Notes:

† $p < 0.10$; * $p < 0.05$; ** $p < 0.01$; *** $p < 0.001$; **** $p < 0.0001$.

Serial entrepreneurs were found to be negatively associated with the amount of money taken out relative to novice entrepreneurs ($p < 0.01$). No significant differences between portfolio and novice entrepreneurs were detected.

Serial entrepreneurs were found to be negatively associated with the amount of money taken out per business relative to novice entrepreneurs ($p < 0.005$). Portfolio entrepreneurs were found to be negatively associated with the amount of money taken out per business relative to novice entrepreneurs ($p < 0.0001$).

Table 6.23   OLS regression relating to the amount of money taken out of business(es) owned standardized by the number of businesses currently owned (total sample)

Independent Variables	Control Model 6i β	Sig	Model 6a β	Sig	Model 6b β	Sig	Model 6c β	Sig
GHK								
Age	-0.09		-0.08		-0.06		-0.08	
Age²	-0.08		-0.07		-0.07		-0.07	
Gender	0.02		0.03		0.03		0.03	
Education	0.16	**	0.17	***	0.18	***	0.18	***
Managerial human capital	0.05		0.05		0.04		0.06	
Managerial capability	0.03		0.04		0.06		0.03	
Technical capability	0.08		0.03		0.07		0.03	
SHK_E								
Entrepreneurial capability	0.15	*	0.13	*	0.16	**	0.13	*
Development	-0.06		-0.05		-0.09		-0.04	
Parent business owners	-0.02		0.01		0.02		0.00	
SHK_V								
Business similarity	-0.18	***	-0.15	**	-0.15	**	-0.15	**
Task similarity	-0.02		-0.02		-0.03		-0.02	
Approval	-0.04		-0.06		-0.05		-0.07	
Welfare	-0.03		-0.06		-0.03		-0.05	
Personal development	0.04		0.07		0.05		0.07	
Independence	0.02		0.01		0.02		0.01	
Financial motives	0.12	*	0.11	*	0.11	*	0.11	*
Reactive motives	0.11	*	0.10	*	0.10	†	0.10	*
Environment								
Expectation of competition	0.00		0.00		0.00		0.00	

	Model 1	Model 2	Model 3	Model 4
Business change	0.06	0.08	0.09 †	0.08
Agriculture	-0.08	-0.08	-0.08	-0.08 †
Manufacturing	-0.02	-0.04	-0.04	-0.04
Construction	-0.09 †	-0.07	-0.07	-0.07
Strategy				
Differentiation strategy	-0.04	-0.03	-0.04	-0.03
Innovation strategy	-0.10 †	-0.08	-0.09	-0.08
Cost-based strategy	-0.04	-0.02	-0.04	-0.03
Firm-specific				
10–49 employees	0.20 ****	0.23 ****	0.24 ****	0.23 ****
50 or more employees	0.12 *	0.15 **	0.14 **	0.15 **
Business 1–5 yrs old	-0.10 †	-0.12 *	-0.11 *	-0.12 *
Business 6–10 yrs old	-0.01	0.00	-0.01	0.01
Purchased business	-0.02	-0.02	-0.01	-0.03
No. of equity partners	0.08	0.06	0.07	0.06
HABITUAL	–	-0.26 ****	–	–
TOTAL	–	–	-0.24 ****	–
HABITUAL$_{FAILED}$	–	–		-0.20 ****
HABITUAL$_{SUCCESSFUL}$	–	–		-0.14 **
HABITUAL$_{MIXED (NO EXIT)}$				-0.27 ****
HABITUAL$_{MIXED (WITH EXIT)}$				-0.03
F-value	3.40 ****	4.39 ****	4.22 ****	4.09 ****
R^2	0.25	0.31	0.30	0.31
Adjusted R^2	0.17	0.24	0.23	0.24
Change in R^2	–	0.06 ****	0.05 ****	0.06 ****
N	364	364	364	364

Note: † $p < 0.10$; * $p < 0.05$; ** $p < 0.01$; *** $p < 0.001$; **** $p < 0.0001$.

173

Table 6.24 Summary of regression results relating to performance for novice and habitual entrepreneurs

Independent variables	Dependent variables							
	Weighted (I)	Weighted (II)	Profit relative to competitors	Employment change[b]	Sales change[c]	Standard of living	Money taken out (I)	Money taken out (II)
GHK								
Age	– –		– –		– –	– – – –	– –	
Age²								
Gender	+						++	
Education							++++	++++
Managerial human capital								
Managerial capability	+++++	+++++	+++				++	
Technical capability	–		– –	– –				
SHK_E								
Entrepreneurial capability	+++++	+++++			+++	++	+++	++
Development							– –	
Parent business owners	–[a]							
SHK_V								
Business similarity								– –
Task similarity								
Approval				– –				
Welfare				+++				
Personal development				+++				
Independence					–			
Financial motives	++	+++					+++	++
Reactive motives							++	++
Environment								
Expectation of competition								
Business change	– –	– –						
Agriculture	– –	– –		–		–	– –	
Manufacturing								

174

	(1)	(2)	(3)	(4)	(5)	(6)	(7)	(8)
Construction							–[a]	–[a]
Strategy								
Differentiation strategy								
Innovation strategy	+						–	–
Cost-based strategy	+						–	–
Firm-specific								
10–49 employees	+	++		++		++	+++++	+++++
50 or more employees			+++++	+++++		+	+++	+++
Business 1–5 yrs old					–		–	–
Business 6–10 yrs old					+			
Purchased business								
No. of equity partners								
HABITUAL	–		–				–	–
TOTAL	–		–				–	–
HABITUAL$_{FAILED}$		–					–	–
HABITUAL$_{SUCCESSFUL}$						– –	–	–
HABITUAL$_{MIXED\ (NO\ EXIT)}$							–	–
HABITUAL$_{MIXED\ (WITH\ EXIT)}$							– – – –	– – – –
Model significance	****	****	***	****	**	****	****	****
R^2	0.23	0.26	0.17	0.20	0.18	0.19	0.35	0.30
Adjusted R^2	0.16	0.19	0.09	0.13	0.09	0.11	0.28	0.23
N	378	378	373	375	322	378	364	364

Notes:

† $p < 0.10$; * $p < 0.05$; ** $p < 0.01$; *** $p < 0.001$; **** $p < 0.0001$.

– Negatively related at $p < 0.10$; – – negatively related at $p < 0.05$; – – – negatively related at $p < 0.01$; – – – – negatively related at $p < 0.001$; – – – – – negatively related at $p < 0.0001$;

+ Positively related at $p < 0.10$; ++ positively related at $p < 0.05$; +++ positively related at $p < 0.01$; ++++ positively related at $p < 0.001$; +++++ positively related at $p < 0.0001$.

[a] Variable significant in the control model only

[b] Employment change was measured in terms of the log of the absolute change in total employment (1996–2001).

[c] Sales change was measured in terms of the percentage change in sales growth between 1996 and 1999. The model with the log of the absolute change in sales was not significant.

Table 6.25 Summary of regression results relating to performance based on habitual entrepreneurs only

Independent variables	Weighted (I)	Weighted (II)	Profit relative to competitors	Employment change[b]	Sales change[c]	Standard of living	Money taken out (I)	Money taken out (II)
GHK								
Age	–		–			– – –	–	
Age²								
Gender	+						+[a]	
Education							+++	++
Managerial human capital	++++	+++++					+	+
Managerial capability					–			
Technical capability	– –			– –	–			
SHK$_E$								
Entrepreneurial capability	+++	+++					++	
Development			+		–		– –	
Parent business owners	–	–	– –					
SHK$_V$								
Business similarity							– – –	– – –
Task similarity							–	
Approval								–
Welfare				+++				
Personal development				+++				+
Independence		+						
Financial motives	+							
Reactive motives								
Environment								
Expectation of competition								
Business change				– –				
Agriculture						– –		+
Manufacturing								

176

	(1)	(2)	(3)	(4)	(5)	(6)	(7)	(8)
Strategy								
Differentiation strategy			++	++			+	
Innovation strategy		−			+++		+++	−a
Cost-based strategy								−a
Firm-specific								
10–49 employees								
50 or more employees	++	+++++	+++++	+++++	+++++	++ +a	+++	+++
Business 1–5 yrs old								
Business 6–10 yrs old								
Purchased business								
No. of equity partners								
PORTFOLIO						+++++	+++++	−−−−−
Model Significance	***	****	*	*	***	*	****	****
R^2	0.27	0.31	0.23	0.23	0.28	0.23	0.42	0.36
Adjusted R^2	0.14	0.19	0.09	0.09	0.13	0.10	0.31	0.24
N	221	221	218	218	194	221	216	216

Notes:

† $p < 0.10$; * $p < 0.05$; ** $p < 0.01$; *** $p < 0.001$; **** $p < 0.0001$.

− Negatively related at $p < 0.10$; − − negatively related at $p < 0.05$; − − − negatively related at $p < 0.01$; − − − − negatively related at $p < 0.001$; − − − − − negatively related at $p < 0.0001$;

+ Positively related at $p < 0.10$; ++ positively related at $p < 0.05$; +++ positively related at $p < 0.01$; ++++ positively related at $p < 0.001$; +++++ positively related at $p < 0.0001$.

a Variable significant in the control model only.

b Employment change was measured in terms of the log of the absolute change in total employment (1996–2001). The model with the percentage change in employment as the dependent variable was not significant.

c Sales change was measured in terms of the log of the absolute change in sales. The model with the percentage change in sales growth between 1996 and 1999 as the dependent variable was not significant.

entrepreneurs reported significantly higher amounts of money taken out, when money taken out was standardized by the number of businesses currently owned, the relationship was completely reversed (consistent with the bivariate analysis). That is, portfolio entrepreneurs reported significantly lower amounts of money taken out per business. With respect to the control variables, education, managerial human capital, entrepreneurial capability, task similarity, motives based on personal development and firm size were positively related to the amount of money taken out per business. Conversely business similarity, approval-based motives and the adoption of an innovation-based business strategy were negatively related to the amount of money taken out per business.

SUMMARY OF FINDINGS

The discussion here is largely based on findings from the multivariate analysis as this type of analysis is deemed to be more robust. Table 6.24 and 6.25 present the nature and strength of the relationship between each variable and the dependent variables relating to the full sample (novice and habitual entrepreneurs) and the subsample of habitual entrepreneurs respectively.

With respect to the full sample, there were a number of significant relationships between the various indicators of business ownership experience and firm performance. All were inverse relationships. In particular being a habitual entrepreneur (as opposed to a novice entrepreneur) was negatively associated with weighted performance (I) and profit relative to competitors. Habitual entrepreneurs who had a majority of failed businesses reported significantly lower performance in terms of weighted performance (I) and weighted performance (II). Further, those habitual entrepreneurs who had not exited from any of the businesses they own were associated with poorer performance relative to competitors.

With regard to entrepreneur performance, habitual entrepreneurs who had a majority of failed businesses were associated with a significantly lower standard of living and lower amounts of money taken out per business owned. However, those habitual entrepreneurs who had a majority of successful businesses and those habitual entrepreneurs who had not exited from any of the businesses they own also reported lower amounts of money taken out per business than novice entrepreneurs. This may suggest either that many habitual entrepreneurs are sitting on poorly performing portfolios or they are reinvesting profits either to grow the business or to start further businesses. Finally, the total number of businesses ever owned was inversely related to the amount of money taken out (II). Overall these findings contrast starkly with the initial prediction that habitual entrepreneurs would outperform their inexperienced counterparts (H_{14a}), as well as that habitual entrepreneurs who had failed would outperform the novices (H_{14c}) along with those who had been successful (H_{14d}).

Among the habitual entrepreneurs being a portfolio entrepreneur was not significantly related to any of the firm performance variables. Being a portfolio entrepreneur was, however, associated with one entrepreneur performance variable. While there was a positive and significant relationship between being a portfolio entrepreneur and the amount of money taken out of a businesses owned (money taken out (I)), this relationship was reversed when the amount of money taken out was standardized by the number of businesses currently owned (money taken out (II)). Consequently there is no support for hypothesis H_{14b}.

CONCLUSION

The purpose of this chapter was to test two hypotheses developed in Chapter 2. Hypothesis H_{14a} suggests that habitual entrepreneurs will report higher levels of performance than novice entrepreneurs, whilst hypothesis H_{14b} suggests that among the habitual entrepreneurs, portfolio entrepreneurs will outperform serial entrepreneurs. These hypotheses were tested for both firm-level and entrepreneur-level performance using both bivariate and multivariate analysis. To test for definitional sensitivities both the business ownership experience variables and the performance were operationalized in a number of ways. With respect to firm performance, indicators included two weighted performance measures (weighted (I) and (II)), profit relative to competitors, employment change and sales change. With respect to entrepreneurial performance their current standard of living compared to when they first started the surveyed business, the total amount of money taken out (money taken out (I)) and amount of money taken out per business owned (money taken out (II)) were used. To capture variations based on different definitions of business ownership experience the following were used: a simple 'habitual or not' dummy variable; a continuous variable capturing the total number of businesses ever owned; and four dummy variables to capture potential differences between those habitual entrepreneurs who had been previous successful and those that had failed. Among the habitual entrepreneurs a distinction was made between portfolio and serial entrepreneurs.

The summary of the findings discussed in the previous section shows that there was no strong support for either of the above hypotheses, irrespective of the method used. If anything the multivariate analysis, which controlled for a variety of variables known to be associated with firm performance, showed that business ownership experience was negatively related to a selection of performance indicators. Interpretation and reflections on these findings is provided in the following chapter.

APPENDIX 6.1

Table 6A.1   *Correlation matrix relating to performance based differences among different types of entrepreneurs (n = 378)*

Pearson correlation	Mean	S.D.	VIF	1	2	3	4
1. Age	−0.49	9.2	1.33	1.00			
2. Age^2	85.44	118.85	1.19	−0.11	1.00		
3. Gender	0.89	0.31	1.30	0.12	−0.02	1.00	
4. Education	0.55	0.93	1.23	−0.08	−0.04	−0.10	1.00
5. Managerial HK	10.46	5.74	1.26	0.20	−0.22	0.08	0.03
6. Managerial capability	0.01	1.00	1.33	−0.01	−0.04	−0.05	−0.13
7. Technical capability	0.02	1.02	1.46	0.03	0.00	0.22	0.06
8. Entrepreneurial capability	−0.08	1.02	1.52	−0.05	0.09	0.10	−0.01
9. Developmental approach	−0.01	0.93	1.43	−0.13	0.01	0.03	−0.01
10. Parent(s) owned business	0.38	0.49	1.19	−0.04	0.09	0.07	0.03
11. Business similarity	0.02	0.98	1.20	0.09	−0.08	−0.15	0.12
12. Task similarity	0.02	0.97	1.10	−0.01	−0.04	−0.03	−0.04
13. Approval	−0.03	0.99	1.15	−0.10	0.10	−0.04	−0.13
14. Welfare	−0.10	0.94	1.31	0.06	0.12	0.06	−0.03
15. Personal development	0.01	1.00	1.48	−0.06	0.03	0.00	0.07
16. Independence	0.05	0.97	1.23	−0.10	−0.04	−0.11	0.09
17. Financial motives	−0.06	0.99	1.13	0.01	−0.09	0.19	−0.06
18. Reactive	−0.04	1.04	1.13	−0.04	−0.01	0.01	0.04
19. Expectation of competition	3.54	1.20	1.12	0.03	−0.13	0.06	−0.08
20. Business change	3.47	0.98	1.21	0.01	0.08	0.16	0.02
21. Agriculture	0.05	0.22	1.20	0.09	0.10	0.05	−0.04
22. Manufacturing	0.12	0.32	1.24	0.08	−0.07	0.10	−0.06
23. Construction	0.09	0.28	1.16	−0.08	0.01	0.11	−0.10
24. Differentiation strategy	0.02	1.01	1.37	−0.11	0.04	0.14	0.11
25. Innovation strategy	−0.02	1.03	1.58	0.03	−0.02	−0.13	0.00
26. Cost-based strategy	−0.09	0.99	1.34	−0.02	−0.02	−0.04	0.14
27. 10–49 employees	0.18	0.39	1.35	0.07	−0.09	0.06	−0.07
28. 50 or more employees	0.03	0.17	1.16	0.01	−0.08	0.06	−0.04
29. Business 1–5 yrs old	0.03	0.18	1.24	−0.17	0.09	−0.12	0.17
30. Business 6–10 yrs old	0.22	0.41	1.28	−0.22	0.06	−0.04	0.05
31. Purchased business	0.14	0.35	1.17	−0.02	−0.03	−0.10	0.01
32. No. of equity partners	1.57	1.06	1.30	0.14	−0.07	−0.02	0.12
33. Habitual	0.58	0.49	1.15	0.03	−0.03	0.06	0.03
34. Total	2.24	1.76	1.16	0.11	0.03	0.08	0.05
35. Habitual failed	0.15	0.36	1.32	0.01	0.00	−0.04	0.00
36. Habitual successful	0.19	0.31	1.19	0.06	−0.03	0.02	−0.06
37. Mixed 1	0.30	0.46	1.43	0.00	0.01	0.06	0.06
38. Mixed 2	0.03	0.17	1.12	−0.05	−0.03	0.06	0.02
39. Serial	0.25	0.43	1.33	0.02	−0.03	−0.09	−0.01
40. Portfolio	0.34	0.47	1.41	0.01	0.00	0.15	0.04

Table 6A.1   continued

Pearson correlation	5	6	7	8	9	10	11
6. Managerial capability	0.15	1.00					
7. Technical capability	0.01	0.01	1.00				
8. Entrepreneurial capability	0.06	−0.06	−0.01	1.00			
9. Developmental approach	0.06	0.21	0.27	0.23	1.00		
10. Parent(s) owned business	−0.13	−0.01	−0.04	0.05	0.02	1.00	
11. Business similarity	0.11	−0.03	−0.13	−0.06	0.02	0.00	1.00
12. Task similarity	−0.07	−0.06	−0.04	−0.01	0.04	−0.09	−0.03
13. Approval	−0.03	0.04	−0.08	0.09	0.02	0.07	−0.07
14. Welfare	−0.12	0.03	−0.08	0.00	0.01	0.22	−0.08
15. Personal development	0.13	0.18	0.19	0.32	0.25	0.07	0.09
16. Independence	0.00	0.07	0.06	0.01	0.13	−0.10	−0.08
17. Financial motives	0.08	0.07	0.07	0.12	0.11	−0.03	−0.05
18. Reactive	−0.09	0.08	−0.01	0.05	0.02	0.06	−0.12
19. Expectation of competition	−0.03	0.03	0.00	0.02	−0.08	−0.02	−0.09
20. Business change	0.05	0.03	0.08	0.07	0.11	0.08	0.01
21. Agriculture	−0.14	−0.11	−0.03	0.03	−0.13	0.18	0.03
22. Manufacturing	0.05	0.02	0.15	0.01	0.07	−0.10	−0.04
23. Construction	0.01	−0.01	0.13	0.00	−0.02	0.03	−0.07
24. Differentiation strategy	−0.05	−0.16	−0.05	−0.06	−0.18	0.02	−0.03
25. Innovation strategy	−0.04	−0.12	−0.12	−0.37	−0.26	−0.05	−0.05
26. Cost-based strategy	0.01	−0.22	−0.09	−0.20	−0.13	0.01	0.13
27. 10–49 employees	0.09	0.07	−0.09	0.07	0.02	0.00	−0.05
28. 50 or more employees	0.01	0.08	0.04	0.04	−0.04	−0.01	0.03
29. Business 1–5 yrs old	−0.05	−0.07	−0.07	0.01	0.07	−0.03	0.05
30. Business 6–10 yrs old	0.08	0.06	−0.12	0.04	0.02	0.01	0.09
31. Purchased business	−0.12	0.04	−0.10	−0.15	−0.09	0.01	−0.06
32. No. of equity partners	0.06	0.02	−0.10	−0.02	−0.03	−0.02	0.05
33. Habitual	0.08	0.05	−0.10	0.02	0.03	0.10	0.13
34. Total	0.04	0.10	−0.03	0.05	−0.05	0.16	0.11
35. Habitual failed	0.07	0.04	−0.03	−0.03	0.02	0.07	−0.06
36. Habitual successful	−0.05	0.06	−0.07	−0.01	−0.06	0.01	0.04
37. Mixed 1	0.07	−0.02	−0.03	0.04	0.08	0.02	0.16
38. Mixed 2	−0.03	0.02	−0.01	0.02	−0.06	0.09	0.00
39. Serial	0.05	−0.07	−0.11	−0.05	0.03	0.07	0.02
40. Portfolio	0.04	0.12	−0.01	0.06	0.00	0.04	0.12

Table 6A.1 continued

Pearson correlation	12	13	14	15	16	17	18
13. Approval	−0.02	1.00					
14. Welfare	0.03	−0.09	1.00				
15. Personal development	0.02	0.05	−0.09	1.00			
16. Independence	0.09	−0.06	−0.01	−0.03	1.00		
17. Financial motives	−0.04	−0.05	−0.03	−0.01	0.00	1.00	
18. Reactive	−0.01	−0.02	0.01	0.00	0.00	−0.02	1.00
19. Expectation of competition	−0.05	0.03	−0.06	−0.05	0.04	0.04	0.03
20. Business change	0.01	0.11	0.02	0.18	−0.06	0.00	−0.07
21. Agriculture	0.01	−0.04	0.21	0.00	−0.03	0.06	0.04
22. Manufacturing	−0.02	−0.09	−0.06	0.10	−0.11	−0.01	−0.10
23. Construction	0.06	0.04	0.01	−0.10	0.12	0.07	−0.04
24. Differentiation strategy	−0.02	0.01	0.18	0.03	−0.19	−0.06	−0.08
25. Innovation strategy	0.03	−0.12	0.05	−0.34	0.11	−0.13	0.08
26. Cost-based strategy	0.05	0.01	−0.19	−0.16	0.09	−0.08	−0.04
27. 10–49 employees	−0.11	−0.01	−0.06	0.08	−0.11	0.02	0.05
28. 50 or more employees	−0.08	0.02	−0.05	0.10	−0.06	−0.04	0.01
29. Business 1–5 yrs old	−0.01	−0.03	−0.03	0.10	0.09	0.00	−0.06
30. Business 6–10 yrs old	0.00	−0.01	0.01	0.05	−0.02	0.03	0.02
31. Purchased business	−0.08	0.01	0.08	−0.13	−0.03	−0.01	0.17
32. No. of equity partners	−0.08	−0.11	0.04	0.00	−0.07	−0.02	0.05
33. Habitual	−0.01	−0.03	−0.07	0.12	−0.07	−0.03	−0.04
34. Total	−0.07	−0.01	0.02	0.10	−0.06	−0.02	−0.04
35. Habitual failed	−0.10	0.05	−0.06	0.02	0.01	0.02	−0.06
36. Habitual successful	0.03	−0.03	0.00	−0.11	−0.04	0.06	−0.05
37. Mixed 1	0.06	−0.08	−0.03	0.17	−0.04	−0.07	0.03
38. Mixed 2	−0.01	0.09	−0.02	0.06	−0.02	−0.03	0.02
39. Serial	−0.01	0.04	−0.05	0.00	0.05	−0.07	−0.11
40. Portfolio	0.00	−0.07	−0.03	0.13	−0.11	0.03	0.06

Table 6A.1   continued

Pearson correlation	19	20	21	22	23	24	25
20. Business change	−0.06	1.00					
21. Agriculture	0.02	0.01	1.00				
22. Manufacturing	0.09	0.14	−0.09	1.00			
23. Construction	0.05	−0.08	−0.07	−0.11	1.00		
24. Differentiation strategy	0.04	0.01	0.10	0.14	−0.02	1.00	
25. Innovation strategy	0.04	−0.28	0.01	−0.10	0.04	−0.01	1.00
26. Cost-based strategy	−0.08	−0.03	−0.06	−0.15	0.02	−0.07	−0.04
27. 10–49 employees	−0.01	0.08	−0.11	0.15	0.02	0.01	−0.10
28. 50 or more employees	0.07	0.11	0.10	0.13	−0.05	−0.02	−0.03
29. Business 1–5 yrs old	−0.01	0.03	0.02	0.02	−0.01	0.18	−0.08
30. Business 6–10 yrs old	−0.14	0.00	−0.04	−0.09	0.00	−0.04	0.01
31. Purchased business	0.11	−0.08	0.04	−0.01	−0.02	0.05	0.09
32. No. of equity partners	0.02	0.10	0.00	0.02	−0.02	−0.10	−0.12
33. Habitual	−0.03	0.09	−0.02	−0.06	0.03	−0.04	−0.09
34. Total	−0.02	0.14	0.03	−0.05	0.03	−0.02	−0.11
35. Habitual failed	−0.06	0.14	0.00	0.05	0.11	−0.07	−0.01
36. Habitual successful	0.07	−0.05	−0.01	0.01	0.01	0.02	0.06
37. Mixed 1	−0.06	0.00	−0.02	−0.13	−0.06	0.00	−0.12
38. Mixed 2	0.07	0.06	0.03	0.04	0.00	0.00	−0.05
39. Serial	0.06	0.01	−0.03	0.02	0.06	−0.06	0.02
40. Portfolio	−0.08	0.08	0.01	−0.09	−0.02	0.02	−0.11

Pearson correlation	26	27	28	29	30	31	32
27. 10–49 employees	−0.01	1.00					
28. 50 or more employees	−0.06	−0.08	1.00				
29. Business 1–5 yrs old	0.03	−0.09	−0.03	1.00			
30. Business 6–10 yrs old	0.01	−0.18	−0.09	−0.10	1.00		
31. Purchased business	0.04	0.02	0.02	0.01	−0.05	1.00	
32. No. of equity partners	0.01	0.26	0.07	0.02	0.06	0.17	1.00
33. Habitual	0.00	0.11	0.08	−0.11	0.07	−0.05	0.00
34. Total	0.00	0.15	0.08	−0.08	−0.01	0.00	0.07
35. Habitual failed	0.03	0.07	0.10	−0.08	0.01	−0.02	0.08
36. Habitual successful	0.01	−0.01	−0.01	−0.02	0.04	0.08	0.03
37. Mixed 1	0.00	0.07	−0.01	−0.03	0.02	−0.10	−0.09
38. Mixed 2	−0.09	0.00	0.06	−0.03	0.02	0.02	0.01
39. Serial	0.06	−0.05	0.01	−0.04	0.07	0.03	−0.01
40. Portfolio	−0.06	0.15	0.08	−0.07	0.00	−0.08	0.01

Note: r has to be 0.101 or higher to be significant at $p < 0.05$ (two-tailed) and r has to be 0.133 or higher to be significant at $p < 0.01$ (two-tailed).

APPENDIX 6.2

*Table 6A.2   Correlation matrix relating to performance based differences
among habitual entrepreneurs (n = 221)*

Pearson correlation	Mean	S.D.	VIF	1	2	3	4
1. Age	−0.28	9.10	1.45				
2. Age²	82.50	118.47	1.27	−0.24			
3. Gender	0.91	0.29	1.41	0.11	−0.09		
4. Education	0.57	0.84	1.31	−0.11	−0.02	−0.08	
5. Managerial HK	10.84	5.79	1.22	0.17	−0.21	0.05	0.05
6. Managerial capability	0.05	0.99	1.44	−0.04	−0.05	−0.03	−0.21
7. Technical capability	−0.07	1.07	1.49	0.07	−0.04	0.23	0.05
8. Entrepreneurial capability	−0.06	1.04	1.67	−0.10	0.07	0.08	0.03
9. Developmental approach	0.01	0.88	1.39	−0.07	0.01	0.06	−0.05
10. Parent(s) owned business	0.42	0.50	1.27	−0.02	0.12	0.06	0.05
11. Business similarity	0.13	0.95	1.23	0.11	−0.08	−0.09	0.16
12. Task similarity	0.01	0.96	1.10	0.01	0.01	−0.03	−0.07
13. Approval	−0.05	1.02	1.23	−0.04	0.07	−0.11	−0.16
14. Welfare	−0.16	0.94	1.41	0.11	0.08	0.08	0.01
15. Personal development	0.10	1.01	1.62	−0.08	0.09	0.01	0.07
16. Independence	−0.01	0.99	1.32	−0.10	−0.08	0.00	0.00
17. Financial motives	−0.08	1.00	1.21	−0.03	−0.11	0.21	−0.11
18. Reactive	−0.08	1.09	1.13	−0.05	−0.01	0.01	0.04
19. Expectation of competition	3.51	1.21	1.16	0.03	−0.13	0.07	−0.04
20. Business change	2.55	0.97	1.31	−0.02	0.12	0.15	−0.01
21. Agriculture	0.05	0.22	1.24	0.01	−0.02	0.07	−0.06
22. Manufacturing	0.10	0.30	1.30	0.10	−0.11	0.11	−0.04
23. Construction	0.10	0.29	1.25	−0.11	−0.02	0.11	−0.09
24. Differentiation strategy	0.05	0.96	1.56	0.04	−0.09	−0.18	−0.16
25. Innovation strategy	0.06	1.04	1.73	−0.02	0.02	0.24	0.01
26. Cost-based strategy	−0.09	0.98	1.42	0.01	0.04	0.00	−0.17
27. 10–49 employees	0.22	0.41	1.49	0.06	−0.13	0.06	−0.04
28. 50 or more employees	0.04	0.20	1.28	0.01	−0.09	0.07	−0.03
29. Business 1–5 yrs old	0.02	0.14	1.36	−0.20	0.15	−0.07	0.11
30. Business 6–10 yrs old	0.24	0.43	1.41	−0.32	0.15	−0.04	0.13
31. Purchased business	0.13	0.33	1.29	0.04	−0.07	−0.16	−0.01
32. No. of equity partners	1.57	1.03	1.42	0.11	−0.05	0.02	0.16
33. Portfolio	0.06	0.50	1.23	−0.01	0.02	0.19	0.04

Table 6A.2   continued

Pearson correlation	5	6	7	8	9	10	11
6. Managerial capability	0.11						
7. Technical capability	0.03	−0.04					
8. Entrepreneurial capability	0.02	−0.01	−0.06				
9. Developmental approach	−0.01	0.12	0.20	0.23			
10. Parent(s) owned business	−0.16	−0.03	0.01	−0.06	0.00		
11. Business similarity	0.14	−0.10	−0.07	0.02	0.05	−0.02	
12. Task similarity	−0.11	−0.02	−0.02	−0.02	0.06	−0.10	−0.08
13. Approval	0.00	0.05	−0.14	0.08	−0.04	0.00	−0.08
14. Welfare	−0.12	0.05	−0.02	0.03	0.03	0.25	−0.15
15. Personal development	0.12	0.14	0.21	0.37	0.24	0.11	0.08
16. Independence	0.03	0.13	0.03	0.03	0.13	−0.11	−0.16
17. Financial motives	0.04	0.05	0.03	0.11	0.07	−0.07	−0.03

Pearson correlation	5	6	7	8	9	10	11
18. Reactive	−0.11	0.05	0.00	0.05	0.02	0.04	−0.03
19. Expectation of competition	−0.02	0.00	−0.01	0.05	−0.09	0.03	−0.06
20. Business change	0.01	0.10	0.08	0.07	0.12	0.11	0.01
21. Agriculture	−0.06	−0.04	−0.01	0.00	−0.03	0.23	0.00
22. Manufacturing	0.10	−0.04	0.12	−0.03	0.02	−0.07	0.01
23. Construction	0.04	−0.04	0.15	−0.02	−0.01	0.01	−0.10
24. Differentiation strategy	0.01	0.25	0.06	0.06	0.27	−0.12	−0.03
25. Innovation strategy	0.06	0.10	0.15	0.42	0.26	0.00	0.01
26. Cost-based strategy	−0.03	0.23	0.03	0.18	0.05	0.00	−0.10
27. 10–49 employees	0.08	0.02	−0.16	0.10	−0.05	−0.03	0.00
28. 50 or more employees	0.02	0.15	0.05	0.06	−0.05	−0.04	0.08
29. Business 1–5 yrs old	−0.08	−0.04	−0.11	0.01	0.08	0.09	0.04
30. Business 6–10 yrs old	−0.02	0.00	−0.08	0.09	0.00	−0.01	0.06
31. Purchased business	−0.06	0.09	−0.17	−0.10	−0.03	0.01	−0.02
32. No. of equity partners	0.02	0.01	−0.06	0.07	−0.04	0.03	0.10
33. Portfolio	−0.01	0.14	0.08	0.08	−0.03	−0.04	0.06

Table 6A.2   continued

Pearson correlation	12	13	14	15	16	17	18
13. Approval	–0.07						
14. Welfare	0.08	–0.19					
15. Personal development	–0.07	0.03	–0.04				
16. Independence	0.09	–0.08	0.08	–0.08			
17. Financial motives	–0.03	–0.10	0.02	–0.06	0.02		
18. Reactive	0.04	–0.05	0.00	0.03	0.01	–0.03	
19. Expectation of competition	–0.04	0.07	–0.03	–0.01	0.09	–0.01	–0.04
20. Business change	–0.09	0.11	0.03	0.20	–0.08	0.02	–0.07
21. Agriculture	0.02	0.00	0.12	0.12	–0.04	0.11	0.04
22. Manufacturing	–0.03	–0.06	–0.04	0.05	–0.13	–0.07	–0.13
23. Construction	0.04	0.04	0.03	–0.11	0.17	0.13	–0.09
24. Differentiation strategy	0.05	0.01	–0.18	–0.05	0.22	0.06	0.05
25. Innovation strategy	–0.10	0.08	–0.03	0.34	–0.07	0.11	–0.08
26. Cost-based strategy	–0.02	–0.02	0.19	0.15	–0.10	0.11	0.05
27. 10–49 employees	–0.08	0.07	–0.07	0.05	–0.11	–0.01	0.01
28. 50 or more employees	–0.05	–0.02	–0.06	0.13	–0.05	–0.05	–0.02
29. Business 1–5 yrs old	0.00	0.00	–0.01	0.14	0.05	–0.01	–0.03
30. Business 6–10 yrs old	–0.01	0.04	0.02	0.06	0.01	0.05	0.07
31. Purchased business	–0.02	0.06	0.08	–0.11	–0.02	–0.02	0.12
32. No. of equity partners	–0.12	–0.11	0.06	0.01	–0.11	–0.02	0.01
33. Portfolio	0.01	–0.09	–0.02	0.09	–0.12	0.08	0.13

Pearson correlation	19	20	21	22	23	24	25
20. Business change	–0.05						
21. Agriculture	–0.01	–0.02					
22. Manufacturing	0.07	0.11	–0.08				
23. Construction	0.08	–0.10	–0.07	–0.11			
24. Differentiation strategy	–0.01	–0.05	–0.10	–0.12	–0.02		
25. Innovation strategy	0.00	0.31	0.08	0.08	–0.01	0.01	
26. Cost-based strategy	0.06	0.06	0.06	0.17	0.00	0.03	0.06
27. 10–49 employees	–0.03	0.09	–0.12	0.12	0.05	0.02	–0.05
28. 50 or more employees	0.10	0.17	0.16	0.16	–0.07	0.01	–0.06
29. Business 1–5 yrs old	0.00	0.13	0.13	–0.05	–0.04	0.22	–0.09
30. Business 6–10 yrs old	–0.13	–0.02	–0.03	–0.05	–0.04	0.04	0.01
31. Purchased business	0.14	0.02	–0.03	0.01	0.02	–0.08	0.13
32. No. of equity partners	0.08	0.08	–0.03	0.08	–0.05	–0.05	–0.13
33. Portfolio	–0.10	0.05	0.03	–0.08	–0.07	0.07	–0.01

Table 6A.2   continued

Pearson correlation	26	27	28	29	30	31	32
27. 10–49 employees	−0.03						
28. 50 or more employees	−0.08	−0.11					
29. Business 1–5 yrs old	−0.12	−0.07	−0.03				
30. Business 6–10 yrs old	0.03	−0.22	−0.12	−0.08			
31. Purchased business	−0.02	0.06	−0.01	0.05	−0.06		
32. No. of equity partners	−0.01	0.30	0.02	0.02	0.02	0.28	
33. Portfolio	−0.09	0.14	0.04	0.02	0.06	0.09	0.02

Note: r has to be 0.132 or higher to be significant at $p < 0.05$ (two-tailed) and r has to be 0.176 or higher to be significant at $p < 0.01$ (two-tailed).

7. Conclusions

INTRODUCTION

This book represents the first systematic study of habitual entrepreneurship. The study has explored the role played by business ownership experience in understanding entrepreneurial behaviour (that is, information search and opportunity identification, pursuit and exploitation) and performance. In particular, the broad research question under study was as follows:

What is the relationship between entrepreneurial experience (business ownership experience), human capital, entrepreneurial behaviour and outcomes?

To address this question, habitual (experienced) and novice (inexperienced) entrepreneurs were compared. In addition, differences between serial entrepreneurs (those who acquired business ownership experience sequentially) and portfolio entrepreneurs (those who acquired business ownership experience concurrently), were examined. By identifying differences between these groups of entrepreneurs a significant source of heterogeneity amongst entrepreneurs, namely the extent and nature of business ownership experience, was identified. While casual observation suggests that entrepreneurs are heterogeneous, many studies have largely ignored this heterogeneity, potentially leading to biased results.

The study also addresses a number of limitations associated with previous research on habitual entrepreneurship. First, by focusing on the entrepreneur and the firm as the unit of analysis, the study avoids a singular focus on the firm at the expense of the entrepreneur. In many smaller businesses the entrepreneur is often the key resource and driver of the organization, and should therefore not be overlooked. Second, the study develops a theoretical framework for the study of habitual entrepreneurship. Previous research has contributed towards but not provided a unifying framework for the study of business ownership experience.

The study is couched within a human capital framework whereby business ownership experience is seen as one element of a broader set of general and specific human capital characteristics of the entrepreneur. By building on and extending human capital theory, (a well-established and respected economic theory) the study offers a fruitful way of viewing entrepreneurs, their behaviour and associated outcomes. Adopting this framework, bivariate and multivariate analyses were conducted to test specific hypotheses. The use of the latter form of analyses offers an advance on previous research in the area because multivariate analysis allows the researcher to control for the effects of dimensions of human capital other than business ownership experience. Consequently, the relative contribution of business ownership experience vis-à-vis other dimensions of human capital was established. Further contributions made by this study will be outlined in the following sections, where the key findings of the study are reflected upon and implications for practitioners and policymakers are presented. In the final section we outline an agenda for further research.

KEY FINDINGS AND INTERPRETATION

To guide discussion of the central findings of the study, Table 7.1 provides a summary of the hypotheses tested based on the multivariate results. The following discussion is organized around four themes. The first three are based on the human capital framework and therefore relate to human capital, behavioural and performance-based differences between the habitual and novice and then serial and portfolio entrepreneurs. When examining the relationship between business ownership experience and behaviour and performance, several control variables were included. There were a number of significant relationships between the control variables and the dependent variables relating to behaviour and performance. These findings are also reported below.

Differences Between Novice and Habitual (Serial and Portfolio) Entrepreneurs Based on Human Capital

In Chapter 2 hypotheses were derived suggesting that besides the extent and nature of their business ownership experience, there would be differences between novice and habitual entrepreneurs (and among the habitual entrepreneurs between serial and portfolio entrepreneurs) in terms of their human capital characteristics. In particular, differences between these entrepreneurs were proposed in terms of their general human capital, entrepreneurship-specific human capital and venture-specific human capital. In Chapter 4 the results relating to the testing of these hypotheses were presented.

With respect to their general human capital characteristics, the results of this study suggest that habitual entrepreneurs are significantly more likely to be men and are less likely to report a high level of perceived technical capability (H_{4a}). Many novice entrepreneurs may have decided to embark on owning a business to exploit and commercialize their technical knowledge. While such technical knowledge may be useful for identifying a business opportunity the first time

Table 7.1   Summary of results

Hypothesis number and description	Multivariate results
H_{1a} Education$_{habitual}$ > Education$_{novice}$	Not supported
H_{1b} Education$_{portfolio}$ > Education$_{serial}$	Not supported
H_{2a} Managerial HK$_{habitual}$ > Managerial HK$_{novice}$	Not supported
H_{2b} Managerial HK$_{portfolio}$ > Managerial HK$_{serial}$	Not supported
H_{3a} Managerial capability$_{habitual}$ > Managerial capability$_{novice}$	Not supported
H_{3b} Managerial capability$_{portfolio}$ > Managerial capability$_{serial}$	Supported
H_{4a} Technical capability$_{habitual}$ < Technical capability$_{novice}$	Supported
H_{4b} Technical capability$_{portfolio}$ < Technical capability$_{serial}$	Not supported
H_{5a} Ent. capability$_{habitual}$ > Ent. capability$_{novice}$	Not supported
H_{5b} Ent. capability$_{portfolio}$ > Ent. capability$_{serial}$	Not supported
H_{6a} Business owner parent$_{habitual}$ > Business owner parent$_{novice}$	Supported
H_{6b} Business owner parent$_{portfolio}$ > Business owner parent$_{serial}$	Not supported
H_{7a} Alertness approach$_{habitual}$ > Alertness approach$_{novice}$	Could not be tested
H_{7b} Alertness approach$_{portfolio}$ > Alertness approach$_{serial}$	Could not be tested
H_{7c} Developmental approach$_{habitual}$ > Developmental approach$_{novice}$	Not supported
H_{7d} Developmental approach$_{portfolio}$ < Developmental approach$_{serial}$	Not supported
H_{8a} Business similarity$_{habitual}$ > Business similarity$_{novice}$	Not supported
H_{8b} Business similarity$_{portfolio}$ > Business similarity$_{serial}$	Not supported
H_{8c} Task similarity$_{habitual}$ > Task similarity$_{novice}$	Not supported
H_{8d} Task similarity$_{portfolio}$ > Task similarity$_{serial}$	Supported
H_{9a} Intrinsic motivation$_{habitual}$ > Intrinsic motivation$_{novice}$	Supported
H_{9b} Intrinsic motivation$_{portfolio}$ < Intrinsic motivation$_{serial}$	Supported
H_{10a} Info. search$_{habitual}$ < Info. search$_{novice}$	Not supported
H_{10b} Info. search$_{portfolio}$ < Info. search$_{serial}$	Not supported
H_{11a} Opp. identification$_{habitual}$ > Opp. identification$_{novice}$	Supported
H_{11b} Opp. identification$_{portfolio}$ > Opp. identification$_{serial}$	Supported
H_{12a} Opp. pursuit$_{habitual}$ > Opp. pursuit$_{novice}$	Supported
H_{12b} Opp. pursuit$_{portfolio}$ > Opp. pursuit$_{serial}$	Supported
H_{13a} Purchase$_{habitual}$ > Purchase$_{novice}$	Not supported
H_{13b} Purchase$_{portfolio}$ < Purchase$_{serial}$	Not supported
H_{14a} Performance$_{habitual}$ > Performance$_{novice}$	Not supported
H_{14b} Performance$_{portfolio}$ > Performance$_{serial}$	Not supported
H_{14c} Performance$_{habitual - successful}$ > Performance$_{novice}$	Not supported
H_{14d} Performance$_{habitual - failed}$ > Performance$_{novice}$	Not supported

round, it may be limited as a source of future opportunities. Habitual entrepreneurs who have been through the experience of identifying and exploiting an opportunity before may be in a better position to realize that technical knowledge may not need to be embodied in the lead entrepreneur; that technical knowledge is not the only source of opportunities and that a broader set of capabilities are required.

Among the habitual entrepreneurs, portfolio entrepreneurs were significantly more likely to be men and report high levels of perceived managerial capability (H_{3b}). The latter finding lends support to the view that portfolio entrepreneurs, who by definition own at least two businesses simultaneously, may appreciate the importance of managerial skills to facilitate multiple business ownership. The managerial capability variable was operationalized in terms of: organizing resources, tasks and people; being able to delegate effectively; and supervising, leading and motivating people. It is not surprising, therefore, that portfolio entrepreneurs were more likely to display these skills. Further supporting this view was the finding relating to one aspect of human capital specific to the venture (other aspects of this dimension of human capital will be discussed below). Portfolio entrepreneurs were significantly more likely than serial entrepreneurs to report task similarity between the surveyed business and their previous main job or business. To facilitate the simultaneous ownership of businesses, portfolio entrepreneurs appear to be more likely to make sure that there is a high level of similarity between their businesses in terms of the knowledge, skills and abilities needed; managerial duties; technical–functional duties; and tasks performed.

With respect to entrepreneurship-specific human capital, there were no significant differences between novice and habitual entrepreneurs, or between serial and portfolio entrepreneurs. One exception was the finding that habitual entrepreneurs could be distinguished from their novice counterparts in many cases by their parental background. Habitual entrepreneurs were significantly more likely to have (or have had) at least one parent who owned a business or businesses. Observing parents during childhood and indirectly experiencing business ownership (vicarious experience) may have the effect of forming a view of business ownership as a way of life, hence inducing continued or multiple business ownership.

Entrepreneurs can also be distinguished in terms of their venture-specific human capital. Evidence suggests that habitual entrepreneurs reported different motivations for business ownership than novice entrepreneurs. With respect to the surveyed businesses, habitual entrepreneurs were significantly more likely to have been motivated by intrinsic reasons than their novice counterparts (H_{9a}). Intrinsic motives relate to interest in and enjoyment derived from the task. One would expect that habitual entrepreneurs must enjoy the experience of owning a business to justify their subsequent or continued ownership. In particular the habitual entrepreneurs in this study were more likely to be motivated by the desire for personal development. Among the habitual entrepreneurs it was hypothesized that serial entrepreneurs would be more likely to be motivated by intrinsic reasons than portfolio entrepreneurs. Empirical evidence provides some support for this hypothesis (H_{9b}). Serial entrepreneurs were significantly more likely to be motivated by independence, which has been identified as an intrinsic motive. This finding lends support to the view discussed in Chapter 2 that serial entrepreneurs are distinct from portfolio entrepreneurs based on their career anchor. However serial entrepreneurs were significantly more likely to be motivated by 'approval' than portfolio entrepreneurs. The approval motive relates largely to the desire to gain recognition and approval from others, and therefore represents an extrinsic motive. This finding questions the suitability of such a broad categorization of motives for entrepreneurship (that is, intrinsic versus extrinsic motives).

The findings suggest that novice and habitual entrepreneurs are distinct from one another because of the level of their business ownership experience as well as other aspects of their human capital. The same applies to serial and portfolio entrepreneurs, who are distinct with regard to the nature of their business ownership experience and other dimensions of their human capital. Collectively these findings strengthen the case for at least controlling for the effects of entrepreneur heterogeneity in future studies by distinguishing between novice and habitual (serial and portfolio) entrepreneurs.

Behavioural differences between novice and habitual (serial and portfolio) entrepreneurs

Hypotheses relating to presumed behavioural differences between the novice and habitual and then serial and portfolio entrepreneurs, were tested in Chapter 5 ($H_{10a, b}$ through to $H_{13a, b}$). Contrary to expectation no significant relationship between business ownership experience and the number of information sources used, or information search intensity (H_{10a}), was detected. However, entrepreneurs with business ownership experience identified more opportunities (H_{11a}). These results did not appear to be sensitive to the use of different measures of business ownership experience (that is, a dummy or a continuous measure of experience). Taken together these findings suggest that habitual entrepreneurs are more efficient in their use of information when identifying business opportunities. With a given amount of information habitual entrepreneurs appear to be more likely to identify an opportunity. This may partly be influenced by the type of information used; though habitual entrepreneurs may not necessarily search for more information, the information sources they use may be different. Indeed, the bivariate results in Chapter 5 show that there were significant differences between novice and habitual entrepreneurs in terms of information sources used and the usefulness of various information sources. In particular habitual entrepreneurs were significantly more likely to have used employees, consultants, financiers and national government sources than their novice counterparts. Further, habitual entrepreneurs found customers and financiers to be significantly less useful in identifying and evaluating opportunities than did novice entrepreneurs.

Although portfolio entrepreneurs did not search for significantly more or less information (H_{10b}), they identified more opportunities over a five-year period than their serial counterparts (H_{11b}). A significantly higher proportion of portfolio rather than serial entrepreneurs had used consultants and technical literature to identify and evaluate business opportunities. Further, portfolio entrepreneurs were significantly more likely than serial entrepreneurs to have found technical literature to be a useful source of information. Consequently, portfolio entrepreneurs appear to be more effective in translating a given amount of information into opportunities, possibly due to the nature of the information they use.

With regard to the pursuit and exploitation of opportunities, habitual entrepreneurs pursued a higher proportion of identified opportunities than novice entrepreneurs. Moreover, portfolio entrepreneurs pursued a higher proportion of opportunities than serial entrepreneurs. Consequently, hypotheses H_{12a} and H_{12b} were supported. However no differences between novice and habitual or serial and portfolio entrepreneurs were detected in terms of the mode of opportunity exploitation with regard to the surveyed businesses.

The findings suggest some behavioural differences between different types of entrepreneurs due to their business ownership experience. Experienced (habitual) entrepreneurs, particularly portfolio entrepreneurs, appear to display greater opportunity identification and pursuit intensity than their novice or serial counterparts.

Performance-based differences between novice and habitual (serial and portfolio) entrepreneurs

The last two hypotheses in Chapter 2 suggested that habitual entrepreneurs would outperform novice entrepreneurs, and that portfolio entrepreneurs would outperform serial entrepreneurs in terms of firm and entrepreneur performance (H_{14a} and H_{14b}). The results relating to this theme presented in Chapter 6 offered no unequivocal support for these hypotheses. Contrary to expectation, the relationship between business ownership experience and performance was negative in some instances. To examine the extent to which the results were influenced by definitional sensitivities a variety of both business ownership experience and performance measures were used.

The multivariate analysis showed that business ownership experience was negatively related to a selection of performance indicators such as weighted performance (I); profit relative to competitors; current standard of living; and money taken out per business owned. The basic premise of the initial hypothesis was that as a result of their experience, habitual entrepreneurs would have had more opportunities to learn and subsequently modify their behaviour favourably to reflect this. However, as discussed in Chapter 2, there are some concerns surrounding the extent to which business ownership experience offers opportunities for learning. Individuals who have been previously successful may suffer from hubris, while those who failed may be in denial: evidence from this study supports this view. Interestingly, even those habitual entrepreneurs who had been previously successful did not outperform novice entrepreneurs. In fact, those habitual entrepreneurs who had been previously successful reported significantly lower profitability relative to competitors. Further, habitual entrepreneurs who had previously 'failed' (in other words had closed or sold businesses because the performance was too low in relation to the entrepreneur's initial expectations or due to a bankruptcy, liquidation or receivership rather than due to an opportunity to realize a capital gain) reported significantly lower standards of living than novice entrepreneurs. With respect to all performance measures, the former group did not outperform their novice counterparts. We can infer that it may be difficult to learn from business ownership failures. The broader implications of these findings, particularly for policymakers, will be discussed below.

Among the habitual entrepreneurs, portfolio entrepreneurs reported that they had taken significantly more money out of the business(es) they owned relative to their serial counterparts. However, per business portfolio entrepreneurs took less money out than serial entrepreneurs. It may be the case that portfolio entrepreneurs own a collection of relatively smaller businesses or take out less money per business because they have (more) equity partners. There were no significant differences between portfolio and serial entrepreneurs in terms of other aspects of performance explored.

Findings relating to the human capital of the entrepreneur

Several human capital characteristics were found to be significantly related to the various themes explored above and are highlighted here. Findings relating to human capital in this study confirm the need to distinguish between various types of human capital. Most notably, general and specific human capital may have different associations with entrepreneurial behaviour (that is, information search and opportunity identification, pursuit and exploitation) and performance.

The number of information sources used and the information search intensity were found to be consistently related to one particular aspect of general human capital, namely managerial capability. Entrepreneurs with higher perceived levels of managerial capability were likely to search for information more intensively, and to use a greater number of information sources. This relationship held for both the full sample and for the sample of habitual entrepreneurs alone. As intimated in Chapter 2 managers have been found to adopt a more systematic mode of information processing relative to entrepreneurs, who are more likely to adopt a heuristic information processing style. This evidence suggests that entrepreneurs who perceive themselves as having a strong managerial capability may be more likely to utilize systematic information processing and therefore rely on more extensive information search strategies. This is consistent with the findings in this study. Interestingly, entrepreneurs who reported higher levels of perceived entrepreneurial capability also sought more information; this is reflected upon below. Overall, it may also be the case that those entrepreneurs with higher levels of managerial and entrepreneurial capability feel that they are in a better position to benefit from information search. Their superior capabilities provide them with the knowledge and/or confidence to not only identify opportunities but also to exploit them. Consequently those entrepreneurs with higher levels of capabilities may appreciate the value of information (because they know how to utilize it) to a greater extent than those with lower levels of the same capabilities.

Among the variables relating to general human capital, the level of technical capability reported by the entrepreneur was also related to information search. In contrast to managerial and entrepreneurial capabilities, entrepreneurs reporting a higher technical capability searched for information less intensively. This may be because entrepreneurs who excel in a particular technical domain remain focused within that domain and, therefore, feel less need to search intensively or are unaware of the need to assess market exigencies.

Two variables relating to entrepreneurship-specific human capital were significantly associated with information search. These were entrepreneurial capability and a positive attitude towards a developmental approach to opportunity identification. Entrepreneurs reporting a high level of entrepreneurial capability were found to search for information more intensively and use a greater number of information sources. This is an interesting finding given our measure of entrepreneurial capability, which included statements relating to an entrepreneur's perceived level of alertness to opportunities.[1] The alertness literature suggests that opportunities are not identified through information search. However, in this study, the entrepreneurs who considered themselves to be alert (those who had high perceived entrepreneurial capability) were more likely to have searched for information intensively. This finding suggests areas for future research and will be discussed below. Entrepreneurs reporting a positive attitude towards a developmental approach to opportunity identification were also found to search for information more intensively. This is not particularly surprising because for entrepreneurs favouring a developmental approach, opportunities are likely to emerge or develop as information becomes available. Information search, in turn, can facilitate the development of opportunities.

Several dimensions of general human capital were found to be significantly associated with opportunity identification intensity (the number of opportunities identified). In particular, younger and male entrepreneurs, and those reporting high levels of managerial capability were associated with greater opportunity identification intensity. Further, for the full sample, but not for the habitual entrepreneur only sample, entrepreneurs with high levels of education and managerial human capital identified more opportunities. These findings suggest that entrepreneurs with higher levels of general human capital appear to be in a better position to identify opportunities. Among the entrepreneurship-specific human capital variables, not surprisingly, entrepreneurs reporting high levels of perceived entrepreneurial capability identified more opportunities. Because the measure of entrepreneurial capability used in this study was based on the entrepreneur's perception of their own capability, the above finding highlights the importance of self-efficacy and self-confidence.

Given the debate relating to whether opportunities can be identified or discovered through search (economic versus Kirznerian approaches), the finding that higher search intensity led to the identification of more opportunities is an important one. Interestingly, the higher the information search intensity, the smaller the proportion of opportunities pursued. This is a potentially important finding for policymakers, given the high proportion of businesses that fail. If greater levels of information allow entrepreneurs to rethink the feasibility of their ideas, it may be a cost-effective way of avoiding business failures if the type of information required can be identified. This issue will be discussed further in the 'Implications for Policymakers and Practitioners' section.

The mode of opportunity exploitation for the surveyed business opportunity was found to be related to a number of general and specific human capital characteristics. In particular, higher levels of managerial human capital, technical capability and entrepreneurial capability were associated with a lower likelihood of purchasing a business. One interpretation of this finding is that entrepreneurs with greater levels of human capital may feel that they have the necessary skills to start a business from scratch. Conversely, entrepreneurs with limited human capital may want to benefit from the existing infrastructure in place in an existing independent business. Advisors to entrepreneurs and financiers may benefit from ensuring an appropriate fit between the human capital of the entrepreneur and the mode of opportunity exploitation selected.

Firm and entrepreneur performance was explored using eight measures. Findings that were broadly consistent across most measures of performance will be discussed here. Consistent with traditional human capital theory, higher levels of education, managerial and entrepreneurial capability were associated with superior performance. Age, however, was associated with lower performance. Furthermore, this relationship appeared to be linear. Building on Gimeno et al., (1997), the age of each respondent was measured in terms of the deviation from the mean age in the sample. Consequently, entrepreneurs below the age of 49 (the mean age of the entrepreneurs in the sample) were likely to underperform in relation to their older counterparts. Entrepreneurs reporting higher levels of technical capability were also found to report lower levels of performance. Once again, this may be because such individuals can be too focused on their technical area of expertise, with insufficient awareness of the need for a broader skill set to achieve superior performance. Indeed, the literature suggests that entrepreneurs need managerial, entrepreneurial and technical capabilities to be successful (for example, Penrose, 1959).

Finally, with respect to venture-specific human capital, the motives for business ownership were found to be related to firm performance. In particular, stronger welfare and personal-development-based motives were associated with superior growth (employment growth in particular). A stronger emphasis on financial motives for business ownership was associated with superior weighted performance and higher levels of money taken out of the business(es) owned.

Overall, the evidence from the study suggests a need to distinguish between different dimensions of human capital, as these various dimensions do not appear to consistently relate to different aspects of the entrepreneurial process and performance in the same way. Further, as Becker (1993) pointed out, human capital can include attributes that have a positive or negative influence on outcomes.

IMPLICATIONS FOR POLICYMAKERS AND PRACTITIONERS

Government intervention to support entrepreneurs and/or their businesses is widespread, particularly in developed countries (Bridge et al., 1998; Deakins, 1999; Storey, 2003). Despite the prevalence of policy initiatives of various forms, there is a continuing debate as to whether government intervention is actually justifiable (Storey, 1982; 1994; Bridge et al., 1998; Holtz-Eakin, 2000). One justification for support is that entrepreneurs and their businesses offer wider economic, social and other benefits and therefore government intervention is warranted to maximize these benefits (Bridge et al., 1998). This rationale has underpinned many policy initiatives which have aimed to increase the pool of entrepreneurs and/or businesses. In practice, however, it is difficult to ensure that such initiatives target those cases (businesses or entrepreneurs) that produce positive benefits for society and that public funds are not used to support 'projects' that would have been undertaken in the absence of support (Storey, 2003).

A key issue in policy development and implementation relates to the identification of the objectives of a particular policy initiative (Storey, 2000). In the absence of clearly specified objectives, the appropriate policy initiative and its subsequent evaluation cannot be established. If the objective of policymakers is to maximize the returns to their investment (Bridge et al., 1998), they may potentially benefit from targeting their financial resources to 'winning businesses' (Storey, 1994) or 'winning entrepreneurs'. One of the purposes of this study was to explore whether a type of 'winning' entrepreneur or entrepreneur with superior performance could be identified. Based on human capital theory, it was expected that experienced (habitual) entrepreneurs would outperform inexperienced novice entrepreneurs and would therefore qualify as 'winning entrepreneurs'. However, if habitual entrepreneurs' businesses generally under-perform, there is a policy choice either to divert scarce resources away from these entrepreneurs or to develop policies that ensure the survival and develop-ment of the businesses owned by them.

The bivariate analysis in this study suggested that habitual entrepreneurs re-ported higher levels of sales growth. However, when a variety of human capital, firm and environment-based factors were controlled for in the multivariate analysis, this finding was not supported. Similarly, while the bivariate analysis suggested that portfolio entrepreneurs outperformed their serial counterparts, this was not supported by the multivariate analysis. Further, pair-wise analysis revealed that neither portfolio nor serial entrepreneurs outperformed novice entrepreneurs in terms of entrepreneur and firm performance.

As intimated earlier, neither those habitual entrepreneurs who had been previ-ously successful, nor those who had previously failed were able to outperform novice entrepreneurs. This finding has implications for the debate surrounding the issue of failure amongst entrepreneurs. It has been argued that as an alterna-tive to many European models, the UK should look to the US model where government intervention is minimal and business failure is an acceptable part of life (Storey, 2004). Some have gone as far as to claim that 'failure is the fuel of success' (Ministry of Economic Affairs, 2001). This claim is consistent with Sitkin's (1992) view that failure may offer an ideal opportunity to reflect on our existing patterns of behaviour and pinpoint aspects of our thinking and behav-iour that need to be modified. Presumably based on these views, policy initiatives have been undertaken to make it easier for entrepreneurs who have failed to start businesses again, such as the Enterprise Act (2002) that has at-tempted to make bankruptcy laws more lenient. However, the evidence in this study suggests caution: experience (positive or negative) may not be the best teacher. Indeed, the basic premise of attribution theory (Heider, 1958; Zucker-man, 1979) is that individuals have a tendency to attribute successes to themselves and failures to external effects, inhibiting unbiased learning. Further, Shepherd (2003) argues that the loss of a business through failure can cause the feeling of grief. This leads to a negative emotional response interfering with the ability to learn from the events surrounding that loss. Policymakers require further information to establish if failure is as valuable as some groups think. Further, they should carefully consider the wider implications of policy initia-tives, such as relaxing bankruptcy laws. Gropp et al. (1997) found that in states where bankruptcy laws were more generous, entrepreneurs faced greater difficulties in raising funds. To overcome biases associated with learning from experience (especially failure), entrepreneurs may require guidance. Even Sitkin (1992) distinguished between failure and 'intelligent failure'. Various steps need to be taken to ensure that entrepreneurs can learn from failure effectively.

Overall, therefore, the recommendation that financial support should be targeted towards certain groups of entrepreneurs based on the level and nature of their business ownership experience cannot be made on the basis of the findings from this study. However, support for entrepreneurs need not be of a financial nature. A distinction has been made between 'hard' financial support and 'soft' support (such as that in the form of information, training, advice and so on) (Bridge et al., 1998; OECD, 1998). While the findings of this study do not allow us to distinguish between novice and habitual (or serial and portfolio) entrepreneurs in terms of performance, a number of findings do suggest differences in terms of their human capital and behaviour. Hence, though policy recommendations relating to 'hard' support cannot be made, the findings of the study have implications for 'soft' support.

The perceived capabilities reported by entrepreneurs were found to be significantly related to performance. In particular, managerial and entrepreneurial capabilities were positively related to performance, while technical capabilities were negatively related. Though there were no significant differences between novice and habitual entrepreneurs with respect to the former two capabilities, novice entrepreneurs reported significantly higher levels of technical capability. Similarly, serial entrepreneurs reported significantly lower levels of managerial capability relative to portfolio entrepreneurs. Policymakers may need to take steps to make entrepreneurs aware of the need for a range of skills, including managerial and entrepreneurial capability. Novice entrepreneurs in particular may need to be made aware that simply being in possession of technical knowledge and a related idea does not guarantee a successful business. Support programmes that allow skills assessment and development may need to be designed. Existing evidence offers only weak support for the view that generic training improves small firm performance (Storey, 2004). However, it has been argued that targeted assistance in such fields as the assessment of business ideas and other business skills allows for better tailoring of services to needs (OECD, 1998). A number of schemes such as The Consultancy Initiative in the UK were designed to offer support in the areas of marketing, business planning, product and service quality, among others. Support in the form of marketing consultancy has been found to be highly effective for certain types of businesses (Wren and Storey, 2002). Though these initiatives have now been terminated, similar schemes targeting the development of managerial and entrepreneurial skills may be introduced.

Habitual entrepreneurs were found to be distinct from novice entrepreneurs in terms of the extent to which they identified opportunities. In a given period, habitual entrepreneurs identified significantly more opportunities than their novice counterparts. Furthermore, among habitual entrepreneurs, portfolio entrepreneurs were associated with significantly higher opportunity identification intensity than serial entrepreneurs. In the short term novice entrepreneurs are restricted in their ability to acquire business ownership experience, which has been found to facilitate opportunity identification. However the results of the study identify additional factors favourably associated with opportunity identification intensity. Higher levels of education, managerial human capital, managerial capability, entrepreneurial capability and information search intensity were all associated with the identification of a greater number of opportunities. If one of the difficulties faced by novice and serial entrepreneurs is in terms of identifying opportunities, steps can be taken to improve various aspects of their human capital identified above. In particular, improving the access to information by novice and serial entrepreneurs may facilitate greater opportunity identification. Higher levels of information search were associated with a higher number of opportunities identified. The evidence in this study showed that though habitual entrepreneurs (and portfolio entrepreneurs) did not search for more information than novice entrepreneurs, they did identify more opportunities. Business ownership experience and information search may, therefore, be substitutes.

Alongside the quantity of information, the nature of the information acquired may also be important. Habitual entrepreneurs, who were able to identify more opportunities than novice entrepreneurs, were more likely to use employees, consultants, financiers, and national government sources to access information. Portfolio entrepreneurs were more likely to use consultants and technical literature as sources of information. Additional research is warranted to explore whether individual external agencies provide or can provide appropriate information (in terms of depth and quality) to entrepreneurs in need of information to identify opportunities. Furthermore, entrepreneurs may benefit from additional network initiatives that allow the exchange of ideas. Habitual entrepreneurs (especially portfolio entrepreneurs) may be able to work in collaboration with novice entrepreneurs to facilitate business opportunity identification. It should be noted at this stage that although habitual (especially portfolio) entrepreneurs were able to identify more opportunities, there is a need for caution in making the recommendation that the information search and opportunity identification practices of these entrepreneurs should be emulated by other groups. While various policy initiatives may be introduced to improve opportunity identification, this would be meaningless if consideration was not given to the value-creating potential of identified opportunities. This study did not examine the value of opportunities identified. The finding that habitual (and portfolio) entrepreneurs did not outperform novice and serial entrepreneurs in terms of the performance of the surveyed business sheds some doubt on the actual quality of opportunities identified by the former group of entrepreneurs. This is an important area for future research and is discussed below.

Our findings raise questions concerning the extent to which policymakers and practitioners should continue to provide general support towards 'nascent' entrepreneurs (those individuals thinking about becoming entrepreneurs) to increase the number of firm owners in an economy (Westhead et al., 2003a, 2005d). Rather, policymakers may benefit from tailoring their assistance to different types of entrepreneur so that firms can grow once they are established. The assets and liabilities of different entrepreneurs need to be considered (Westhead et al., 2005a, d). For example, while habitual entrepreneurs may have the inclination and ability to identify opportunities, they appear to be lacking the skills to successfully exploit them. Our analysis has identified issues relating to how and to what extent policymakers and practitioners should adopt different approaches to the support of novice, serial and portfolio entrepreneurs. Additional research and debate are required, however, to help develop policy responses to these issues.

FUTURE RESEARCH

While the research presented in this book has drawn attention to the importance of examining different types of entrepreneurs, it is evident that it is not possible to examine all aspects of the habitual entrepreneurship phenomenon in one study. This section discusses an agenda for further research. The dimensions of this research agenda concern: the need for further examination of the nature of opportunities; information search and human capital; the need to go beyond a focus on a single entrepreneur to consider entrepreneurial teams; the need to revisit measures of habitual entrepreneurship; the scope for a broader appreciation of the contexts in which habitual entrepreneurship may occur; and sources of data.

The nature of opportunities

While certain groups of entrepreneurs (habitual entrepreneurs and in particular portfolio entrepreneurs) may identify a greater number of opportunities in a given period, this provides minimal insight as to the nature and value of identified opportunities. This offers avenues for future research. There is considerable debate surrounding how the value of an opportunity can be assessed, and much of this debate stems from contrasting views of what constitutes an entrepreneurial opportunity. Shane and Venkataraman (2000: 220) use Casson's (1982) definition of entrepreneurial opportunities: 'those situations in which new goods, services, raw materials, and organizing methods can be introduced and sold at greater than their cost of production'. Conversely Singh (2001) argues that this definition represents a *post hoc* view, based on criteria stipulating profitability as a requirement for entrepreneurial opportunities. It can be argued that such *post hoc* approaches do not control for confounding factors (such as environment, mode of exploitation, managerial expertise and so on), which can influence the performance of the venture. Instead, ways of assessing the opportunity *ex ante* may need to be used.

Fiet and Migliore (2001) and Fiet et al. (2003) used a panel to rank ideas based on the panel's assessment of whether the opportunity represented a concept that could create and sustain a competitive advantage. Such an approach, while desirable, was not feasible for the current study as the method is extremely time-consuming, costly, and is also based on the panel's subjective opinion. Chandler and Hanks (1994) used a six-item scale to measure the quality of an opportunity. This scale, however, was based largely on the respondents' views of the competitive environment and the venture's ability to sustain a competitive advantage. It did not, however, provide details as to whether the opportunity had the capacity to create a competitive advantage in the first place. Alternative ways of assessing the value of an opportunity may include the amount of initial finance used (Cooper et al., 1995) and the use of partners, as these indicate the willingness of other parties to be involved in the venture, presumably because it is deemed viable. Cooper et al. (1994) argued that ventures with higher levels or proportions of external financing can represent the more promising propositions that passed the screening of lenders and investors. Finally, there is growing recognition that the nature of opportunities identified and pursued by entrepreneurs, particularly in terms of the degree of innovation involved, is worthy of greater consideration (Fiet, 2002; Shepherd and DeTienne, 2005). Ucbasaran et al. (2006) demonstrate significant differences between novice, serial and portfolio entrepreneurs' ability to identify and exploit innovative opportunities. In particular, the level of innovation reported by portfolio entrepreneurs was significantly higher than the other groups.

Information Search

In this study, the entrepreneurs who considered themselves to be alert (those who had high entrepreneurial capability) were more likely to have searched for information intensively. This finding suggests areas for further research; there is a need to explore the relationship between information search and alertness. While Kirzner (1973) argued that systematic search for information would not lead to an opportunity, the entrepreneur still needs to be alert to, or alerted by information to, opportunities. Future research may benefit from a distinction between a systematic search for information and scanning the informational environment with no particular opportunity in mind. Scanning may allow the entrepreneur to piece together disparate information to generate an idea even though there was no idea from the outset. This suggests that the opportunity identification stage itself may involve a number of stages, such as scanning the informational environment, the actual idea stage and then systematic search to refine the idea.

Leveraging human capital

Business ownership experience has been viewed as one aspect of human capital specific to entrepreneurship. Future researchers may benefit from examining the extent to which business ownership experience is a substitute, or complementary to, other dimensions of human capital. For example, experience may amplify the effects of other aspects of human capital, such as managerial human capital and education. The use of interaction variables between business ownership experience and other human capital characteristics may prove useful. By exploring the extent to which business ownership experience acts as a moderator or mediator variable (Cohen et al., 2003), possible substitutes for business ownership experience may be identified. Studies such as that by Chandler and Hanks (1998), where the substitutability of human capital and financial capital were examined, may act as a useful guide.

This study did not consider finance-related issues. In many cases experienced entrepreneurs may have been able to accumulate financial resources or due to their track record are in a better position to acquire funds (Shane and Khurana, 2003; Wright, et al. 1997b). Cressy (1996) argues that human capital factors are correlated with both start-up performance (measured in terms of survival) and financial assets, which can give the false impression that initial finance is a determinant of performance and that start-ups are finance-constrained. Cressy shows, however, that human capital is the 'true' determinant of survival and that the correlation between financial capital and survival is spurious. Further research exploring the relative importance of human capital and financial capital in relation to alternative performance measures is warranted. In addition, the reluctance by some venture capitalists to provide funds to those entrepreneurs that they have funded before (Wright et al., 1997b) is also an area worthy of further examination. Further, the extent to which venture capitalists change their contractual and monitoring arrangements for habitual entrepreneurs, and the implications for opportunity identification and pursuit as well as performance, warrant attention. Does the nature of monitoring become more lax and do the nature of opportunities become more risky?

Entrepreneurial Teams

This study relied on the responses from a single entrepreneur and hence examined the notions of human capital, opportunity recognition and information search from this perspective. In many cases entrepreneurs use partners to establish or purchase their ventures since this can provide both complementary human capital as well as access to greater internal financial resources. In this study, teams were involved in 34 per cent of ventures involving novice entrepreneurs, 36 per cent involving serial entrepreneurs and 41 per cent involving portfolio entrepreneurs. While the study relied on the main entrepreneur as the key informant (as someone who is aware of all aspects of the business), data collected from partners could have been used to verify information relating to the business and to provide different perspectives. This is an area for further research.

We know little about the composition of the teams in ventures involving novice and habitual entrepreneurs. Habitual entrepreneurs may be more adept at constructing teams with complementary skills. What is the nature of this complementarity? For example, is opportunity identification carried out by one individual with other team members involved in its evaluation and exploitation, or is opportunity identification a team effort? To what extent are any differences between novice and habitual entrepreneurs in these respects the result of learning or of 'better' initial behaviour?

A further issue concerns the extent to which habitual entrepreneurs maintain the same team of partners in successive ventures. To what extent do habitual entrepreneurs change their partners? Why do these changes occur? Do they occur because of conflicts in the team or because individuals' objectives begin to diverge? A related issue concerns the implications of team member entry and exit as ventures develop (Ucbasaran et al., 2003a; Vanaelst et al., 2006; Vohora et al., 2004). This phenomenon poses problems in cross-sectional studies analysing the roles of teams in ventures owned by different types of entrepreneurs. Further research could usefully examine the process of developing teams by novice and habitual entrepreneurs.

Measures of Habitual Entrepreneurship

There is further scope for the consideration of different measures of habitual entrepreneurship. Building on the human capital framework developed in this study, Ucbasaran et al. (2003c) focus on the cognitive dimensions of human capital. Just like the aspects of human capital described in the current study, cognition is also likely to be associated with behaviour and performance. Though studies have suggested that entrepreneurs possess different cognitive characteristics from other groups, especially managers (for example, Busenitz and Barney, 1997), there has been limited investigation into the extent to which cognitive heterogeneity exists among entrepreneurs. Adopting this central tenet Ucbasaran (2004b) develops a typology of entrepreneurs. A distinction between 'experienced' and 'expert' habitual entrepreneurs and between 'pure' and 'transient' novice entrepreneurs is proposed. While some novice entrepreneurs have no intention of becoming a habitual entrepreneur, others do. Only 22 per cent of novice entrepreneurs in the sample used for this study reported that they intended to establish or purchase a business in the future. Accordingly, while 'pure' novice entrepreneurs represent the group of novice entrepreneurs that will remain one-time entrepreneurs, 'transient' novice entrepreneurs will at least attempt to become habitual entrepreneurs. These two types of novice entrepreneur may display different cognitive characteristics. Further, a distinction is made between 'experienced' and 'expert' entrepreneurs. While both groups have the benefit of experience, expert entrepreneurs are more effective due to their cognitive characteristics, which allow them to learn effectively from their experiences. In contrast 'experienced' habitual entrepreneurs may be subject to cognitive biases and limitations. Longitudinal studies can allow us to determine the extent to which the cognitive characteristics of an entrepreneur can predict future behaviour and performance.

A simplistic though not yet utilized definition of an expert habitual entrepreneur could be one who has owned three or more successful businesses. One of the potential problems with defining a habitual entrepreneur in terms of two business ownership experiences is that it does not control for luck and external factors. An entrepreneur may have been successful due to factors outside his or her doing the first time, creating an initial stock of wealth for another business. This second business may therefore be 'protected' by a buffer of financial resources. Therefore, to be considered a successful habitual entrepreneur or an 'expert' entrepreneur, one may benefit from using a rule of three successful businesses. However, even this is somewhat arbitrary and there may be a need to experiment with alternative definitions of expert entrepreneurs. More importantly, however, examining the cognitive characteristics of 'expert' habitual entrepreneurs in comparison to other groups may be a promising area of future research with important implications for policymakers and practitioners.

Contexts for Habitual Entrepreneurship

This study adopted a categorization of different types of entrepreneur based on the establishment of the ownership of a venture. A number of alternative contexts are available. Considering this additional heterogeneity, the categorization of types of entrepreneurs presented in Chapter 1 can be developed to offer an extended categorization of entrepreneurs (Table 7.2). One option could be to use the notion of self-employment. Indeed, some databases of self-employment contain measures to identify multiple periods of self-employment activity (Flores-Romero, 2006; Flores-Romero and Blackburn, 2006). However, there is some concern about the extent to which self-employment captures entrepreneurial opportunity identification and exploitation. Though there is likely to be

Table 7.2   An extended categorization of the nature of entrepreneurship by type of entrepreneur

Nature of entrepreneurship		Single activity	Multiple activity	
		Novice entrepreneurs	Habitual entrepreneurs	
			Sequential Serial entrepreneurs	*Simultaneous* Portfolio entrepreneurs
Involving no new legal entity	**Self-employment**	Novice self-employed	Serial self-employed	Portfolio self-employed
Involving new business(es)	*De novo* **business**	Novice founders	Serial founders	Portfolio founders
	Spinout (including corporate and university spinouts)	Novice spinout entrepreneurs	Serial spinout entrepreneurs	Portfolio spinout entrepreneurs
Involving existing business(es)	**Purchase (including buy-outs/buy-ins)**	Novice acquirers	Serial acquirers (e.g. secondary MBOs/MBIs)	Portfolio acquirers (e.g. leveraged build-ups)
	Corporate entrepreneurship	Novice corporate entrepreneurs	Serial corporate entrepreneurs	Portfolio corporate entrepreneurs

heterogeneity amongst business owners in terms of how 'entrepreneurial' they are, there is a well-established tradition of viewing ownership and entrepreneurship as complementary (Fama and Jensen, 1983; Hawley, 1907).

In this study, we considered whether ownership came about through start-up or acquisition. Further comparative exploration is required of the process of opportunity identification and pursuit where habitual entrepreneurship takes place through start-up or acquisition. Using case studies, Ucbasaran et al. (2003b) found notable differences between habitual-acquirer and habitual-starter entrepreneurs with respect to their motivations and strategies towards opportunity identification and exploitation.

The analysis may also be extended to other potentially important contexts. For example, there has been growing attention to the generation of spin-out companies from universities based on academic inventions (Shane, 2003; Vohora et al., 2004). An area of research and policy concern has been the extent to which these ventures are able to generate wealth and how this can be achieved (Lambert, 2003; Lockett and Wright, 2005). A key distinguishing aspect relates to the notion that academics starting businesses may have fewer capabilities to generate growth than those entrepreneurs emerging from a commercial environment. A further aspect concerns the quality of the support provided to these entrepreneurs and the potential need to bring in surrogate entrepreneurs from outside the university in order to access the missing human capital required for commercial success (Franklin, et al., 2001). While there has been limited work on opportunity identification in academic entrepreneurship (Vohora et al., 2004), this has not considered whether academic entrepreneurs who create more than one spin-out company experience beneficial learning effects. As the phenomenon of academic entrepreneurship develops, there is a need for further research that examines these issues. For example, do habitual academic entrepreneurs coming from a non-commercial environment learn differently from habitual entrepreneurs coming from a commercial environment (after controlling for other factors)?

This study has also focused on issues relating to the habitual ownership of more than one business, either simultaneously or over time. A further context where examination of the role of human capital in the opportunity identification and pursuit process is warranted concerns the case of secondary management buy-outs and buy-ins of the same company. Secondary management buy-outs and buy-ins involve the refinancing and repurchase of an initial buy-out or buy-in. In a secondary management buy-out, typically some or all of the management team remain, increasing their equity stake significantly as the original financiers are replaced by a new set (Wright et al., 2000). In a secondary management buy-in, a new external team may be involved in the purchase of the initial buy-out or buy-in. These transactions have become an increasingly important part of the private equity and buy-out market internationally (CMBOR, 2005) and pose important research and policy questions. A central question concerns the identification of the opportunity for creating further returns in the second deal, especially where the management and the initial set of financiers have taken actions to generate gains in the first buy-out or buy-in. For example, in the case of Maccess, the first buy-out enabled management to establish the business as an independent entity after it had previously been part of a larger group but the venture capital financiers imposed tight restrictions on their ability to take entrepreneurial decisions. The second buy-out of Maccess enabled the same management team to obtain a larger equity stake and more discretion to pursue growth opportunities through acquisition (Robbie and Wright, 1990). However, these actions created trading problems for the firm, which had to be rescued and restructured with the senior management being replaced. These types of habitual entrepreneurs raise further research questions. For example, are the opportunities in the second deal related mainly to the use of debt to fund the transaction, so that when this is reimbursed through cash flows the new owners can achieve significant gains, or are they related to the identification of new areas for organic growth that could not have been realized previously?

A related type of management buy-out or buy-in concerns the leveraged build-up (LBU). In these cases, entrepreneurs create a group of companies through a series of acquisitions based on an initial management buy-out or buy-in, with the private equity financiers typically providing additional finance to enable these purchases. This kind of portfolio entrepreneurship activity raises interesting questions concerning the human capital and opportunity identification behaviour of the entrepreneurs concerned. To what extent do these portfolios represent financial transactions where the opportunity involves consolidating fragmented sectors to create a larger group that can be sold subsequently? To what extent do the entrepreneurs involved possess expertise in identifying, acquiring and integrating acquisitions versus expertise in growing businesses organically? To what extent are the gains obtained due to creating economies of scale and scope or to arbitraging the difference between the typically lower purchase price earnings multiple paid for a smaller firm and the larger exit price earnings multiple that can be obtained from selling a larger group?

Data Sources

The study relied largely on data obtained through questionnaires. The subjective nature of this information can be particularly problematic when it comes to the performance of the business. While it can be insightful to examine performance from the perspective of the entrepreneur, it makes it difficult to compare businesses with each other. For example, each owner may view two businesses reporting similar levels of profitability very differently. In their study of business exits, Gimeno et al. (1997) demonstrated that entrepreneurs had different thresholds of performance depending to some extent on their human capital. In particular, entrepreneurs with superior levels of human capital were more likely to exit from a business at a given level of performance, as they tended to have higher expectations. This issue may be particularly important when trying to compare the performance of novice entrepreneurs with habitual entrepreneurs. Given differing views on what levels of business performance are acceptable, subjective measures of performance can be problematic, especially those relating to satisfaction. Ideally, objective data relating to the performance of the surveyed businesses would be collected and compared with the subjective indicators of performance reported by the entrepreneurs. Unfortunately, these kinds of data are not widely available publicly and many business owners are reluctant to disclose financial performance data (such as the level of profit).

This study relied largely on data from a cross-sectional survey. While surveys offer a number of advantages, they can be limited in terms of their ability to capture details relating to the 'why' and 'how' aspects of a phenomenon. Future studies may benefit from the use of in-depth case studies (Ucbasaran et al., 2003b). In particular, while this study examined the nature of business ownership experiences of habitual entrepreneurs to some extent, much more is needed. Case studies can be used to examine each business owned by an entrepreneur and to identify the motivations, opportunity identification process and performance relating to each business. Case studies may provide insights into the extent to which learning takes place between ventures owned by habitual entrepreneurs. Further, longitudinal case studies may help to overcome problems of endogeneity associated with cross-sectional studies.

Longitudinal studies (using case studies or longitudinal datasets) offer the advantage of being able to establish causal relationships between human capital, entrepreneurial behaviour and performance. Longitudinal studies monitoring the 'stock' of skills and experience of each type of entrepreneur, and the 'flows' across the entrepreneur categories, would provide rich process and contextual evidence. For example, they could explore the characteristics and skills associated with novice entrepreneurs who are able to transform into serial or portfolio entrepreneurs. Also, studies might focus on the initiation processes leading to the ownership of subsequent ventures by experienced entrepreneurs, and why they accept or reject particular types of deals. Similarly, there is a need to understand how serial and portfolio entrepreneurs learn from their previous business ownership experiences. For the purposes of understanding wealth creation, there is a need to analyse the 'quality', rather than just the 'quantity' of prior business ownership experience. In addition, there is a need for research that analyses the total economic contribution of novice, serial and portfolio entrepreneurs to local and national economies.

CONCLUSION

This study has explored the relationship between business ownership experience, human capital, entrepreneurial behaviour and performance. In so doing, differences between novice and habitual entrepreneurs on these dimensions have been established. Further, among habitual entrepreneurs, it has been shown that serial and portfolio entrepreneurs differ in their human capital profile and behaviour. Consequently, the study has sought to enhance our understanding of the heterogeneity of entrepreneurs by utilizing a human capital framework. Beyond this contribution, the study has also identified a number of human capital characteristics of entrepreneurs that are associated with firm and entrepreneur performance. It is evident that there remains considerable further scope to develop understanding of the heterogeneity of entrepreneurial experience.

On the basis of these empirical findings, a number of policy implications and recommendations have been presented. While the evidence in this study did not allow us to prescribe financial support towards a particular group of entrepreneurs, it did lead to suggestions for 'soft' support. In particular, recent moves towards supporting entrepreneurs who have failed were questioned. Based on relationships between various dimensions of human capital and performance, recommendations for making available tailored training for entrepreneurs were presented. Further, given the positive relationship between information search and opportunity identification, improving access to various sources of information was suggested. Finally, while the study has made some progress, the suggestions for future research identified in this chapter indicate that there remains considerable scope for further understanding the contribution of habitual entrepreneurs to entrepreneurial behaviour and performance.

NOTE

1. The reader is reminded of the distinction between the entrepreneurial capability measure and the alertness measures. The latter measures related to an attitude towards opportunity identification but was dropped due to low reliability. The former, however, related to the entrepreneur's self-perceived ability to identify and exploit opportunities. The two measures are, therefore, distinct.

References

Aiken, L.S. and S.G. West (1991), *Multiple Regression: Testing and Interpreting Interactions*, Newbury Park, CA: Sage.

Aldrich, H. (1999), *Organizations Evolving*, London: Sage.

Aldrich, H. and E.R. Auster (1986), 'Even dwarfs started small: liabilities of age and size and their strategic implications', in B. Staw and L.L. Cummings (eds), *Research in Organization Behavior*, vol. 8, Greenwich, Conn: JAI Press, pp. 165–98.

Alvarez, S. and L. Busenitz (2001), 'The entrepreneurship of resource-based theory', *Journal of Management*, **27**, 755–76.

Amabile, T.M., K.G. Hill, B.A. Hennesey and E.M. Tighe (1994), 'The work preference inventory: assessing intrinsic and extrinsic motivational orientations', *Journal of Personality and Social Psychology*, **66**, 950–67.

Amit, R., L. Glosten and E. Muller (1993), 'Challenges to theory development in entrepreneurship research', *Journal of Management Studies*, **30**, 815–34.

Amit, R., E. Mueller and L. Cockburn (1995), 'Opportunity costs and entrepreneurial activity', *Journal of Business Venturing*, **10**, 95–106.

Ardichvili, A., R. Cardozo and S. Ray (2003), 'A theory of entrepreneurial opportunity identification and development', *Journal of Business Venturing*, **18**, 105–23.

Bandura, A. (1982), 'The psychology of chance encounters and life paths', *American Psychologist*, **37**, 747–55.

Bandura, A. (1991), 'Social cognitive theory of self-regulation', *Organizational Behavior and Human Decision Processes*, **50**, 248–87.

Bandura, A. (1995), 'Perceived self-efficacy', in A.S.R. Manstead and M. Hewstone (eds), *The Blackwell Encyclopaedia of Social Psychology*, Oxford: Blackwell Publishers Ltd, pp. 434–6.

Baron, R.M. and D.A. Kenny (1986), 'The moderator-mediator distinction in social psychological research: conceptual, strategic, and statistical considerations', *Journal of Personality and Social Psychology*, **51**, 1173–82.

Bates, T. (1990), 'Entrepreneur human capital inputs and small firm longevity', *Review of Economics and Statistics*, **72**, 551–9.

Bates, T. (1995), 'Analysis of survival rates among franchise and independent small business start-ups', *Journal of Small Business Management*, **33**, 26–36.

Bates, T. (1998), 'Survival patterns among newcomers to franchising', *Journal of Business Venturing*, **13**, 113–30.

Baumol, W.J. (1968), 'Entrepreneurship in economic theory', *American Economic Review*, **58**, 64–71.

Bazerman, M.H. (1990), *Judgement in Managerial Decision Making*, 2nd edition, New York: John Wiley and Sons.

Becker, G.S. (1975), *Human Capital*, New York: National Bureau of Economic Research.

Becker, G.S. (1993), 'Nobel lecture: the economic way of looking at behavior', *The Journal of Political Economy*, **101**, 385–409.

Begley, T. and D. Boyd (1987), 'Characteristics associated with performance in entrepreneurial firms and smaller businesses', *Journal of Business Venturing*, **2**, 79–93.

Bird, B.J. (1992), 'The operation of intentions in time: The emergence of the new venture', *Entrepreneurship Theory and Practice*, **17**, 11–21.

Birley, S. and S. Stockley (2000), 'Entrepreneurial teams and venture growth', in D.L. Sexton and H. Landström (eds), *The Blackwell Handbook of Entrepreneurship*, Oxford: Blackwell.

Birley, S. and P. Westhead (1990a), 'Private business sales environments in the United Kingdom', *Journal of Business Venturing*, **5**, 349–73.

Birley, S. and P. Westhead (1990b), 'Growth and performance contrasts between "types" of small firms', *Strategic Management Journal*, **11**, 535–57.

Birley, S. and P. Westhead (1993a), 'The owner-managers exit route', in H. Klandt (ed), *Entrepreneurship and Business Development*, Aldershot: Avebury, pp. 123–40.

Birley, S. and P. Westhead (1993b), 'A comparison of new businesses established by "novice" and "habitual" founders in Great Britain', *International Small Business Journal*, **12**, 8–60.

Birley, S. and P. Westhead (1994), 'A taxonomy of business start-up reasons and their impact on firm growth and size', *Journal of Business Venturing*, **9**, 7–31.

Bridge, S., K. O'Neilland S. Cromie (1998), *Understanding Enterprise, Entrepreneurship and Small Business*. Basingstoke: Macmillan Press Ltd.

Brown, T.E. and B.A. Kirchhoff (1997), 'Resource acquisition self-efficacy: measuring entrepreneurs' growth ambitions', in P.D. Reynolds, W.D. Carter, P. Davidsson, W.B. Gartnerand P. McDougall (eds), *Frontiers in Entrepreneurship Research*, Wellesley, MA: Babson College, pp. 59–60.

Brüderl, J., P. Preisendorfer and R. Zeigler (1992), 'Survival chances of newly founded business organizations', *American Sociological Review*, **57**, 227–42.

Busenitz, L.W. and J.B. Barney (1997), 'Differences between entrepreneurs and managers in large organisations: biases and heuristics in strategic decision-making', *Journal of Business Venturing*, **12**, 9–30.

Busenitz, L.W. and C. Lau (1996), 'A cross-cultural cognitive model of new venture creation', *Entrepreneurship Theory and Practice*, **20**, 25–39.

Bygrave, W.D. (1993), 'Theory building in the entrepreneurship paradigm', *Journal of Business Venturing*, **8**, 255–80.

Campbell, D.T. (1955), 'The informant in quantitative research', *American Journal of Sociology*, **60**, 339–42.

Caplan, B. (1999), 'The Austrian search for realistic foundations', *Southern Economic Journal*, **65**, 823–38.

Carroll, G. and E. Mosakowski (1987), 'The career dynamics of self-employment', *Administrative Science Quarterly*, **32**, 570–89.

Casson, M. (1982), *The Entrepreneur: An Economic Theory*, Oxford: Martin Robertson.

Castanias, R.P. and C.E. Helfat (1991), 'Managerial resources and rents', *Journal of Management*, **17**, 155–71.

Castanias, R.P. and C.E. Helfat (1992), 'Managerial and windfall rents in the market for corporate control', *Journal of Economic Behavior and Organization*, **18**, 153–84.

Castanias, R.P. and C.E. Helfat (2001), 'The managerial rents model: theory and empirical analysis', *Journal of Management*, **27**, 661–78.

Caves, R. (1988), 'Industrial organization and new findings on the turnover and mobility of firms', *Journal of Economic Literature*, **36**, 1947–82.

Chandler, G.N. (1996), 'Business similarity as a moderator of the relationship between pre-ownership experience and venture performance', *Entrepreneurship Theory and Practice*, **20**, 51–65.

Chandler, G. and S.H. Hanks (1993), 'Measuring the performance of emerging businesses: a validation study', *Journal of Business Venturing*, **8**, 391–408.

Chandler, G. and S.H. Hanks (1994), 'Market attractiveness, resource-based capabilities, venture strategies, and venture performance', *Journal of Business Venturing*, **9**, 331–49.

Chandler, G. and S.H. Hanks (1998), 'An examination of the substitutability of founders human and financial capital in emerging business ventures', *Journal of Business Venturing*, **13**, 353–69.

Chandler, G.N. and E. Jansen (1992), 'The founder's self-assessed competence and venture performance', *Journal of Business Venturing*, **7**, 223–36.

CMBOR (2005), *Management Buy-Outs: Quarterly Review*, Autumn. Nottingham: Centre for Management Buy-Out Research.

Cohen, J., P. Cohen, S.G. West and L.S. Aiken (2003), *Applied Multiple Regression / Correlation Analysis for the Behavioral Social Sciences*, 3rd edition, Mahwah, NJ: Lawrence Erlbaum Associates.

Cooper, A.C. (1993), 'Challenges in predicting new firm performance', *Journal of Business Venturing*, **8**, 241–53.

Cooper, A.C. and K.W. Artz (1995), 'Determinants of satisfaction for entrepreneurs', *Journal of Business Venturing*, **10**, 439–57.

Cooper, A.C.and W.C. Dunkelberg (1986), 'Entrepreneurship and paths to business ownership', *Strategic Management Journal*, **7**, 53–68.

Cooper, A.C., T.B. Folta and C. Woo (1995), 'Entrepreneurial information search', *Journal of Business Venturing*, **10**, 107–120.

Cooper, A.C., F.J. Gimeno-Gascon and C. Woo (1994), 'Initial human and financial capital predictors of new venture performance', *Journal of Business Venturing*, **9**, 371–95.

Cooper, A.C., C. Woo and W. Dunkelberg (1988), 'Entrepreneurs' perceived chances of success', *Journal of Business Venturing*, **3**, 97–108.

Cooper, A.C. Woo and W. Dunkelberg (1989), 'Entrepreneurship and the initial size of firms', *Journal of Business Venturing*, **4**, 317–32.

Cressy, R. (1996), 'Are business start-ups debt-rationed?' *The Economic Journal*, **106**, 1253–70.

Cross, M. (1981), *New Firm Formation and Regional Development*, London: Gower.

Cuevas, J.G. (1994), 'Towards a taxonomy of entrepreneurial theories', *International Small Business Journal*, **12**, 77–88.

Curran, J., R. Blackburn and A. Woods (1991), *Profiles of Small Enterprise in the Service Sector*, Kingston: Kingston University, ESRC Research on Small Service Sector Enterprise.

Davidsson, P. and J. Wiklund (2001), 'Level of analysis in entrepreneurship research practice and suggestions for the future', *Entrepreneurship Theory and Practice*, **25**, 81–100.

Day, R.R. (1987), 'The general theory of disequilibrium economics and of economic evolution', in J. Batten, D. Casti and B. Johansson (eds), *Economic Evolution and Structural Adjustment*, Berlin: Springer, pp. 46–63.

Deakins, D. (1999), *Entrepreneurship and Small Firms*, 2nd edition, Berkshire: McGraw-Hill.

Deci, E.L. (1992a), 'On the nature and functions of motivation theories', *Psychological Science*, **3**, 167–71.

Deci, E.L. (1992b), 'The relation of interest to motivation of behavior: a self-determination theory perspective', in K. Renninger, S. Hidi and A. Krapp (eds), *The Role of Interest in Learning and Development*, Hillsdale, NJ: Erlbaum, pp. 43–70.

Delmar, F. (2000), 'The psychology of the entrepreneur', in S. Carter and D. Jones-Evan (eds), *Enterprise and Small Business*, Essex: Financial Times–Prentice Hall, pp. 132–54.

Department of Trade and Industry (2004), *A Government Action Plan for Small*

Business. Making the UK the Best Place in the World to Start and Grow a Business: The Evidence Base, London: DTI, Small Business Service.

Diamantopolous, A. and S. Hart (1993), 'Linking market orientation and company performance: preliminary evidence on Kohli and Jaworski's framework', *Journal of Strategic Marketing*, **1**, 93–121.

Donckels, R., B. Dupont and P. Michel (1987), 'Multiple business starters. Who? Why? What?', *Journal of Small Business and Entrepreneurship*, **5**, 48–63.

Eisenhardt, K.M. and J.A. Martin (2000), 'Dynamic capabilities: what are they?' *Strategic Management Journal*, **21**, 1105–21.

Enterprise Act (2002), London: HMSO. Can be downloaded from www.dti.gov. uk/ccp/enterpriseact/intro.htm.

Evans, D.S. and L. Leighton (1989), 'Some empirical aspects of entrepreneurship', *American Economic Review*, **9**, 519–35.

Fama, E. and M. Jensen (1983), 'Separation of ownership and control', *Journal of Law and Economics*, **26**, 301–25.

Fazio, R., M. Powell and P. Herr (1983), 'Towards a process model of the attitude-behavior relation', *Journal of Personality and Social Psychology*, **44**, 723–35.

Fiet, J.O. (1996), 'The informational basis for entrepreneurial discovery', *Small Business Economics*, **8**, 419–30.

Fiet, J.O. (2002), *The Systematic Search for Entrepreneurial Discoveries*, Westport, Conn: Quorum Books.

Fiet, J.O., M. Gupta and W.I. Norton (2003), 'Evaluating the wealth creating potential of venture ideas', Paper presented at the Babson Kauffman Entrepreneurship Research Conference, Babson College, MA: Wellesley, June.

Fiet, J.O. and P.J. Migliore (2001), 'The testing of a model of entrepreneurial discovery by aspiring entrepreneurs', in W.D. Bygrave, E. Autio, C. Brush, P. Davidsson, P. Green, P. Reynolds and, H.J. Sapienza (eds), *Frontiers of Entrepreneurship Research 2001*, Wellesley, MA: Babson College.

Fiske, S.T. and S.E. Taylor (1991), *Social Cognition*, 2nd edition, Singapore: McGraw-Hill.

Flores-Romero, M.G. (2006), 'An empirical investigation into the job generation capacity of serial entrepreneurs', paper presented at the Exit and Serial Entrepreneurship Workshop, Jena, Max Plank Institute, January.

Flores-Romero, M.G. and R. Blackburn (2006), 'Is entrepreneurship more about stocking with a firm or about running several of them?', paper presented at the Exit and Serial Entrepreneurship Workshop, Jena, Max Plank Institute, January.

Forbes, D. (2005), 'Are some entrepreneurs more overconfident than others?' *Journal of Business Venturing*, **20**, 623–40.

Franklin, S., M. Wright and A. Lockett (2001), 'Academic and surrogate entrepreneurs in university spin-out companies', *Journal of Technology Transfer*, **26**, 127–41.

Gaglio, C.M. (1997), 'Opportunity identification: review, critique and suggested research directions', in J.A. Katz (ed), *Advances in Entrepreneurship, Firm Emergence and Growth*, vol. 3, Greenwich, CA: JAI Press, pp. 119–38.

Gaglio, C.M. and J.A. Katz (2001), 'The psychological basis of opportunity identification: entrepreneurial alertness', *Small Business Economics*, **16**, 95–111.

Gartner, W.B. (1985), 'A conceptual framework for describing the phenomenon of new venture creation', *Academy of Management Review*, **10**, 696–706.

Gartner, W.B. (1988), '"Who is the entrepreneur?" is the wrong question', *American Journal of Small Business*, **12**, 11–32.

Gartner, W.B. (1990), 'What are we talking about when we talk about entrepreneurship', *Journal of Business Venturing*, **5**, 15–28.

Gartner, W.B. (2001), 'Is there an elephant in entrepreneurship? Blind assumptions in theory development', *Entrepreneurship Theory and Practice*, **25**, 27–40.

Gavron, R., M. Cowling, G. Holtham and A. Westall (1998), *The Entrepreneurial Society*, London: Institute of Public Policy Research.

Gerowski, P. (1995), 'What do we know about entry?' *International Journal of Industrial Organization*, **13**, 421–40.

Gilad, B., S. Kaish and J. Ronen (1989), 'Information, search, and entrepreneurship: a pilot study', *The Journal of Behavioural Economics*, **18**, 217–35.

Gimeno, J., T. Folta, A. Cooper and C. Woo (1997), 'Survival of the fittest? Entrepreneurial human capital and the persistence of underperforming firms', *Administrative Science Quarterly*, **42**, 750–83.

Gist, M.E. (1987), 'Self-efficacy: implications for organizational behavior and human resource management', *Academy of Management Review*, **12**, 472–86.

Gray, C. (1993), 'Stages of growth and entrepreneurial career motivation', in F. Chittenden, M. Robertson and I. Marshall (eds), *Small Firms: Recession and Recovery*, London: Paul Chapman Publishing, pp. 149–59.

Greene, P.G., C. Brush and M. Hart (1999), 'The corporate venture champion: a resource-based approach to role and process', *Entrepreneurship Theory and Practice*, **23**, 103–22.

Greene, P.G. and T.E. Brown (1997), 'Resource needs and the dynamic capitalism typology', *Journal of Business Venturing*, **12**, 161–73.

Gropp, R., J.K. Scholtz and M.J. White (1997), 'Personal bankruptcy and credit supply and demand', *Quarterly Journal of Economics*, **112**, 217–51.

Hair, J.F., R.E. Anderson, R.L. Tatham and W.C. Black (1995), *Multivariate Data Analysis*, 4th edition, Englewood Cliffs, NJ: Prentice Hall.

Hall, P. (1995), 'Habitual owners of small businesses', in F. Chittenden, M.

Robertson and I. Marshall (eds), *Small Firms: Partnerships for Growth*. London: Paul Chapman Publishing, pp. 217–30.

Hart, M.M., P.G. Greene and C.G. Brush (1997), 'Leveraging resources: building an organisation on an entrepreneurial resource base', in P.D. Reynolds, W.D. Carter, P. Davidsson, W.B. Gartner and P. McDougall (eds), *Frontiers in Entrepreneurship Research*, Wellesley, MA: Babson College, pp. 347–48.

Harvey, M. and R. Evans (1995), 'Strategic windows in the entrepreneurial process', *Journal of Business Venturing*, **10**, 331–47.

Hausman, J.A. (1978), 'Specification tests in econometrics', *Econometrica*, **46**, 1251–71.

Hausman, J.A. (1983), 'Specification and estimation of simultaneous equation models', in Z. Griliches and M.D. Intriligator (eds), *Handbook of Econometrics*, vol. I, Amsterdam: North Holland, pp. 391–448.

Hawley, F.B. (1907), *Enterprise and the Productive Process*, New York: G.P. Putnam's Sons.

Hayek, F. (1945), 'The use of knowledge in society', *American Economic Review*, **35**, 519–30.

Heider, F. (1958), *The Psychology of Interpersonal Relations*. New York: Wiley.

Herron, L. and H. Sapienza (1992), 'The entrepreneur and the initiation of new venture launch activities', *Entrepreneurship Theory and Practice*, **17**, 49–55.

Hillerbrand, E. (1989), 'Cognitive differences between experts and novices: implications for group supervision', *Journal of Counselling and Development*, **67**, 293–96.

Hills, G.E., G.T. Lumpkin and R.P. Singh (1997), 'Opportunity recognition: perceptions and behaviours of entrepreneurs', in P.D. Reynolds, W.D. Carter, P. Davidsson, W.B. Gartner and P. McDougall (eds), *Frontiers in Entrepreneurship Research*, Wellesley, MA: Babson College, pp. 168–82.

Hitt, M., R.D. Ireland, M. Camp and D.L. Sexton (2001), 'Guest editors' introduction to the special issue on strategic entrepreneurship: entrepreneurial strategies for wealth creation', *Strategic Management Journal*, **22**, 479–91.

Holtz-Eakin, D. (2000), 'Public policy toward entrepreneurship', *Small Business Economics*, **15**, 283–91.

Hoy, F. and D. Hellriegel (1982), 'The Killman and Herden model of organizational effectiveness criteria for small business managers', *Academy of Management Journal*, **25**, 3087–322.

Jacoby, J., M. Morrin, G. Johar, Z. Gurhan, A. Kuss and D. Mazursky (2001), 'Training novice investors to become more expert: the role of information accessing strategy', *The Journal of Psychology and Financial Markets*, **2**, 69–79.

Jovanovic, B. (1982), 'Selection and the evolution of industry', *Econometrica*, **50**, 649–70.

Kahneman, D. and D. Lovallo (1994), 'Timid choices and bold forecasts: a cognitive perspective on risk taking', *Management Science*, **39**, 17–31.

Kaish, S. and B. Gilad (1991), 'Characteristics of opportunities search of entrepreneurs versus executives: sources, interests, general alertness', *Journal of Business Venturing*, **6**, 45–61.

Katz, J.A. (1994), 'Modelling entrepreneurial career progressions: concepts and considerations', *Entrepreneurship Theory and Practice*, **19**, 23–39.

Katz, J.A. and W.B. Gartner (1988), 'Properties of emerging organizations', *Academy of Management Review*, **13**, 429–41.

Keasey, K. and Watson, R. (1991), 'The state of the art of small firm failure prediction: achievements and prognosis', *International Small Business Journal*, **9**, 11–29.

Kirzner, I.M. (1973), *Competition and Entrepreneurship*, Chicago: University of Chicago Press.

Kirzner, I.M. (1997), 'Entrepreneurial discovery and the competitive market process: an Austrian approach', *Journal of Economic Literature*, **35**, 60–85.

Kolvereid, L. and E. Bullvåg (1993), 'Novices versus experienced founders: an exploratory investigation', in S. Birley, I. MacMillan and S. Subramony (eds), *Entrepreneurship Research: Global Perspectives*, Amsterdam: Elsevier Science Publishers, pp. 275–85.

Krueger, N. (1993), 'The impact of prior entrepreneurial exposure on perceptions of new venture feasibility and desirability', *Entrepreneurship Theory and Practice*, **19**, 5–21.

Krueger, N. and D.V. Brazeal (1994), 'Entrepreneurial potential and potential entrepreneurs', *Entrepreneurship Theory and Practice*, **18**, 91–104.

Kumar, N., L.W. Stern and J.W. Anderson (1993), 'Conducting interorganizational research using key informants', *Academy of Management Journal*, **36**, 1663–51.

Lambert, R. (2003), *Lambert Review of Business–University Collaboration*, London: HMSO.

Lockett, A. and M. Wright (2005), 'Resources, capabilities, risk capital and the creation of university spin-out companies', *Research Policy*, **34**, 1043–57.

Long, W. and W.E. McMullan (1984), 'Mapping the new venture opportunity identification process', in J.A. Hornaday, F.A. Tardley, J.A. Timmons and K.H. Vesper (eds), *Frontiers of Entrepreneurship Research*, Wellesley, MA: Babson College, pp. 567–91.

Lord, R.G. and K.J. Maher (1990), 'Alternative information-processing models and their implications for theory, research, and practice', *Academy of Management Review*, **15**, 9–28.

Louis M.R. and R.I. Sutton (1991), 'Switching cognitive gears: from habits of mind to active thinking', *Human Relations*, **44**, 55–76.

Low, M.B. (2001), 'The adolescence of entrepreneurship research: specification of purpose', *Entrepreneurship Theory and Practice*, **25**, 17–26.

Low, M.B. and I.C. MacMillan (1988), 'Entrepreneurship: past research and future challenges', *Journal of Management*, **14**, 139–62.

McGrath, R.G. (1999), 'Falling forward: real options reasoning and entrepreneurial failure', *Academy of Management Review*, **24**, 13–30.

McGrath, R.G. and I.C. MacMillan (2000), *The Entrepreneurial Mindset*, Boston, MA: Harvard Business School Press.

MacMillan I.C. (1986), 'To really learn about entrepreneurship, let's study habitual entrepreneurs', *Journal of Business Venturing*, **1**, 241–43.

MacMillan, I., R. Siegel and P.N. Narasimha (1985), 'Criteria used by venture capitalists to evaluate new venture proposals', *Journal of Business Venturing*, **1**, 119–29.

Marshal, A. (1920), *Principles of Economics*, 8th edition, reset 1949. London: MacMillan.

Mincer, J. (1974), *Schooling, Experience and Earnings*, New York: Columbia University Press (for NBER).

Ministry of Economic Affairs (2001), Seminar on business failure, The Hague, The Netherlands, 10–11 May.

Minniti, M. and W.B. Bygrave (2001), 'A dynamic model of entrepreneurial learning', *Entrepreneurship: Theory and Practice*, **25**, 5–16.

Mintzberg, H. (1988), 'The simple structure' in J.B. Quinn, H. Mintzbergand R.M. James (eds), *The Strategy Process: Concepts, Contexts and Cases*, Englewood Cliffs, NJ: Prentice Hall.

Mintzberg, H. and J.A. Waters (1982), 'Tracking strategy in an entrepreneurial firm', *Academy of Management Journal*, **25**, 465–99.

Mitchell, R.K., L. Busenitz, T. Lant, P. McDougall, E. Morse and J.B. Smith (2002), 'Toward a theory of entrepreneurial cognition: rethinking the people side of entrepreneurship research', *Entrepreneurship: Theory and Practice*, **27**, 93–105.

Mosakowski, E. (1993), 'A resource-based perspective on the dynamic strategy-performance relationship: an empirical examination of the focus and differentiation strategies in entrepreneurial firms', *Journal of Management*, **19**, 819–39.

Naman, J.L. and D.P. Slevin (1993), 'Entrepreneurship and the concept of fit: A model and empirical tests', *Strategic Management Journal*, **14**, 137–53.

Nisbett, R. and L. Ross (1980), *Human Inferences: Strategies and Shortcomings of Social Judgement*, Englewood Cliffs, NJ: Prentice-Hall.

Office for National Statistics (1999), *PA 1003 Commerce, Energy and Industry:*

Size Analysis of the United Kingdom Businesses, London: Office for National Statistics.

Organisation for Economic Co-Operation and Development (OECD) (1998), *Fostering Entrepreneurship*, Paris: Organisation for Economic Co-Operation and Development.

Palich, L.E. and D.R. Bagby (1995), 'Using cognitive theory to explain entrepreneurial risk taking: challenging conventional wisdom', *Journal of Business Venturing*, **10**, 425–38.

Parkhouse, S. (2005), 'Dragon back in her den', *The Observer* (Business), 11 December, p. 10.

Penrose, E.T. (1959), *The Theory of Growth of the Firm*, Oxford: Oxford University Press.

Reuber, A.R. and E. Fischer (1999), 'Understanding the consequences of founders' experience', *Journal of Small Business Management*, **37**, 30–45.

Reynolds, P.D. (1987), 'New firms: societal contribution versus potential', *Journal of Business Venturing*, **2**, 231–46.

Reynolds, P.D. (1997), 'Who starts new firms? Preliminary explorations of firms-in-gestation', *Small Business Economics*, **9**, 449–62.

Reynolds, P., D.J. Storey and P. Westhead (1994), 'Cross-national comparisons of the variation in new firm formation rates', *Regional Studies*, **28**, 443–56.

Robbie, K. and M. Wright, (1990), 'The case of Maccess' in S. Taylor and S. Turley (eds), *Cases in Financial Accounting*, Deddington: Philip Allan.

Robbie, K.and M. Wright (1996), *Management Buy-Ins: Entrepreneurship, Active Investors and Corporate Restructuring*, Manchester: Manchester University Press.

Robbie, K., M. Wright and C. Ennew (1993), 'Management buy-outs from receivership', *Omega, International Journal of Management Science*, **21**, 519–30.

Robinson, P.B., D.V. Stimpson, J.C. Huefner and H.K. Hunt (1991), 'An attitude approach to the prediction of entrepreneurship', *Entrepreneurship Theory and Practice*, **15**, 13–31.

Robson, C. (1993), *Real World Research: A Resource for Social Scientists and Practitioner Researchers*, Oxford: Blackwell.

Ronstadt (1986), 'Exit, stage left: why entrepreneurs end their entrepreneurial careers before retirement', *Journal of Business Venturing*, **1**, 323–38.

Ronstadt, R. (1988), 'The corridor principal and entrepreneurial time', *Journal of Business Venturing*, **1**, 295–306.

Rosa, P. (1998), 'Entrepreneurial processes of business cluster formation and growth by "habitual" entrepreneurs', *Entrepreneurship Theory and Practice*, **22**, 43–61.

Rosa, P. and D. Hamilton (1994), 'Gender and ownership in UK small firms', *Entrepreneurship Theory and Practice*, **18**, 11–27.

Rosa, P. and M.G. Scott (1998), *Entrepreneurial Performance and 'Habitual' Entrepreneurs: Processes of Business Cluster Formation and Growth*. Stirling: Department of Entrepreneurship, University of Stirling.

Salkind, N.J. (2000), *Exploring Research*, 4th edition. Englewood Cliffs, NJ: Prentice Hall.

Sanberg, W.R. (1986), *New Venture Performance: The Role of Strategy and Industry Structure*, Lexington, MA: Lexington Books.

Sarasvathy, S.D. (2001), 'Causation and effectuation: towards a theoretical shift from economic inevitability to entrepreneurial contingency', *Academy of Management Review*, **26**, 243–88.

Schein, E.H. (1978), *Career Dynamics: Matching Individual and Organizational Needs*, Reading, MA: Addison-Wesley.

Scheinberg, S. and I.C. MacMillan (1988), 'An 11 country study of motivations to start a business', in B.A. Kirchhoff, W.A. Long, W.E. McMullan, K.H. Vesper and W.E. Wetzel, Jr. (eds), *Frontiers in Entrepreneurship Research*, Wellesley, MA: Babson College, pp. 669–87.

Schollhammer, H. (1991), 'Incidence and determinants of multiple entrepreneurship', in N.C. Churchill, W.D. Bygrave, J.G. Covin, D.L. Sexton, D.P. Slevin, K.H. Vesper and W.E. Wetzel (eds), *Frontiers of Entrepreneurship Research 1991*, Wellesley, MA: Babson College, pp. 11–24.

Schumpeter, J.A. (1934), 'The Theory of Economic Development', *Harvard Economic Studies*, Cambridge, MA: Harvard University.

Scott, M. and P. Rosa (1996), 'Has firm level analysis reached its limits?' *International Small Business Journal*, **14**, 81–9.

Sexton, E.A. and P.B. Robinson (1989), 'The economic and demographic determinants of self-employment', in R.H. Brockhaus (ed), *Frontiers of Entrepreneurship Research*, Wellesley, MA: Babson College, pp. 28–42.

Shane, S. (2000), 'Prior knowledge and the discovery of entrepreneurial opportunities', *Organization Science*, **11**, 448–69.

Shane, S. (2003), *Academic Entrepreneurship*. Cheltenham: Edward Elgar.

Shane, S. and K. Khurana (2003), 'Career experience and firm founding', *Industrial and Corporate Change*, **12**, 519–44.

Shane, S. and S. Venkataraman (2000), 'The promise of entrepreneurship as a field of research', *Academy of Management Review*, **25**, 217–26.

Shanteau, J. (1992), 'Competence in experts: the role of task characteristics', *Organizational behaviour and Human Decision Processes*, **53**, 252–66.

Shepherd, D.A. (2003), 'Learning from business failure: propositions of grief recovery for the self-employed', *Academy of Management Review*, **28**, 318–29.

Shepherd, D.A. and D.R. DeTienne (2005), 'Prior knowledge, potential financial reward, and opportunity identification', *Entrepreneurship Theory and Practice*, **29**, 91–112.

Shook, C.L., R.L. Priem and J.E. McGee (2003), 'Venture creation and the enterprising individual: a review and synthesis', *Journal of Management*, **29**, 379–99.

Simon, H.A. (1973), 'The structure of ill–structured problems', *Artificial Intelligence*, **4**, 181–201.

Singh, R.P. (2001), 'A comment on developing the field of entrepreneurship through the study of opportunity recognition and exploitation', *Academy of Management Review*, **26**, 10–12.

Sitkin, S.B. (1992), 'Learning through failure: the strategy of small losses', *Research in Organizational Behavior*, **14**, 231–66.

Spence, M.T. and M. Brucks (1997), 'The moderating effects of problem characteristics on experts' and novices' judgement', *Journal of Marketing Research*, **37**, 233–47.

Spinelli, S. and S. Birley (1996), 'Towards a theory of conflict in the franchise system', *Journal of Business Venturing*, **11**, 329–42.

Starr, J. and W.B. Bygrave (1991), 'The assets and liabilities of prior start-up experience: an exploratory study of multiple venture entrepreneurs' in N.C. Churchill, W.D. Bygrave, J.G. Covin, D.L. Sexton, D.P. Slevin, K.H. Vesper and W.E. Wetzel (eds), *Frontiers of Entrepreneurship Research 1991*, Wellesley, MA: Babson College, pp. 213–27.

Stevenson, H. and J.C. Jarillo (1990), 'A paradigm of entrepreneurship: Entrepreneurial management', *Strategic Management Journal*, **11**, 17–27.

Stigler, G.J. (1961), 'The economics of information', *The Journal of Political Economy*, **LXIX**, 213–25.

Stinchcombe, A.L. (1965), 'Social structure and organizations', in J.G. March (ed.), *Handbook of Organizations*, Chicago: Rand McNally, pp. 153–93.

Stokes, D. and R. Blackburn (2002), 'Learning the hard way: the lessons of owner-managers who have closed their businesses', *Journal of Small Business and Enterprise Development*, **9**, 17–27.

Storey, D.J. (1982), *Entrepreneurship and the New Firm*, London: Croom Helm.

Storey, D.J. (1994), *Understanding the Small Business Sector*. London: Routledge.

Storey, D.J. (2000), 'Six steps to heaven: evaluating the impact of public policies to support small businesses in developed economies' in D.L. Sexton and H. Landström (eds), *The Blackwell Handbook of Entrepreneurship*, Malden, MA: Blackwell Publishing Ltd, pp. 176–94.

Storey, D.J. (2003), 'Entrepreneurship, small and medium sized enterprises and public policies', in Z.J. Acs and D.B. Audretsch (eds), *Handbook of Entrepreneurship Research: An Interdisciplinary Survey and Introduction*, Dordrecht, The Netherlands: Kluwer, pp. 473–511.

Storey, D.J. (2004), 'Exploring the link, among small firms, between management training and firm performance: a comparison between the UK and other OECD countries', *International Journal of Human Resource Management*, **14**, 112–30.

Taylor, R. (1999), 'The small firm as a temporary coalition', *Entrepreneurship and Regional Development*, **11**, 1–19.

Teece, D.J., G. Pisano and A. Shuen (1997), 'Dynamic capabilities and strategic management', *Strategic Management Journal*, **18**, 509–33.

Thompson, A.A. and A.J. Strickland (1989), *Strategic Management: Concepts and Cases*, Plano, TX: Business Publications Inc.

Timmons, J.A., D.F. Muzyka, H.H. Stevenson and W.D. Bygrave (1987), 'Opportunity recognition: the core of entrepreneurship', in N.C. Churchill (ed), *Frontiers in Entrepreneurship Research*, Wellesley, MA: Babson College, pp. 109–23.

Tversky, A. and D. Kahneman (1986), 'Rational choice and the framing of decisions', *Journal of Business*, **59**, 251–94.

Ucbasaran, D. (2004a), *Business Ownership Experience, Entrepreneurial Behaviour and Performance: Novice, Habitual, Serial and Portfolio Entrepreneurs*. Unpublished doctoral thesis, Nottingham University Business School.

Ucbasaran, D. (2004b), 'Opportunity identification behavior by different types of entrepreneurs', in J. Butler (ed), *Opportunity Identification and Entrepreneurial Behavior*, Greenwich, CA: IAP, Research in Entrepreneurship and Management Series, pp. 75–98.

Ucbasaran, D., A. Lockett, M. Wright and P. Westhead (2003a), 'Entrepreneurial founder teams: Factors associated with team member entry and exit', *Entrepreneurship Theory and Practice*, **28**, 107–28.

Ucbasaran, D., M. Wright and P. Westhead (2003b), 'A longitudinal study of habitual entrepreneurs: starters and acquirers', *Entrepreneurship and Regional Development*, **15**, 207–28.

Ucbasaran, D., M. Wright, P. Westhead and L. Busenitz (2003c), 'The impact of entrepreneurial experience on opportunity identification and exploitation: habitual and novice entrepreneurs', in J.A. Katz and D.A. Shepherd (eds), *Advances in Entrepreneurship, Firm Emergence and Growth: Cognitive Approaches to Entrepreneurship*, **6**, 231–63.

Ucbasaran, D., P. Westhead and M. Wright (2001), 'The focus of entrepreneurial research: contextual and process issues', *Entrepreneurship Theory and Practice*, **25**, 57–80.

Ucbasaran, D., P. Westhead and M. Wright (2006), 'Entrepreneurial entry, exit and re-entry: opportunity identification and pursuit', paper presented at the Exit and Serial Entrepreneurship Workshop, Jena, Max Plank Institute, January.

Vanaelst, I., B. Clarysse, M. Wright, A. Lockett, N. Moray and R. S'Jegers

(2006), 'Entrepreneurial team development in academic spin-outs: an examination of team heterogeneity', *Entrepreneurship Theory and Practice*, **30**, 249–72.

Venkataraman, S. (1997), 'The distinctive domain of entrepreneurship research: an editor's perspective', in J.A. Katz (ed), *Advances in Entrepreneurship, Firm Emergence and Growth*, Greenwich, CA: JAI Press, **3**, 119–38.

Venkataraman, S. and I.C. MacMillan (1997), 'Choice of organizational mode in new business development: theory and propositions', in D.L. Sexton and R.W. Smilor (eds), *Entrepreneurship 2000*, Chicago, IL: Upstart Publishing Company, pp. 151–66.

Vohora, A., M. Wright and A. Lockett (2004), 'Critical junctures in the growth in university high-tech spinout companies', *Research Policy*, **33**, 147–75.

Ward, T., S. Smithand J. Vaid (eds) (1997), *Creative Thought: An Investigation of Conceptual Structures and Processes*, Washington, DC: American Psychological Association.

Westhead, P. (1995), 'Survival and employment growth contrasts between types of owner-managed high-technology firms', *Entrepreneurship Theory and Practice*, **20**, 5–27.

Westhead, P. and M. Cowling (1998), 'Family firm research: the need for a methodological rethink', *Entrepreneurship Theory and Practice*, **23**, 31–56.

Westhead, P. and A. Moyes (1992), 'Reflections on Thatcher's Britain: evidence from new production firm registrations 1980–1988', *Entrepreneurship and Regional Development*, **4**, 21–56.

Westhead, P. and M. Wright (1998a), 'Novice, portfolio and serial founders: Are they different?', *Journal of Business Venturing*, **13**, 173–204.

Westhead, P. and M. Wright (1998b), 'Novice, portfolio and serial founders in rural and urban areas', *Entrepreneurship Theory and Practice*, **22**, 63–100.

Westhead, P. and M. Wright (1999), 'Contributions of novice, portfolio and serial founders in rural and urban areas', *Regional Studies*, **33**, 157–73.

Westhead, P. and M. Wright (eds) (2000), *Advances in Entrepreneurship*. Aldershot: Edward Elgar Publishing Ltd.

Westhead, P., D. Ucbasaran and M. Wright (2003a), 'Differences between private firms owned by novice, serial and portfolio entrepreneurs: implications for policy-makers and practitioners', *Regional Studies*, **37**, 187–200.

Westhead, P., D. Ucbasaran, M. Wright and F. Martin (2003b), *Habitual Entrepreneurs in Scotland: Characteristics, Search Processes, Learning and Performance – Summary Report*, Glasgow: Scottish Enterprise. A copy of the full report can be downloaded from www.scottish-enterprise.com in the Research and Publications section.

Westhead, P., D. Ucbasaran and M. Wright (2005a), 'Policy toward novice, serial and portfolio entrepreneurs', *Environment and Planning C: Government and Policy*, **22**, 779–98.

Westhead, P., D. Ucbasaran and M. Wright (2005b), 'Experience and cognition: do novice, serial and portfolio entrepreneurs differ?' *International Small Business Journal*, **23**, 72–98.

Westhead, P., D. Ucbasaran and M. Wright (2005c), 'Decisions, actions, and performance: novice, serial and portfolio entrepreneurs differ?', *Journal of Small Business Management*, **43**, 393–417.

Westhead, P., D. Ucbasaran, M. Wright and M. Binks (2005d), 'Policy toward novice, serial and portfolio entrepreneurs', *Small Business Economics*, **25**, 109–32.

Wheatley, C. (2004), 'Portrait of a serial entrepreneur', *Real Business*, October.

Witt, U. (1998), 'Imagination and leadership – the neglected dimension of an evolutionary theory of the firm', *Journal of Economic Behavior and Organization*, **35**, 161–77.

Woo, C.Y., A.C. Cooper and W.C. Dunkelberg (1991), 'The development and interpretation of entrepreneurial typologies', *Journal of Business Venturing*, **6**, 93–114.

Wood, R. and A. Bandura (1989), 'Social cognitive theory of organizational management', *Academy of Management Review*, **14**, 361–84.

Wren, C. and D.J. Storey (2002), 'Evaluating the effect of soft business support upon small firm performance', *Oxford Economic Papers*, **54**, 334–65.

Wright, M., K. Robbie and M. Albrighton (2000), 'Secondary management buy-outs and buy-ins', *International Journal of Entrepreneurial Behavior and Research*, **6**, 21–40.

Wright, M., K. Robbie and C. Ennew (1997a), 'Serial entrepreneurs', *British Journal of Management*, **8**, 251–68.

Wright, M., K. Robbie and C. Ennew (1997b), 'Venture capitalists and serial entrepreneurs', *Journal of Business Venturing*, **12**, 227–49.

Wright, M., K. Robbie, S. Thompson and P. Wong (1995), 'Management buy-outs in the short and long term', *Journal of Business Finance and Accounting*, **22**, 461–82.

Wright, M., S. Thompson and K. Robbie (1992), 'Venture capital and management-led, leveraged buy-outs: a European perspective', *Journal of Business Venturing*, **7**, 47–71.

Wright, M., P. Westhead and J. Sohl (1998), 'Editors' introduction: habitual entrepreneurs and angel investors' *Entrepreneurship Theory and Practice*, **22**, 1–9.

Wright, M., N. Wilson and K. Robbie (1996), 'The longer term effects of management-led buyouts', *Journal of Entrepreneurial and Small Business Finance*, **5**, 213–34.

Zahra, S.A. (1993), 'Environment, corporate entrepreneurship, and financial performance: a taxonomic approach', *Journal of Business Venturing*, **8**, 319–40.

Zuckerman, M. (1979), 'Attribution of success and failure revisited, and the motivational bias is alive and well in attribution theory', *Journal of Personality*, **47**, 245–87.

Index